More Praise for *The Compassionate Life*

"The more who read him, the better the world will be. Inspiring and encouraging."

—*Kirkus Reviews* (starred review)

"Cultivating the virtue of compassion is a requirement for optimum health, as well as for improving the state of the world. This book will help you do both—it is good medicine for our time."

—Andrew Weil, MD, author of *Healthy Aging*

"This book is a marvelous act of generosity: a wise, beautiful, triumphant reminder of our human goodness."

—Jack Kornfield, PhD, author of *A Path with Heart*

"Writing in a friendly, upbeat voice, Barasch is never pious as he ponders the meaning of compassion, its healing properties, and the wisdom of the compassionate…Melding accessible reportage with spiritual quest, Barasch's stirring account is thought-provoking and inspiring.

—*Publishers Weekly* (starred review)

"Refreshingly real, beyond right or left, just straight to the center of the human heart. If you want to help save the world today, then give someone—anyone—this startling, truthful, and passionate book."

—Arianna Huffington, cofounder and editor in chief, *The Huffington Post*

"Describing how compassion unfolds in ordinary lives and transforms them is Barasch's great gift. Elegant, erudite, and profoundly gentle: his book is a shimmering jewel."

—Larry Dossey, MD, author of *Healing Words*

"Makes a powerful case for a world of kindness, generosity, and love. Barasch develops sophisticated social theory that challenges the paralyzing cynicism that is the 'common sense' of our age."

—Rabbi Michael Lerner, editor, *Tikkun* magazine, and author of *The Left Hand of God*

"If I had to pick one skill that was most important for a negotiator—meaning everyone, every day—it would be the ability to put yourself in the other side's shoes. In this extraordinary book, Marc Barasch helps us understand why and how."

—William Ury, PhD, coauthor of *Getting to Yes*

"I have read the book twice—once from an intellectual perspective and the second time from my heart—and I was doubly rewarded by its wisdom. I heartily recommend it to anyone who wants to understand why the compassionate life is the answer—and who wants to learn how to live it."

—Bernie Siegel, MD, author of *Love, Medicine, and Miracles*

Praise for *The Healing Path*

"For its honesty, style, and wise wariness about cures, it's a book that could help all of us deal with both bodily illness and the soul sickness of our lives."

—Thomas Moore, author of *Care of the Soul* and *Soul Mates*

'This book is a masterful, awesome feat—an unnervingly accurate reframing of the nature of wounding and task of becoming whole."

—Rachel Naomi Remen, MD, author of *Kitchen Table Wisdom*

"An epic, provocative study...sharp, witty prose, filled with metaphor and fresh language...[A]rgues for important redefinitions of not just disease and cure, but also for the validity of the human imagination."

—*San Antonio Express-News*

"Scholarly and wise, poignant and funny…it rings of the authenticity that is the very hallmark of healing. A classic in the burgeoning field of body-mind medicine."

—Joan Borysenko, PhD, author of
Minding the Body, Mending the Mind

"*The Healing Path* is the most engrossing, challenging, and empowering book on this topic I have ever read. Barasch's honest, literate portrayal of his personal journey and the healing journeys of others, combined with his thorough citation of biomedical references, make this a unique contribution to the medical literature on healing."

—*Alternative Therapies in Health and Medicine*

Praise for *Remarkable Recovery*

"Thrilling!"

—*Newsweek*

"Even skeptics will enjoy the documented stories of unbelievable recoveries…With each astounding discovery, you can't put this book down."

—*San Francisco Chronicle*

"Here is a book I have made it a point to read and reread. In the darkness and uncertainty that accompanies cancer, this book gave me hope. It was a guiding light on a sometimes starless night and will forever maintain a cherished place on my bookshelf."

—Banda Seri Begawan (cancer patient)

Praise for *Healing Dreams*

"Provocative and thoughtful…one of the most compelling and convincing accounts of the significance of dreams. *Healing Dreams* is distinguished by the author's reluctance to claim to have the answers—his ego takes a backseat to the evidence—and by the quality of his prose…Barasch has the gift of making readers want to journey with him."

—*Publishers Weekly*

"In his fascinating, well-organized and lucid book, Marc Ian Barasch carries us along with him on a brave night journey through the dream world…It never fails to capture the reader's interest thanks to Barasch's own enthusiasm, his profound research, and his poet's eye for the heart of the matter… In these days of journalistic sensationalism and excess, Barasch remains an honest reporter with a respectful tone of gentle inquiry into the mystery of his subject. This book is as wise and healing as a dream."

    —*Washington Post Book World*

"Marc Barasch is a daring thinker, a mesmerizing writer, and a fully conscious human being who never fails to take us on an eye-opening romp through our own minds. As with all his work, *Healing Dreams* has transformative power; the reader emerges not only illumined but more intensely alive."

    —Hara Marano, editor at large, *Psychology Today*

"Marc Barasch is the Nabokov of contemporary dream writers. He gives his dreams and those of others voices that speak intimately, powerfully, and unforgettably. The power to profoundly enhance our appreciation of reality is the gift of dreams and the gift of this fine book. Read it if you want to live a bigger, more vivid life."

    —Gayle Delaney, PhD, founding president, International Association for the Study of Dreams, and author of *All About Dreams*

"In all my years o°f working in the field of human potential there are perhaps only a dozen books that I would accord the status of 'critically innovative.' This is one! *Healing Dreams* could mark a revolution in the study of consciousness and its capacities."

    —Jean Houston, PhD, author of *A Mythic Life* and *The Possible Human*

THE COMPASSIONATE LIFE

WALKING THE PATH OF KINDNESS

Marc Ian Barasch

BK

Berrett–Koehler Publishers, Inc.
San Francisco
a BK Life book

Berrett-Koehler Publishers, Inc.
235 Montgomery Street, Suite 650, San Francisco, CA 94104-2916
Tel: (415) 288-0260 Fax: (415) 362-2512 www.bkconnection.com

Ordering Information

Quantity sales. Special discounts are available on quantity purchases by corporations, associations, and others. For details, contact the "Special Sales Department" at the Berrett-Koehler address above.

Individual sales. Berrett-Koehler publications are available through most bookstores. They can also be ordered directly from Berrett-Koehler:
Tel: (800) 929-2929; Fax: (802) 864-7626; www.bkconnection.com.

Orders for college textbook/course adoption use. Please contact Berrett-Koehler:
Tel: (800) 929-2929; Fax: (802) 864-7626.

Orders by U.S. trade bookstores and wholesalers. Please contact Ingram Publisher Services, Tel: (800) 509-4887; Fax: (800) 838-1149; E-mail: customer.service@ ingrampublisherservices.com; or visit www.ingrampublisherservices.com/Ordering for details about electronic ordering.

Berrett-Koehler and the BK logo are registered trademarks of Berrett-Koehler Publishers, Inc.

Printed in the United States of America

Berrett-Koehler books are printed on long-lasting acid-free paper. When it is available, we choose paper that has been manufactured by environmentally responsible processes. These may include using trees grown in sustainable forests, incorporating recycled paper, minimizing chlorine in bleaching, or recycling the energy produced at the paper mill.

Library of Congress Cataloging-in-Publication Data
Barasch, Marc.
    The compassionate life : walking the path of kindness / Marc Ian Barasch.
        p. cm.
    Includes bibliographical references and index.
    ISBN 978-1-57675-756-7 (pbk. : alk. paper)
    1. Compassion. I. Title.
BJ1475.B37 2009
177'.7—dc22

                                                                    2009007605

14 13 12 11 10 09   10 9 8 7 6 5 4 3 2 1

Interior design and composition by Gary Palmatier, Ideas to Images.
Elizabeth von Radics, copyeditor; Mike Mollett, proofreader; Medea Minnich, indexer.

To the givers

The heart sees, the heart hears, the heart speaks,
the heart walks, the heart falls, the heart rejoices,
the heart cries out, the heart comforts, the heart suffers,
the heart surrenders, the heart errs, the heart trembles,
the heart awakens...

—The Midrash

CONTENTS

PREFACE

I am thankful that thorns have roses.

—Alphonse Karr

Ｅ VERY NOW AND THEN, I'LL MEET AN ESCAPEE, SOMEONE WHO has broken free of self-centeredness and lit out for the territory of compassion. You've met them, too, those people who seem to emit a steady stream of, for want of a better word, love-vibes. As soon as you come within range, you feel embraced, accepted for who you are. For those of us who suspect that you rarely get something for nothing, such geniality can be discomfiting. Yet it feels so good to be around them. They stand there, radiating photons of goodwill, and despite yourself you beam back, and the world, in a twinkling, changes.

I appreciate these compassion-mongers, even marvel at them. But I've rarely thought that I could be one of them. Sure, I've tried to live a benign life, putting my shoulder to the wheel for peace, justice, and Mother Earth. Like most people, I adore my offspring, even when they drive me crazy; love my parents, despite the corkscrew of childhood; dote on my siblings (though there *is* that scrapbook of old slights); and treasure my friends (even if they sometimes let me down). Conventional wisdom wouldn't fault me for saving the best stuff for my nearest and dearest and giving the rest of humanity the leftovers.

Thus it is, say the sages, that the harvest of kindness—of kindredness—is winnowed down to a precious few grains. For at the center of all spiritual traditions is the beacon of a truly radical proposal: Open your heart to everybody. *Every*body.

Is this even possible?

Nelson Mandela once remarked that he befriended his jailers, those grim, khaki-clad overseers of his decades of hard labor in a limestone quarry, by "exploiting their good qualities." Asked if he believed all people were kind at their core, he responded, "There is no doubt whatsoever, provided you are able to arouse their inherent goodness." If that sounds like wishful thinking, well, he actually did it.

NOT THAT MANDELA, OR ANYONE IN HIS OR HER RIGHT mind, would claim it was easy. Compassion isn't simply opening a spigot and coating everything in a treacly, all-purpose goo. It requires a gut hunch that whatever I do unto others, I do unto myself. It calls for appreciating not only what comforts us but what pierces us. (*Compassion* comes from the Latin *cum patior,* "to suffer with," while *apathy*—literally, "not to suffer"—connotes a heart benumbed).

Even among those in what are known as the caring professions, I've seen a credo posted on office doors and bulletin boards:

People are unreasonable, illogical, and self-centered.
   Love them anyway.

If you do good, people will accuse you of selfish, ulterior motives.
   Do good anyway.

The kindness you show today will be forgotten tomorrow
   Be kind anyway.

Why bother? Sure, it's better to offer a hand than turn a blind eye. And if you're trying to get to heaven, it's probably the route with the fewest traffic delays. But there's another reason: A compassionate life is more fulfilling. It's only when the ego bows out that the curtain rises on real life. That it's more blessed to give than to receive is not some moral nostrum, they say, but a prescription for authentic joy.

Did I really believe that? I'm ever on guard against disillusion; I don't want to be shocked if my better angels turn out to have size 12 clay feet. Today the world stirs with hope for some new upward arc, for a kinder epoch. The need to turn away from cynicism and toward each other has never been clearer. But we still live on a planet where thirty thousand kids die in poverty each day while we obsess over our calories. We go to work in the morning with every good intention even as our diligence stokes an iron giant that is grinding up the earth. The crises exceed the grasp of our polity, challenging the reach of our human potential.

This book began as a personal investigation. I wanted to know what it takes to overcome that I-me-mine I'm convinced ruins everything, to sweeten my tongue, change my jealous mind, think of other people first, just to see what happens. Spiritual teachers throughout history have insisted we each possess the requisite piece of equipment: one standard-issue human heart. It is not a case of being born with the right disposition but of cultivating, like diligent, sweat-stained gardeners, the kernel of benevolence that is our birthright.

I intended on my journey to break bread with the saints (or some reasonable facsimile). But I also needed to sit down with a man of violence because once, in a bitter argument with my ex-wife, I'd pounded the wall and was appalled to see I'd put my fist through plaster. Compassion is easy enough in a vacuum, but what happens when what's hardest to bear is right up in your face?

My inquiry grew into a years-long quest to develop that persuasion of mind that paves the way for authentic conviction. I found myself being persuaded—maybe more than I'd expected—by examples and exemplars, by theology and neurobiology, by my own forays into the deep backcountry of human kindness. Conviction crept up on me, almost without my noticing. It went from a fairy tale, a just-so story, to what-if, to a tentative but persistent yes. I felt, after a while, I'd been given a pair of magic glasses with lenses that see only the good in people—if I could just remember to put them on.

The Circle of Compassion

*If one completes the journey to one's own heart,
one will find oneself in the heart of everyone else.*

—Father Thomas Keating

WHEN I WAS IN MY TWENTIES, MY BUDDHIST TEACHER tricked me into taking a vow of universal compassion. Using some spiritual sleight of hand, he made it appear that I could aspire to a tender concern for everybody, even putting their welfare before my own.

Fat chance, I thought. But in his wily way, he framed this vow—the *bodhisattva's* promise to live for others—as a case of enlightened self-interest. It was not, he told me, a matter of wearing a one-size-fits-all hair shirt. I was taking the vow for my own good. It would give me some leverage to pry loose, finger by finger, the claustrophobic monkey-grip of ego, would give the heart a little breathing room. By treating others generously, I might find them responding in kind. I felt I was being made privy to an ancient secret: *To attain your own human potential, be mindful of everyone else's.*

At some point in my vow ceremony, a casual affair held in a rocky field, it *did* seem as if my vision suddenly cleared. I glimpsed, like a sky swept clean of clouds, everyone's innate okayness. Years later I still marvel at the spiritual chutzpah of the liturgy: *However innumerable are beings, I vow to save them all.* Hardly knowing what I was doing, I'd planted myself in a millennia-old tradition that claims you can love all without preconditions, exclusionary clauses, or bottom lines, that says life isn't *quid pro quo* but *quid pro bono.*

To my surprise the vow hadn't made me feel obligated, but liberated from my own suffocating strictures, from the narrowness of my concerns. It was as if I'd been waiting for a signal, a green light to step onto the crosswalk to the opposite curb, some goad to be compassionate not out of blind craving for virtue but because it seemed the only genuinely interesting thing to do with my life.

I had so often assumed life was about magnifying myself (for the greater good, of course), but now that seemed like the wrong end of the telescope: It made everyone else look small. I soon took a job running a residential therapeutic community in exchange for room and board, surprised at my ability to care for the walking wounded. I stopped thinking so much about how others had let me down, broken my heart, failed to anticipate my needs or take my oh-so-unique sensitivities into account. I began striving to see—and even nourish—other people's possibilities, receiving in return those surprise concoctions the human spirit dishes out when it feels accepted and at ease.

But there came a point on my journey when I stumbled badly and fell far: a dire illness, an interminable recovery, penury, loneliness, and despair. Friends clucked in sympathy but stepped gingerly over the body. Family didn't do much better. I had a soul-curdling realization: The people you love (and who ostensibly love you) may not be there when you need them most. I got through it—the kindness of strangers and all—but I was soon back to squinting at people through my cool fisheye, seeing their preening vanity, their intellectual shortfalls, their ethical squishiness. It took time to realize that my shortsightedness was taking a toll, let alone that there was anything I could do about it.

Finding my way back to meditation helped. Nothing like getting a good, long look at myself (and funny how much I looked like everyone else). I noticed how often my social trade-offs were more about getting than giving, how many of *my* thoughts revolved in geosynchronous orbit around Planet Numero Uno. Still my teacher had insisted that one thing was certain: Despite seeing all the ego's pitfalls and pratfalls, real *bodhisattvas* make friends with themselves. Everyone, he said, possessed some worth past quantifying or qualifying, some value beyond judgment or fine-tuning—and that included oneself.

To love your neighbor *as yourself,* after all, is the great injunction of every religion. But what does loving yourself *mean*? It's one thing to say it; it's another to know it in your bones. The spiritual consensus seems to be that it's like learning to love anyone: You start by getting to know them. The side benefit is that to know yourself is also to know the person sitting next to you and the one halfway around the world. "Read thyself," wrote philosopher Thomas Hobbes. "Whosoever looketh into himself...shall know what are the thoughts and passions of all other men."

Still, having looketh'd into myself, I can't say I loveth all I see. I *have* read myself, and there in oversized type it says: *petty, suspicious, greedy, vain, jealous, lazy, stingy, dull* (and that's just on the page; there's more between the lines). That I also reckon myself magnanimous, conscientious, loyal, thrifty, brave, and intermittently humble is beside the point. It's not enough to offset scourging self-judgment with some roll call of compensatory pluses. We have to take ourselves (and one another) whole. The Dalai Lama points out that the Tibetan term for compassion, *tsewa,* generally means "love of others," but "one can have that feeling toward oneself as well. It is a state of mind where you extend how you relate to yourself toward others." If it's true that what goes around comes around, compassion is about nothing if not love's tendency to circulate.

And radiate. Alexander Pope (poet of the "eternal sunshine of the spotless mind") envisioned compassion as a series of concentric circles rippling outward:

> Self-love but serves the virtuous mind to wake,
> As the small pebble stirs the peaceful lake;
> ...Friend, parent, neighbor, first it will embrace;
> His country next; and next all human race.

It sounds great. (It *is* great.) But for many of us there's a nagging doubt that this whole compassion routine could edge into self-effacement—into loving others *instead* of ourselves, giving away the store until the shelves are bare. The usual formula is first to stockpile some extra self-esteem—*then* you can afford to be generous. That isn't quite how nineteenth-century religious philosopher Søren Kierkegaard saw it. The commandment to love thy neighbor was to him a divine burglary that "as with a pick, wrenches open the lock of self-love and wrests it away from the person." *Oh, great.* What about looking out for number one? Isn't it prudent to follow that flight attendant's advisory: "First place the mask over your own nose and mouth, tightening the straps to begin the flow of oxygen"? We're of no use to anyone if we're passed out in our seat from hypoxia.

It's a hard balance to strike. If I am not for myself, who will be? But if I am only for myself, what am I? There is a growing sense in our society, left, right, and center, that the balance has woozily tipped, that our obsession with seamless self-contentment has occluded our caring. Our cultural default setting has become *get your own needs met.* Our psychosocial mean temperature, I've heard clinicians say, is "people-friendly narcissism." Our therapeutic model focuses so much on strengthening the ego-self that it omits what psychologists call the "self-in-relation." (One group of mostly female psychologists has proposed "openness to mutual influence" as a more reliable barometer of mental health than self-esteem.)

Self-esteem remains our all-purpose buzzword, a stock phrase in therapists' offices, corporate training modules, even elementary school curricula. Psychologist Abraham Maslow coined the term in 1940 after observing a monkey colony in a Madison, Wisconsin, zoo. He was fascinated by the cockiness of the troupe's dominant alphas and the social benefits they accrued, reminiscent of socially successful people. His concept of self-esteem had its origins in the alpha's great cry of triumphal self-love: I *am* somebody—and you're not. Far from simple self-affirmation, this self-esteem was more akin to that sense of self that made Frank Sinatra sing how swell it was to be king of the hill.

What Maslow failed to stress was the social dimension. Even in a primate colony—especially so—no ape is an island: Modern primatologists point out that an alpha animal, contrary to its reputation as solitary lord of all it surveys, is thickly enmeshed in a social web, dependent on the reciprocities of group life. Maslow's paragon of the "self-actualized" person ("authentic, individuated, productive" with "a surprising amount of detachment from people in general") begins to sound less like a social creature than a self-pollinating flower.

Taking potshots at Maslow may be a little unfair. At a time when psychology was obsessed with what goes wrong in the psyche, Maslow championed the things that go right. He was an exuberant advocate of human potential when most shrinks spent their fifty-minute hours chronicling pathology. And he did posit that self-actualization would inevitably produce a sense of responsibility for others. But his emphasis on personal growth as the be-all helped spawn a national cottage industry devoted to building a better me, an enhanced self-to-the-tenth-power with a full entitlement of psychospiritual fabulousness. Not such an awful idea, I suppose, but, as the song goes, *Is that all there is?*

I dropped in on a human potential workshop recently. There was plenty of talk about self-empowerment and self-realization, self-efficacy and peak performance, but compassion didn't rate a second billing on the marquee. It made me wonder what sort of selfhood we're seeking: the self that gets its needs met but is never fulfilled, or the self that gives abundantly yet is never empty? Instead of self-discovery, what about *other*-discovery, our real terra incognita?

"The American way is to first feel good about yourself," says Benedictine monk Thomas Keating, "and then feel good about others. But spiritual traditions say it's the other way around—that you develop a sense of goodness by giving of yourself."

I'VE BEEN AN AUDREY HEPBURN FAN SINCE I WAS A BOY WITH my first major movie-star crush, all the more when I discovered that the adorable gamine of *Breakfast at Tiffany's* was also a great humanitarian. I once came across a nugget of her philosophy while waiting in the dentist's office. A fashion magazine had asked for her beauty tips, and she'd replied with her favorite poem (by the great wit Sam Levenson):

> For attractive lips, speak words of kindness.
> For lovely eyes, seek out the good in people.
> For a slim figure, share your food with the hungry.
> For poise, walk with the knowledge you never walk alone.
> If you ever need a helping hand, you'll find one
>   at the end of each of your arms.

This homily, a sort of Saint Francis prayer for the Maybelline set, is a graceful rebuttal to the fetish of self-improvement. Instead of being all about me, it's about us; instead of getting and having, it's about giving and then giving some more. Saint Francis himself went beyond mere charity. The son of a rich clothier, he gave up wealth and privilege to dress in rags and hang out with lepers. This was taking kindness to an extreme few of us would find attainable, let alone remotely appealing. But compassion has a certain down-and-dirty quality and a more than casual familiarity with the soul's darker, draftier labyrinths.

At its root meaning of "to suffer with," compassion challenges our tendency to flinch away from life's too-tender parts, whether those parts belong to us or to others. I know this much: When I acknowledge my own pain, I am much less squeamish about drawing nearer to yours. I seem to acquire my compassion piecemeal, hurt by hurt. After a bad sprain and time spent on crutches, I became more sympathetic to those who hobble with canes and walkers.

Perhaps Saint Thomas Aquinas was not so far off when he claimed that no one becomes compassionate unless he suffers. I take this less as a mandate for medieval masochism than a call to embrace our own actual experience. I've become suspicious of the unblemished life. Maybe the heart must be broken, like a child's prize honeycomb, for the real sweetness to come out. Although something inside us yearns to walk on air, never touching the ground, compassion brings us down to earth. It has been likened to the lotus, whose exquisite, fragrant blossom grows out of the muck and the mire.

The Buddha, the jewel in the lotus himself, didn't start out in the mud. He was raised like a hothouse flower, living the cosseted life of a pampered young prince. His royal parents, fearing a prophecy that he would grow up to become a spiritual teacher instead of a king, confined him within high castle walls, surrounded by every luxury. The lame, the sick, and the down-and-out were banished from sight. It wasn't that his parents were afraid that their son would be shocked by the sight of suffering (after all, he was to be a battle-hardened feudal monarch) but that he would *respond* to it. They were afraid, in other words, that their son might become compassionate.

One day the prince secretly ventured outside. He stumbled first upon a diseased beggar, then a dead man. The walls that had separated him from the world-as-it-is crumbled. Indeed, the castle might be thought of as a metaphorical ego-structure: Don't we often try to secure happiness by fortifying ourselves against imperfection? When the Buddha proclaimed his First Noble Truth, *dukha* ("dissatisfactoriness"), he was pointing to the dissatisfaction of ego-driven existence. In the end his enlightenment was to accept everything and everyone as they are, not in relation to some feel-good agenda; to sit down for the full meal of life; and to stop trying to eat around the broccoli.

When I first took my vows and embarked on the path, I assumed that after *x* years of diligent meditation I'd be a wise man with a small secret smile, wafting clear and calm through my own inner space. Lovingkindness would be a spin-off technology from my private moon shot. But after some time spent trying to attain escape velocity, I noticed that most spiritual teachings regard compassion as the main event—*the* path to enlightenment, the way to slice through self-deception and small thoughts. "Spiritual practice is not just about feeling peaceful and happy," a Buddhist lama once told me, "but being willing to give up your own comfort to help someone else. Unless there's some sacrifice for others, it's just meditation by remote control!"

*W*HAT DO WE MEAN BY *COMPASSION*? THE WORD ITSELF is one among many used to describe the profundity of human connection, but it's the only one, I'd submit, that implies kindness without condition. *Empathy,* for example, refers to our ability to feel and perceive from another's viewpoint. But acutely sensing someone's feelings can also be disturbing (the plight of the "oversensitive"), leading as easily to drawing back as to reaching out. *Sympathy* is famously tenderhearted but can remain at arm's length (think "sympathy card" or "I sympathize with your concerns, but..."). Even when it comes to altruism, the noblest self-sacrifice can be merely parochial, reserved for one's family or the insiders of one's religion or nation, too often at outsiders' expense.

Then, of course, there's the heart's miracle potion of *love.* "All, everything that I understand," exclaimed Leo Tolstoy, "I understand only because I love." Love to him was not just romance's quickened pulse but the plangency of some universal heartbeat—a distinction that, in our eagerness, we often brush right past. We crave love's fierce attachment, its irresistible force of gravity. Next to the possessive throb of desire (*yo quiero* in Spanish means "I love" *and* "I want"), kindness can sound like weak tea.

But with great love often comes great exclusivity. In the chivalric love story of Tristan and Isolde, Tristan's heart is said to be "sealed and locked from all the world save her alone." Kierkegaard referred to erotic love as "the very peak of self-esteem, the *I* intoxicated in the *other I....* This united *I* selfishly cuts itself off from everyone else." Yet just as self-love can lead to either self-absorption or the discovery of common humanity, so can romantic love spiral inward or blossom out, make us hoarders of private happiness or philanthropists of the heart. To talk of love as a singular phenomenon reflects more the parsimonious limits of language than the complex facts on the ground.

I once fell in love with a beautiful, brilliant young woman who came into my life like Cupid's sledgehammer—right between the eyes. I was like a dazed cartoon character with twittering bluebirds circling my head. Amazingly, my feelings were reciprocated—or so it seemed. As she later explained with remarkable patience, what I'd taken for the romantic real deal was to her just budding friendly affection. When I'd gotten over my embarrassment, I had to laugh. I'd misinterpreted her every gesture, word, and look, seizing on parts to construct a whole picture more to my liking.

This kind of love is a long day's journey from compassion (I certainly hadn't taken *her* feelings into account) and from those emotional commitments we share with those we love and who, thankfully, love us back. But I am amazed, reflecting on it, at the complex palette of emotions with which I had painted this non-affair. It wasn't just lust at first sight. I'd felt a profound sense of cherishing toward someone I hardly knew. I'd seen in pristine focus a perfect (and I mean *perfect*) stranger's unique goodness. William Blake's observation, "Love to faults is always blind / Always is to a joy inclined," was on full display. (In one British study, when a person in a brain scanner was shown a photo of his beloved, the neocortical regions associated with judgment shut down, going dark as a Broadway theater on a Monday.)

This bestowal of value on another, seeing him or her in a supernal best light, is a strong component of not only romance but compassion. Faced with love's many nuances, the Greeks wisely concocted a whole spectrum of terms to describe it, from *storge* (tenderness) to *erotike* (sexual desire) to such fortunate grace notes as *eunoia* (benevolence). Science is bearing out the distinctions. A study of college students in the grip of hot new romances showed unique activity deep in the limbic system—activity that differed markedly from the neural signatures of long-term relationship and friendship. (In other studies lust, passion, and long-term attachment have been shown to have differing brain chemistries.)

When I was in the throes of my big crush, I'd also noted a yearning to care for, to do for—that sense of almost maternal nurturing that lovers, male and female alike, feel toward each other when they call each other "baby." Indeed, the type of love most often cited as an analogy for compassion is mother-love itself. The Hebrew word for compassion, *rachamim,* is the plural of the word for womb. Christianity's most tender image is the pietà. Said the Buddha: "Like a mother who protects her child, her only child, with her own life, one should cultivate a heart of unlimited love and compassion toward all living beings." Science has recently shown how the interactions between mother and child—all the soft stroking, gazing, vocalizations, and nurturance of infancy—become the basis for all subsequent relatedness. (Says Allan N. Schore of the University of California [UCLA]: "Our brains are physically wired to develop in tandem with another's through emotional communication, beginning before words are spoken.")

Researchers who study maternal attachment have zeroed in on oxytocin, a master hormone in mother/infant bonding. Intriguingly, oxytocin is also implicated in the experience of falling in love. Released when we touch, it also functions as a sex hormone in both females and males. Does oxytocin make the world go round?

A friend of mine, a specialist in international conflict resolution, described an incident that made me wonder. He'd been summoned to a meeting of political opponents whose bitterness was virtually paralyzing a government. Communication had broken down completely along with all trust. The high tension in the room, he said, was enough to electrocute you. But in the midst of one angry exchange, a baby who had eluded the child-care services crawled out onto the floor between them.

"Suddenly these men who were on the verge of throttling each other got this *awww* look in their eyes," he recalls. "I've never seen a situation turn around faster. Hardened positions seemed to melt. People made concessions. It was like someone had slipped them a drug."

This in effect might have been the case. "In the presence of a baby," notes neuroscientist Sue Carter of Chicago's Psychiatric Institute, "both males and females will produce oxytocin, leading to tender, maternal-like feelings.* How might this translate into other sorts of social attachment?" Given that, as Carter points out, a single exposure to oxytocin can make a lifelong change in the brain," it's not a trivial question. Some suspect that oxytocin is the genesis of "helper's high," those glowing feelings of warmth and well-being described by almost everyone who does volunteer work. A group of UCLA researchers is studying the link between oxytocin and the emotion they call "love of humanity," wondering if the hormone might be the actual milk of human kindness.

Here science approaches the view of love proclaimed in the mystical traditions. According to the Sufis, the feelings we have for family, friends, and lovers all are aspects of divine love. The narrowest affection can lead even to the universal mystery they call the Beloved. In an essay titled "My Heart Can Take On Any Appearance," Islamic sage Ibn El-Arabi proclaimed the highest love to be "like the love of lovers, except that instead of loving

---

*Interestingly, it has been reported that when male chimps are on the verge of mutual aggression, one will sometimes snatch a baby from its mother's arms and brandish it before his rival, which seems to abruptly defuse the conflict. Is it a form of hostage-taking or an instinctual gesture that catalyzes a sort of hormonal truce?

the phenomenon, I love the Essential. A purpose of human love is to demonstrate ultimate, real love." High romance or doing-the-laundry love, simple affection or mad crushes, maybe all are prismatic beams of a single transforming light.

I HAVE A FEW FRIENDS WHO EMBODY THIS BRAND OF BENEFICENT love some researchers refer to as "generativity." I got to know Alicia and Paul (not their real names) when I was teetering at the edge of a private cliffhanger. Though they barely knew me, they showed up one day with a check that pulled me back from the brink. No strings, they assured me as I stammered my thanks. I didn't have to do good with it, reciprocate in any way, or even, they joked, have dinner with them. It wasn't just the sum—several months' food and rent—that startled me but the clear sense I got of the givers' unencumbered hearts.

Over the years we've become close friends. Alicia and Paul live on a hilltop bordered by redwood forest with their three kids, a cockatoo, an ancient desert tortoise, a once-feral cat, a snake, and a pet rat—all of whom gather around their large breakfast table each morning and seem to get along famously. The family is both well off and deeply well intentioned. They save swatches of rain forest; they build schools and teach in them; they take political refugees into their home; they plant community gardens. The last time I saw her, Alicia had just received her massage certification so she could give hospice patients the tenderness of her touch.

I sat in their kitchen one recent morning, looking out on a vista that was almost absurdly breathtaking—mist-shrouded valleys undulating like bumps in a lush green carpet, rolling to the edge of a silvery sea. Paul wandered in for breakfast. Soon, so did a pet rooster, its spurs clicking regally over the ochre tiles until, abandoning all dignity, it leaped onto his lap. "It's spooky," said Paul. "Even our animals are nice." He wasn't bragging, just bemused. He doesn't see himself as particularly compassionate, he tells me, just lucky: lucky to have made enough money to be able to give some away; lucky to have met his wife.

"Philanthropy's not that hard," he said. "Learning how to be really kind to people—that's more elusive. Alicia's sort of a genius in that department."

I can attest to it. She makes you feel so favored—as if you'd done something extraordinary by simply existing—that you can't help but osmose a little of whatever she has and try to pass it along. Alicia, I'd always assumed, was one of those from-the-cradle love-bugs, born with some extra endowment of solar warmth.

"You've got to be kidding," she says. If anything, she insists, she was "born sad, not sweet," an anxious, self-enclosed kid. It was her mother, a "kind of saintly" woman with an eighth-grade education, who got through her shell. "She flat-out taught me compassion. She said that life's greatest joy was to 'pull the beauty out of people' because that makes your life beautiful, too. She was rock-solid in her devotion to other people. She'd be there for the superannoying person no one else wanted to be around, take care of the one who'd landed in the biggest mess." At age eighty-five, Alicia's mother still corresponds weekly with dozens of people in varying degrees of muddle and distress, people who, Alicia says, "count on her letters to help them hold on.

"I'm not at all like her," Alicia claims. "I'm much more critical of people. Mom kept saying the secret was just to take a genuine interest in others—just ask them questions, want to know how they are, really. I'd try that and it would feel good, so I'd do it some more. Step by step I got to see how wonderful that sensation is of serving others." Alicia also credits her kids, a few books, and sundry gurus. But she says it wasn't until she met Tommy that it all came together.

Tommy had AIDS. He had no money, no place to stay, and less than a year to live. "Well, it seemed so obvious," says Alicia. "Not just to say, 'Gee, I'm so sorry, good luck'; but, '*Duh!* you can stay *here.*'" Alicia and her family and a group of friends agreed to divide up the tasks. "I assigned myself to care for him physically—give him massages, that kind of thing. I found I just loved it. When you see the suffering a person's enduring, there's no way you *can't* respond. It takes you beyond yourself. Suddenly, all those judgments you'd make if you just met them at a party evaporate. You're stripped down to two people doing their best to partake of this mystery."

Tommy had been walking with a cane when they first met him. Six months later he was a quadriplegic. "But," says Alicia, "god, was he fun! He had this sparkly, devilish, bad-boy quality. Even when he was really sick, he'd want to go down to Baja and throw some big soirée, so we'd organize this whole elaborate caravan of his friends and our friends and IVs and wheelchairs and just *do* it. You think you've loved before, but this kind of thing opens your heart a thousand times."

Alicia's weekly hospice work grew out of that experience. At fifty-two she still has that lean, blond California-girl look, her shoulders tan and muscular from paddling in the surf. It's easy to imagine her strong hands kneading the failing flesh and comforting the helpless. But aren't there times, I press her, when she wonders why she's putting herself through this, when she thinks of other things she could be doing—times she feels repulsed?

"I would have thought so," she says, "but the worse it got, somehow the more I felt attracted. After all the surgeries, the bodies look like battlefields. You feel the loneliness of that person whose skin is falling off, who has tubes coming in and out of everywhere. And still, behind this war-torn shell, you feel the incredible strength of humanity. It may sound strange or corny, but there's nothing more heavenly than connecting with that."

Alicia's no sentimental pushover. She describes one of her charges who was "frankly an asshole, and the fact that he was dying hardly softened that one bit. He ticked me off something terrible." But she's learned to do something when she feels cornered: to "clear away evaluation and just rest someplace that doesn't have all those opinionated *voices* in it. When you do that, out comes this love that melts people—not melts who they are but who they *aren't*. Finding that is just like finding yourself. It makes you feel great." She laughs. "I swear, it's a totally *selfish* thing."

While we've been talking, the phone has been ringing—and ringing. Somebody wants something. Alicia gets up to answer. "If we can't help each other, what's the point?" she says. "Everything else gets kinda old after a while."

I'm not trying to sell you on Alicia and Paul as Mother Teresa and Mahatma Gandhi. They've had rough patches like any couple; they're spiritually unfancy folk. They enjoy their bounty with a contagious joie de vivre. You could quibble that, sure, it's easy to open your heart in the lap of luxury; but I've met insanely wealthy people who are more miserable than Midas.

Besides which, I know another family that's just like Alicia and Paul's except they're living a gritty existence barely above the poverty line. If 90 percent of life is showing up, they go the other 20. Their door is always open, even though the weathered porch is sagging. There's always a pot of chili on the stove. Their small living room feels crowded with conviviality. You can stay a few nights on the fraying couch if cat dander and dog hair don't bother you too much. They take care of jobs and kids and ailing grandparents and friends' troubles and community causes, and when I ask them how they do it, they say, "Do what?"

Folks like these have basically eliminated any option of pretending that I don't know what we can be for each other. I know I could stand to be kinder, more generous, fiercer in cleaving to the good, true, and beautiful. I've been pondering something Saint John of the Cross wrote: "Where you find no love, put love, and you will find love." It could be worth a shot.

ROOTS, BRANCHES, AND
THE CLEAR BLUE SKY

*Therefore I say, grant reason to any animal with social and
sexual instincts, and yet with passion, he must have conscience.*

—Charles Darwin

S OMETIMES WHEN THE WORLD SEEMS A LOVELORN PLACE,
I contemplate a snapshot over my desk of two bonobo apes
hugging and kissing with lush abandon, and I perk right up. I'm
inspired by these fellow primates whose social life is, in the words
of one zoologist, "ruled by compassion." They are, I like to think,
a reminder not only of where we come from but of what sort of
creature we are at heart.

It isn't the usual picture of our evolutionary heritage. The official family portrait that science hangs over the mantelpiece depicts
us as brainy, aggression-prone apes driven by selfish instincts and
constrained (at best) by a thin thread of culture. It's only lately that
some scientists are stressing the more benign traits we share with
higher primates: conciliation, nurturance, our flair for alliance—
and especially empathy. More than superior smarts and a talent
for predation, it may be our ability to sense what others are feeling

that has put us on evolution's fast track—and will be the saving grace that keeps our stock rolling.

Charles Darwin himself, great chronicler of the "struggle for existence," found in animals the ancient taproot of our goodness. In their instinct for "mutual aid," he saw the moral lineaments of human society. His writings are filled with admiring accounts of animal reciprocity, cooperation, and even *love*—a word, shunned by most evolutionary biologists, that appears some ninety-five times in the *Descent of Man* (against only two entries for *survival of the fittest*). Darwin beheld in even the humblest mammal the origins of the Golden Rule: Their "strong sexual, parental, and social instincts," he suggested, "give rise to 'do unto others as yourself' and 'love thy neighbor as thyself.'" Our ancestral line, contrary to its selfish-gene reputation, has given us a startling capacity to care deeply about what happens to each other.

To understand the mysteries of our makeup, science has looked to the creatures closest to the original prototype. On that branch of the tree upon which we perch, there's nobody here but us anthropoids—you and me, gorillas and orangutans, chimps and bonobos—aka the great apes.

The family resemblance has always been unmistakable, but genomics has confirmed the patrimony: We're not just similar to chimps—we share with them a downright cousinish 99.4 percent of our DNA. A 2003 report to the National Academy of Sciences, issued some 130 years after the publication of the *Descent of Man,* argued that because we are "only slightly remodeled chimpanzee-like apes," we should expand *Le Club Humaine* to include some more low-brow members.

If that happened—and taxonomically it just might—it would be a big boost for animal advocates who regard apes as cognizant, feeling beings who deserve some designation of personhood ("extending the circle of compassion," as Jane Goodall puts it, "to our closest living relatives").

Others find the genomic hoopla overblown. "A banana's got 30 percent of human DNA," huffed one biologist, "but I find it hard to believe a banana is 30 percent as conscious as I am." Others still—and not just fundamentalists slapping *Evolution's Just a Theory* stickers on Alabama schoolbooks—find the kinship unsettling, seeing in chimps' proclivity for mayhem a dim omen for the human prospect.

The world has always been divided between those who believe we're basically kind and those who say we're basically cutthroat. Is compassion a fundamental human instinct, or does it depend on putting a lid on our inner chimp? I decided I'd best go to the source on that one.

*T*HE GEORGIA WOODS, MAJESTIC AND MIASMIC, SUGGEST THE primeval forest of our origins. The racket emanating from the white and ochre Quonsets clumped in its midst only adds to the impression. Faint hoots, shrieks, grunts, and an occasional piercing scream punctuate the humid air as I near the barbed-wire-topped enclosure of the Yerkes National Primate Research Center.

I'm met by Frans de Waal, a lanky, quizzical zoologist in blue jeans and wire rims who directs the center's Living Links program. In books like *Chimpanzee Politics* and *Our Inner Ape,* de Waal has taken a witty and penetrating look at the evolutionary bases of human behavior, from the loftiest altruism to the most lowdown maneuvering. De Waal has found in chimps, who peeled off from our shared common ancestor a few million years ago, clues to the interplay between selfishness and kindliness that keeps our own species scratching its head.

We clamber up to his mission control center, a makeshift-looking yellow tower with a bird's-eye view of the chimp colony.

The creatures below, formally known as *Pan troglodytes,* go about their daily business amid spare furnishings done in Late Neoprimate: a few plastic barrels to climb and perch on, some big rubber tires for swinging, and a freestanding 8-foot wall for privacy (especially for secret trysts between subordinate males and wandering prize females).

At first it seems like not much is really happening, but it's only my naive eye. De Waal, as attuned to the chimp social whirl as a gossip columnist for the *Troglodyte Times,* knows all, sees all, reporting every interaction in a complex code of numbers and letters on his PalmPilot. He points out some females off in one corner, picking through each other's fur, as essential a chimp social grace as a kaffeeklatsch. "And look, over there," he says, gesturing at two roistering juveniles. "They're laughing." Sure enough, their wide-open mouths, upturned lips, and soft chuckling as they tickle and tumble are so recognizable it would be impossible to call it anything else.

I've never been so close before to large primates without a distracting contingent of screaming kids and parents clasping melting Mr. Frostees. When a female chimp climbs up on a barrel for a better look at me, it's just the two of us. Receiving the full attention of an intelligent nonhuman is an unanticipated shock to the system, a thrill along the nerves. No casual passerby on a city street would regard me with such frank and unwavering curiosity. De Waal says that chimp empathy is more an expression of instinct than intellect ("Chim*pun*zees," he says with a trace of his native Dutch accent, "don't *neet* to have an *idee*"), but I imagine I see wheels turning behind those brown eyes, a cogitation however rudimentary.

Suddenly, she scampers down with a *waaa!* as the alpha male makes a stagey entrance, his fur bristling as if charged by a static field. Sheer charisma's not enough: He's set one of the orange canisters on its side and rolls it before him like an engine of war, pounding it loudly. It has the desired effect of shock and awe.

"Can you hear? They're all making submissive sounds," de Waal says, and indeed there's a din of high-pitched hooting reminiscent of Cheetah in the old Tarzan movies, followed by subservient "pant-grunts": *yesboss, yesboss, yesboss.*

Boisterous just doesn't describe this guy ("Björn," says de Waal helpfully). Every gesture is outsized and histrionic; he's part panjandrum, part Tasmanian devil. He galumphs through the enclave, noising off, seizing the topmost perch (an alpha must be His Highness), filling every inch of social space with his Songs of Myself while his subjects howl his praise. He rolls his juggernaut through the compound at speed, beating it as rhythmically as a tom-tom. *Thump-thump, thump! Thump-de-thump, thump, thump!*

"Maybe says something about the origins of drumming," de Waal suggests mildly. He clues me in to an ongoing struggle for dominance between Björn and the number two male, Socrates (aka Socko), each courting the allegiance of a third male, whose loyalty's up for grabs. Socko, cunning and ever politic, grooms Björn, occasionally ducking his head—the ape equivalent of genuflecting to kiss the ring—even as he covets the throne. If Björn were overthrown by some act of *lèse majesté,* Socko would grab the same reins of rank, declaring himself Supreme Orange Plastic Barrel Roller and incumbent Dearest Breeder. It's a bit depressing and all too human to contemplate. These guys are as likely to live in egalitarian, compassionate harmony as to randomly type out *The Tempest* (or, more to the point, *Richard III*).

While Jane Goodall has emphasized chimps' more charming side, other researchers have stressed their talent for deceit (especially sexual sneakiness), violence (up to serial killing), theft, battery, infanticide, cannibalism, and intergroup warfare. But chimps also exhibit what we think of as human virtues: aid to the weak, sharing of resources, and social rules that reward good citizens with extra grooming and punish bad guys with ostracism. De Waal has eloquently described how the toughest rivals will reconcile after a fight, stretching out their hands to each other, smiling, kissing, and hugging; or how a bystander to a battle will sling a comforting arm around the shoulder of a victim (he calls this "consolation behavior")—all suggesting that empathy is a 30-million-year-old habit unbroken since the hominoid dawn-time.

*B*UT IF THERE ARE GANDHIS AMBLING AROUND THE PRIMATE world, they'd turn up among the bonobos. Regarded until the 1930s as "pygmy chimps," bonobos are now recognized as *Pan paniscus,* a species of strikingly different character. Robert Yerkes, the primate center's founder, had in the 1920s unwittingly kept among his chimp population a bonobo he'd dubbed Prince Chim, whose gentle, thoughtful temperament so enraptured Yerkes that he hailed him as an "intellectual genius." (While the colony's chimps tended to shred books for amusement, Prince Chim would sit delicately paging through one as if trying to understand what humans saw in it.)

Many decades later de Waal, dubbing bonobos "the forgotten ape," meticulously chronicled not only their high intelligence but their conciliatory customs. His own disposition is so amiable, his speech so measured and considered, it's easy to forget what a relentless infighter he's been for his theories. He tells me he has made his largely male colleagues deeply uncomfortable by pointing out that this decidedly nonmacho species can claim just as much kinship to us as the chest-beating chimps. But unlike the bellicose trogs, when bonobos meet a potential rival group it's less like a battle than a tea party (often a rather erotic one, a simian

Déjeuner sur l'herbe), As the bonobo males hang back standoff-
ishly, females will approach the opposing tribe's bravos to do the
peacemaking—usually some variant of sleeping with the enemy.*
Conflicts inside bonobo groups often end through the efforts of
females, who will interpose themselves between rivalrous males
like so many United Nations blue helmets.

De Waal says he feels a little responsible for "bonobos being
idealized as peacenik hippies next to the bad-guy chimps." But
he expresses more regret that the bonobo wasn't studied earlier
for clues to the origins of human behavior. If bonobos instead
of chimps had been taken as the prehuman model, the killer-
ape crowd would never have gotten such traction. The scientific
premises about our primate inheritance—and hence our modern
assumptions about our basic nature—might have stressed equality
of the sexes, familial bonds, and peacemaking rather than male
dominance hierarchies and naked aggression.

Primatologists are finding in the bonobos evidence that it is
not tooth-and-nail competition but conciliation, cuddling, and
cooperation that may be the central organizing principle of human
evolution. "Survival of the kindest," de Waal calls it. "Could it be,"
he wonders, "that the bonobo is cognitively specialized to read
emotions and to take the point of view of others? In short, is the
bonobo the most empathic ape?"

---

*To say nothing of sleeping with their friends: Bonobos of both genders are,
in a word, rather sweetly slutty. They'll do it solo or in an erotically contorted,
polymorphous cluster. (The original swingers, they've been observed in fla-
grante delicto while hanging from a branch.) Unlike all other primates except
you-know-who, they French kiss with osculating abandon and have sex face-to-
face. Much of it isn't exactly sex as we understand it, though, but quick, erotically
tinged assurances of affiliation, affection, and conciliation—what one scientist
calls "full-body hugging." De Waal has a standard shibboleth: "The chimpanzee
resolves sexual issues with power, and the bonobos resolve power issues with sex."

It is a heretical position, not only in singling out bonobos for such a distinction but for attributing empathy to an animal in the first place. Empathy has often been considered a uniquely human capacity, requiring a human level of intellect. Thomas H. Huxley, known as "Darwin's Bulldog" for his ferocious early championing of natural selection ("ruthless self-assertion," he wrote, by which "the strongest...tread down the weaker"), maintained that our ability to feel compassion and to act for the benefit of others depended on the unique power of human rationality for "curbing the instincts of savagery."

But clearly not all animal instincts are savage; many are rather tender. Should we assume we're so much more empathetic than, say, a bonobo just because we have more cognitive firepower? (Indeed we often behave as though we've *lost* touch with our innate kindness. Our very ability to govern our feelings enables us to overrule our natural sympathies.) At its most basic level, empathy is a form of largely mindless and nearly automatic resonance. Its likely origins can be found in the evolutionary biology of parenthood. The animal mother who proved most sensitive to the needs of her offspring was most likely to ensure their survival, a capacity marked in natural selection's double-plus column—and reinforced by strong emotion. A human mother's gut-level response to her baby's four-alarm cry is an experience likely shared by a cat anxious to get to her squeaking kittens or a father bird's rushing to stuff a fledgling's mouth.

Infant animals, from their side, survive by *evoking* empathy, signaling their vital needs with dependent, "adorable" helplessness to which parents are hardwired to succumb. Adults of many species mimic infantile behavior when they want to elicit sympathy from others. Even a formidable male chimp defeated in a dominance struggle will sit in the dust pouting, emitting the occasional sorrowing yelp, reaching out so pitiably that eventually another chimp can't bear it and comes to comfort him.

Signals of distress are powerful stimuli for the empathic response, suggestive of *compassion*'s primal meaning, "to suffer with." This can lead to animal behavior that appears startlingly simpatico. In a study conducted in 1964, a group of psychiatrists at Northwestern University trained rhesus monkeys to pull a chain to get a reward of their favored food. But when the same chain was rigged to deliver not only food but also a nasty shock to a monkey in an adjacent cage, the others soon refused to yank it. The desire to avoid seeing, hearing, and feeling the distress of a companion overrode the desire to eat. One particular rhesus went without food for twelve days rather than pull the chain.

In the early 1990s, Italian neuroscientists pinpointed a mechanism in the primate brain that might form the primitive basis for the empathic response. They discovered specialized neurons in macaque monkeys' premotor cortex (the brain area that plans and executes physical tasks) that had a unique property: These cells would fire not only when the animal performed a specific movement but also when it watched the *experimenter* perform the same action.

For example, if a monkey had previously plucked a raisin from a tray and then watched the experimenter's hand pick up a raisin, the same neuron would fire in its brain in both cases. These "mirror neurons," as they were quickly dubbed, seemed to act as an internal reflection of another creature's experience. Primates appear to have a brain mechanism dedicated to empathy's basic motto: I feel *you* in *me*.

Mirror neurons have now been found in the human brain, a largely unheralded discovery whose implications are sparking a quiet scientific revolution. "Mirror neurons will do for psychology what DNA did for biology," asserts neurobiologist Vilayanur S. Ramachandran, director of the University of California's Center for Brain and Cognition. "They will provide a unifying framework for a host of mental abilities that have hitherto remained mysterious."

One of these abilities is surely empathy. One study showed that the same cells that light up when a person's finger is jabbed with a pin also light up when someone *else's* finger is pricked. We've all experienced this effect. We wince when we see someone stub her toe and hop painfully on one foot. We've been there. A parent takes her child to the pediatrician for a vaccination, then involuntarily flinches when the needle jabs. She can't stand to see him hurt.

Mirror neurons, writes one scientist, "suggest that an archaic kind of sociality, one which does not distinguish between self and other, is woven into the primate brain." Just as our brain is said to have a primitive "grammar nugget" that enables us to acquire the hallowed complexities of language, perhaps we have a "Golden Rule nugget" containing the neurological ground rules for compassion itself. Mirror neurons may help produce the most primitive form of empathic response, which researchers call "emotional contagion." You've heard it loud and clear if you've ever gone to a G-rated matinee. Someone's child starts to cry, and all toddlers within siren range promptly join in the wailing. It's not that they consciously worry about the other child. The other kid's distress simply triggers a similar distress in them, just as we burst out laughing when others laugh, or one person's fear can flare suddenly through a crowd.

Is emotional contagion the reason that animals respond in ways that seem to be empathic? My friend's new puppy, sitting in her lap as we chat one afternoon, suddenly gives her a hard nip. "Ow!" she yells, raising her finger sternly. "No!" The dog jerks his

head back for a minute in surprise, then lunges at her again with
his sharp baby teeth, clearly having a great time.

"Watch this," she tells me. "Something they taught us in dog-
training class."

She mimes crying. *"Boo-hoo,"* she weeps softly, piteously, putting her hands over her eyes and peeking out from between her
fingers. *"Boo-hoo-hoo."* I am incredulous when the dog instantly
stops biting, looks quizzically into her eyes, then clambers toward
her face to lick it, whining in what sounds like sympathy and performing what certainly looks like an attempt to comfort her. What
is puppy love?

Whatever it is, it may not be so far from ape empathy. In
The Ape and the Sushi Master, Frans de Waal tells the story of a
researcher in early-twentieth-century Moscow who raised a mis-
chievous chimp named Yoni, whom she could never lure from the
roof with any system of rewards, even his favorite foods. Finally
she hit on a foolproof technique:

> If I pretend to be crying, close my eyes and weep, Yoni immediately
> stops his play or any other activities, quickly runs over to me...from
> where I could not drive him down despite my persistent calls and
> entreaties. He hastily runs around me, as if looking for the offender;
> looking at my face, he tenderly takes my chin in his palm, lightly
> touches my face with this finger...

In this account the chimp does not respond to her distress signal only by becoming distressed himself but by acting to protect
and comfort her. Though it could be argued that this too is simply
a way to remove an aversive stimulus, it does look suspiciously
close to actual empathy, compassion's cornerstone.

Thomas Aquinas could have been describing the empathic
instincts of, say, a rhesus when he wrote: "From the very fact that
a person takes pity on anyone, it follows that another's distress

grieves him…" But he added a critical coda: "One grieves or sorrows for another's distress, in so far as one looks upon another's distress as one's own…*because it makes them realize the same may happen to themselves* [emphasis added]." Here empathy jumps the track to include cognition—an ability to mentally walk a mile in someone else's moccasins.

Moral theorists from Aristotle onward have argued that this is why compassion is a singularly human characteristic. Alone among creatures, our exceptionally large, complex brains give us the logical skills for moral reasoning and the imagination to place ourselves in another's circumstances (psychologists call this "perspective-taking" or "cognitive empathy"). We are moved to care about others because we can put ourselves in their predicament.

Researcher Carolyn Zahn-Waxler, a psychologist at the National Institute of Mental Health, has identified the first stirrings of true empathic behavior in children between one and two years old. Here, for example, is how a twenty-one-month-old child responded when his mother pretended to be sad: peering into her face to determine what was wrong; looking concerned; giving her a hug while making "consoling sounds." Intriguingly, in some of the sessions that took place in peoples' homes, Zahn-Waxler also found that the family dog responded as quickly and effusively as the child to the "distressed" parent, whining and licking and looking distressed. So what, if anything, was the difference between the dog's response and the child's?

Zahn-Waxler thinks a child at this age begins to realize that others are similar to *but distinct from* himself. At that momentous juncture, she writes, "indiscriminate emotional contagion is superseded by cognitive empathy, a willed and knowing stepping into the role of the other." Now the heart's blind, automatic response (that "archaic sociality which does not distinguish between self and other") is augmented by the insight that, in the words of philosopher Paul Ricoeur, "the other is also a self."* Mother is not just an extension of me. A two-year-old may ask an upset parent, "What's wrong, Mommy? Why are you crying? Can I help?" True, he may try to soothe away the upset because it is disturbing *him,* but now he will also try to *understand.* It is the beginning of moral reasoning—the capability to see past oneself and into the heart of another.

The word *empathy* is a translation of the German *Einfuhlung,* a term coined in 1903 by a student of aesthetics named Theodore Lipps. He was searching for a way to express the strangely intimate emotional connection that arises between a viewer and an onstage performer. He used the example of watching an acrobat stepping across a high wire, that moment of breathless suspension when audience members gasp as if they themselves were teetering on a tightrope, the sense of, as Lipps described it, "I feel myself inside of him."

Lipps defined empathy as an "inner participation...in foreign experiences." Cognitive scientists refer to this ability to read another's feelings, thoughts, or intentions as a "theory of mind" (or just by the shorthand "mind-reading"). When a friend tells us her sister has fallen seriously ill, we feel heart-stricken. We can imagine the anxiety she must feel in the pit of our own stomach; we can sense her helplessness at being unable to take a loved one's pain away. When she announces her sister has recovered, we rejoice with her at the news. It is generally held that animals,

---

*Interestingly, the only creatures capable of so-called cognitive empathy seem to be those that are also able to recognize their own image in the mirror: humans, dolphins, elephants, and the great apes. (Bonobos will even drape themselves in banana-leaf shawls and strut back and forth, preening. A macaque monkey, however, will attack its own image as if it were a rival.) Does it take a "self" to fully imagine an "other"?

even higher primates, cannot feel such "true" empathy, let alone compassion, because they are unable to *think* themselves into another's situation.

*W*HAT, THEN, ARE WE TO MAKE OF KANZI THE BONOBO? Raised from infancy by psychobiologist Sue Savage-Rumbaugh, who literally co-parented him with an adoptive bonobo mother, he has shown what might be interpreted as cognitive empathy. Once, for example, attempting to open a jar of cherries by throwing it on the ground, Kanzi accidentally bounced the jar off the leg of his keeper, who screamed in pain and grabbed her knee. Kanzi, seeming to assume that she had hurt her hand, grasped her palm and gently turned it over, inspecting the skin. Noticing an old scar, he moved her hand in the direction of a water canteen. When the woman verbally asked what he wanted (Kanzi has shown a remarkable level of language comprehension), he pointed to the canteen and then to her old injury, as if urging her to douse her hand with water. As she did so, Kanzi tried to wash her wound.

Can an ape get inside your head? It could be argued that Kanzi didn't have a full-blown understanding of his keeper's needs: Cooling water was what *he* would have wanted if *he'd* had a painful scrape. (Apes have been observed cleaning wounds in the wild with water, though usually with their own saliva.) But his behavior seemed consistent with a central human moral tenet: *Do unto others as you would have them do unto you.* He was at least standing on the threshold of "perspective-taking"—the ability to see the world through another's eyes, a hallmark of human compassion.

Kanzi is thought by some to be standing at humanity's very doorstep. When Darwin, speaking of the dawning of the human moral sense, proclaimed, "We also differ from the lower animals in the power of expressing our desires by words, which thus become a guide to the aid required and bestowed," he hadn't reckoned with an ape who seems not only to have the rudiments of morality but also speech—albeit an artificial visual language known as Yerkish. Kanzi began learning Yerkish's hundreds of abstract colored symbols (called lexigrams) when he was a baby clambering around his mother during researchers' fruitless attempts to teach her. Shocked scientists soon realized that Kanzi was acquiring language exactly in the way a human infant does, simply by being exposed to it. The bonobo brain, they've since concluded, has an innate, downright freaky capacity for language.

Kanzi (Swahili for "buried treasure") has been adjudged in tests to have the linguistic competence of a human child. He is bilingual (trilingual, if you count Ape). He understands two thousand to three thousand English words. He has even jammed on keyboards with rock legend Peter Gabriel. Here, I thought, is an ape worth talking to: I needed some questions answered.

After several months of negotiation ("Barbara *Walters* asked, and we said no," an official informed me), my interview request was unexpectedly granted. I was instructed to take a certain highway to the far outskirts of Atlanta, turn off at an anonymous black mailbox, and drive through a series of electrically controlled gates.

My host, a resident cognitive scientist named Bill Fields, pulls up to meet me in one of the little jeeps they use to tool around the 50 wooded acres of the Language Research Center. We head straight to the language room, where Fields shows me a panel of hundreds of 1-inch squares embossed with colored symbols. When he presses one lexigram symbol and then another, the images flash on a nearby plasma screen and Fields's own recorded voice booms out in a cheerful southern drawl, "Me!...Want!...More!...Grapes!"

Some of the Yerkish symbols are relatively straightforward. "Grapes" is a red *G* with stylized bunches hanging from it; the outline of a house stands for a log cabin on the property. But overall the chart looks like a frieze of abstract geometry.

The sign for "Squirrel," for example, is a purple circle with an X and a squiggle. "Visitor" is a triangle topped with a round circle. A few images stand for purely abstract concepts: "Yesterday" is a shadowed white moon over a dark pyramid, and other equally recondite symbols mean "Now" or "Later" (bonobos apparently have a sense of past, present, and future). It's taken research assistants as long as a year to attain the measure of Yerkish fluency that for some bonobos is now second nature.

Fields lets a few of Kanzi's relations into the lab and plants me by a Plexiglas window to observe. Bonobos' appearance is often described as "gracile": long legs, narrow shoulders, high foreheads. Unlike the beetle-browed chimps with their alternately adorable, ribald, or saturnine look, bonobo features seem, well...*sincere*. Each has a mat of black hair with a natural part running neatly down the middle, like some lost tribe of Borscht Belt comedians. They spend a surprising amount of time walking upright, arms swinging at their sides in a gait that eerily resembles computer animations of the skeleton of Lucy, our 3.5-million-year-old *Australopithecus* ancestor.

Watching them, I immediately sense how like us these creatures are. The young ones begin showing off for the stranger. One juvenile puts a black plastic garbage bag over his head and scuttles about comically. Then he drapes it over himself like a cloak, climbs up the mesh of his cage, and jumps down, looking for all the world like a kid playing Batman. A bonobo baby named Nyota peers up at me and executes a few perfect little standing backflips, then clambers up to a ledge and sits in a fair imitation of Rodin's statue *The Thinker,* one hand parked pensively under his chin (and the other absently grasping his crotch).

I watch as Kanzi's grown-up sister, Panbanisha, swipes a brush through her hair, then runs it down her fur (there seems to be a difference—at least to her). She ambles over to her attendant, Liz, a strong-looking woman with a stoic, forbearing expression, then pulls off the young woman's sneakers and begins gently scraping under her toenails with a tiny stick, as intent as any manicurist. Any doubt that hair salons and nail parlor franchises are attributable to primate grooming instincts vanishes.

Panbanisha glances at me occasionally, poking a few desultory lexigrams on her electronic panel. I'm hoping she'll say "Do Unto Others" or maybe just "Two Legs Good, Four Legs Bad," but she seems to regard me as room service, requesting repeatedly that I bring her more grapes and peanuts and her favorite, lemon ice.

Unlike de Waal's Chimpville, I can see that the Land of Bonobia is more of a let's-all-hang-out-together place. It seems as much interspecies commune as animal research colony. Fields walks in, effusive with praise. "Panbanisha, you are so beautiful!" he exclaims, though I see only a large hairy creature with sagging dugs and a genital swelling. She grins from ear to ear. Her son, catching her mood, does a little capering dance.

"Each bonobo shares the feeling of the group," Fields tells me. "Bonobos are happy only when *everybody's* happy." He describes an orangutan named Mari who had lost her arms and preferred to spend most of her time outdoors. "All the bonobos would refuse to eat a bite until we put Mari's meal together and served it to her out there. Then Panbanisha would insist we bring a blanket out to Mari at night."

Fields thinks we can learn a thing or two about social mores from the bonobos. "They always want conflict resolved—immediately, if possible," he notes. Studying bonobo conciliation—the "biology of forgiveness in nonhuman primates," as he puts it—

might yield clues about "why we desire to forgive or be forgiven, and how to encourage it." The bonobos' remarkably sensitive responses to one another—what Fields terms "empathic elaboration"—could answer fundamental questions, he says, about "the universality of empathy: How much is innate, how much determined by cultural filters?"

When I ask him if the apes might be learning empathy from being around people, he responds, "I learn it from them." All the time spent among them has made him an interspecies egalitarian. When I mention a bonobo has just bared its fangs at me, he's mildly put out. "Fangs? They're incisors," he snorts. "*Fangs?* Then *we* have fangs, too!"

Finally, Fields takes me to meet Kanzi in his outdoor cage. I stand a few feet away, while the two of them communicate using a portable Yerkish chart—making introductions, says Fields, who supplements his own symbol-pointing with inaudible words. It's a private conversation: Fields whispers; Kanzi cocks his ear carefully. Fields whispers again; Kanzi casually taps some lexigrams. Fields explains that Kanzi wants me to sit on a stool, that he's not comfortable having me stand over him—a matter of ape etiquette.

I sit, taking note of Kanzi's hirsute arms, thick as fenceposts, with their massive, arboreal triceps. Bonobos are astoundingly strong, and though this is a peaceable kingdom, they can occasionally be aggressive.* Fields has only half a middle finger on one

---

*Frans de Waal notes, "All animals are competitive...There would obviously be no need for peacemaking if they lived in perfect harmony." He acknowledges that bonobos sometimes catch and eat prey, but he points out this is feeding, not aggression. He cites a 2007 experiment in which apes were presented with a platform from which they could obtain food if they worked together to pull it closer. "The presence of food," writes de Waal, "normally induces rivalry [in chimps], but the bonobos engaged in sexual contact, played together, and happily shared the food side by side. The chimpanzees, in contrast, were unable to overcome their competition long enough to obtain the treat."

hand—the outcome, he explains vaguely, of a rare Pan Homo dis-
pute. But as I hang out with the famously literate ape, I'm struck by
a clear unscientific impression: Kanzi has good vibes.

Kanzi points to a few more symbols, shooting me an impenetrable glance. Fields tells me that Kanzi has indicated he wants to
watch Fields and me "Chase."

"He wants to see who's dominant," Fields says. "He wants me
to jump on you and play-bite you, to chase and tickle. But it's too
hot and buggy for *that*." I feign a look of bitter disappointment.

Later, Fields and I sit in his cramped office, which is lined
from floor to ceiling with tapes and CDs of thousands of hours
of bonobo observation, a fraction of twenty-five years of data collection. Fields enumerates some of Kanzi's other cognitive feats.
With a little training, Kanzi has proven nearly as adept as our early
ancestors at toolmaking. He can knap stone "knives" by knock-
ing two rocks together, choosing the sharpest flake by testing the
edge with his tongue and lips, then using the crude blade to saw
through a piece of tough hide covering a box of goodies. Fields
shows me some footage on his laptop. Sure enough, there's Kanzi,
flaking one of his flint shivs. Then Fields fast-forwards to show me
footage of another ape named P-Suke, who was "wild caught" and
never taught language.

"Now watch," Fields says. The same rocks are placed in P-Suke's
hands. He lets them fall from his grasp. The ape's hands are then
manually guided to knock the stones together. He stares down,
blank and uncomprehending, letting them roll from his fingers.
And so it goes. P-Suke just holds the two rocks and does nothing.
It's dark at the head of the stairs: He hasn't got a clue. No amount of
coaxing or training makes the light go on. For five *years* they have
been trying to teach P-Suke to do what Kanzi managed to learn in
a matter of hours.

"Why is that?" I ask Fields, baffled. He silently reaches over, takes a pen from his desk, lifts it in the air, and plops it on top of a notebook. Then he glances at me. I realize I'm supposed to understand, but I feel a bit like P-Suke: The point eludes me.

"How is tool manipulation different from the manipulation of symbols in language?" Fields asks rhetorically. "The answer is *not much*. Language, culture, and tools are like the Father, the Son, and the Holy Ghost: They're aspects of the same thing."

Suddenly a realization dawns, and it feels a little stunning. Kanzi, due to his facility with one system of symbols—language—can catch on to the skill and perhaps even the *concept* of toolmaking that characterized early man. Kanzi has acquired a different *mind* than P-Suke, a symbol-using mind; and that has brought him a new way of—for want of a more cautious term—thinking about the world.

Kanzi was just a regular Joe Bonobo until he was handed (or seized for himself) the tools of symbolic thinking. "The primate brain is the hardware. Culture is the operating system," Fields says. "I can run a simple system on my computer hardware, like DOS 1.0, or I can run Windows, or I can run Linux. Kanzi's operating system has become different from P-Suke's; Kanzi's brain can now run the genera of culture."

*F*IELDS'S APPROACH IS, IT'S SAFE TO SAY, UNCONVENTIONAL. His take on the bonobo world is that of an ethnographer, he says, a student of culture; and the notion that animals can have culture has been one of anthropology's great divides. Animals are said to have only "species-specific behaviors"—instinctual, genetically fixed, nearly as preprogrammed as robots. Sure, chimps can be trained to mimic culture—to dress in street clothes or grimace in mock garrulity on the Chimp Channel. But to say that apes are affected by culture beyond minor ways observed in the wild—differences in the way one group uses a twig to filch red ants, say, or slight variations in handclasps during grooming—remains somewhat heretical.*

Unlike de Waal, Jane Goodall, Dian Fossey, Biruté Galdikas, and other primate researchers who observe apes' "natural" behavior, the scientists at the Language Research Center have shifted their focus from what an ape brain does to what an ape brain *can* do. Fields describes the center as a "Pan-Homo Culture" where two types of primates with large vocabularies and the capacity for symbolic thought can share an uncommon meeting ground.

"When it comes to big-brained primates," Fields tells me, harping on a favored theme, "whether us or them, there almost *is* no species-specific behavior. A large, complex brain is not much restrained by the genome. What feedback from the envi-

---

*This truism is changing. In 2004 a landmark paper chronicled the social modification of what are usually considered hardwired traits among baboons. Dominant male baboons are normally highly aggressive, harassing and attacking females and low-ranking males to climb the social ladder. But one troupe of baboons in Kenya suffered a unique catastrophe: Its most aggressive males—dominant alphas who had, with typical belligerence, claimed the exclusive right to forage in a nearby garbage dump—had eaten some discarded meat tainted with bovine tuberculosis and promptly died. The remaining group members, consisting of subordinate males who'd lost out on the brawls over garbage goodies, together with all the females and their children, had undergone, in the words of *New York Times* science journalist Natalie Angier, "a cultural swing toward pacifism, a relaxing of the usually parlous baboon hierarchy, and a willingness to use affection and mutual grooming rather than threats, swipes and bites..." This shift toward distinctly more bonobian-sounding social relations has now persisted for two decades, even though the original kinder-and-gentler male survivors have either died or drifted away. New males who join the group seem to absorb the unusual norms. One scientist expressed amazement that it was not merely a change in a rote behavior—in, say, a way of cracking nuts—that was being transmitted, but "an attitude...the social ethos of the group." The implications for human culture can scarcely be overstated. "If baboons can do it," as Frans de Waal put it, "why not us?"

ronment—from culture—can do to the neurological substrates is almost limitless."

He's conjuring a radical view of evolution, of the remarkable potential of primate brains to, in effect, shape themselves. I feel a surge of hope; I also get the willies. I think of us at *our* evolutionary juncture, trying not to fall behind our own learning curve, looking for the sweet spot between smart and heart, extending our right hand to each other with the left still at each other's throats. That our collective push-me-pull-you sorely needs to evolve toward a better game is a no-brainer.

On the way home, I can't help seeing the world in Primate-Vision. The airport is a captive colony, perfect for observing hominoid behavior. There's a pair-bonded couple keeping a tolerant, protective eye on their playful juveniles. In front of me, in a long, slow line, is an irritable middle-aged alpha. When his mate says, "Put the ticket in your jacket pocket, Sid," the old silverback rears up and growls loudly, "It *is* in my jacket pocket. You *saw* me put it in. *Quit* your damn nagging!" The female hangs her head, speaks softly, soothingly, grooming some lint from his rumpled sports coat.

This effect lasts for weeks. It was hard not to think *display behavior* as I acted extra-gregarious at a party, impressing some and leaving others cold (*social hierarchy*); as I got into a political argument, pushing way too hard to win (*dominance conflict*), then apologizing (*conciliation*) for any boorishness; as I caught myself deferentially ducking my head (*submission, ugh!*) to someone I thought of as a better writer; as I provided a soft shoulder (*consolation*) to a friend with marital problems. My social finesse seemed disconcertingly undergirded with apely agendas. How many of my little daily transactions are tainted by trying to maximize rank, secure a better food supply, and maneuver for breeding privileges?

How many are out of pure human generosity, compassion, and sensitivity to others?

But in the weeks and the months that followed, I found myself most haunted by the memory of P-Suke—a by no means stupid, just typical *Pan paniscus* with an unstretched mind—and Kanzi, who through some culture-induced mental alchemy has become a sort of *Pan sapiens*. In what ways am I, are we all, like P-Suke, the stones of full cognizance just rolling from our grip? In what ways are we like Kanzi, tweaking our operating system to new levels of understanding? Kanzi is said to have more brain than he needs to succeed in his environmental niche. So do we—though I wonder if we have enough heart? When de Waal says that the bonobos' "greatest intellectual achievement is not tool use but sensitivity to others," I wish I could feel with full certainty that the same applies to us.

If our spiritual traditions are any clue, we have been trying since forever to reroute or suppress our aggressive circuits and reinforce our caring ones. We assume that our course of development runs from childhood to adulthood; but spiritual teachers have always claimed there is a superseding path, if we choose to take it, which leads to higher consciousness. What else is the extraordinary compassion of the saints but proof-of-concept that we can bootstrap our primate inheritance to its optimum capacity for kindness? That heritage has already endowed us with more compassionate traits than selfish ones: nurturance of family, emotional commitment to friends, sympathy, affection, a sense of fairness and empathy, forgiveness, maybe even altruism. Whether you believe your Maker to be the Good Lord or Darwin's Blind Watchmaker, they've been working from a similar schematic—one with built-in capacities for modification and much room for improvement.

It may sound silly to say, but my short time with the bonobos has made me more trusting of the instinctual foundations of my own unruly emotional life, has given me a certain confidence in our good nature. Sure, maybe the good stuff is alloyed with chimply cunning, and my impulses are more often fight-or-flight than unconditional love. But hey, I'm riding on a vintage primate chassis: I'm just glad to know that a responsive heart comes standard and preinstalled.

A famous chimp named Washoe, the first to use American Sign Language, once leaped over a dangerous high-voltage fence to pull a newly arrived chimp from the water, risking her life for an individual she'd known only a few hours. And chimps fear and *despise* water. Here, surely, are clues to the roots of compassion, if not—who knows?—its o'er-spreading branches, and the clear blue sky. Researcher Roger Fouts describes how Washoe, who had lost both her offspring as infants, reacted when a keeper told her that her own newborn had just died. Looking deep into the grieving woman's eyes, Washoe signed, "Cry," tracing on her own cheek the path a tear would take down a human's (chimps don't shed tears). Then Washoe signed, "Please Person Hug."

We've come so very far from Washoe in our astonishing, lonely odyssey of 2 million years. But our journey to realizing full humanity may have just begun. Meanwhile, if I had my druthers, I'd engrave *Please Person Hug* on the Great Seal, put the lexigram for "Grapes" in one eagle talon and "Chase-Tickle" in the other— just as an experiment, to see where we might go from there, just to see how far we could take it.

EMPATHY: YOU IN ME, ME IN YOU

See yourself in others
Then whom can you hurt?
What harm can you do?

—The Buddha

I ONCE SPENT A DAY SHADOWING THE DALAI LAMA. IT WAS ONE of his early visits to the United States, and I was covering him for the local paper, but that was just my alibi. I wanted to take his measure, to see for myself what this incarnation of Avalokiteśvara, the deity of compassion, was really like when the rubber sandals met the road.

He struck me as bright and curious—an exceptionally *nice* man—but a living Buddha? Yet as the day wore on, it crept up on me: His caring never seemed to waver. He emanated a steady warmth without gaps, moods, or slipups. I watched him meet with the mayor of Denver, a stogie-chomping old pol whose small talk inched dutifully over the official terrain of tourism and molybdenum mining. The Dalai Lama stood listening, duck-footed, hands folded, eyebrows cocked, his trademark smile hovering somewhere near delight. Hizzoner presented His Holiness with a picture book of the state's Rocky Mountain wonders, the sort you'd pick up at an airport gift shop. The Dalai Lama accepted happily, sitting down to leaf through it with what appeared to be genuine interest. When he came upon a color plate of a bighorn sheep, he told the mayor warmly, "We have this kind in *our* mountains, too!"

They chatted awhile, and before long the doughty old pol had cracked a smile, was heard to chortle; he *liked* this golden-skinned man in the maroon robes. He looked crestfallen when an aide whispered to him about a waiting appointment and a city to run.

As the Dalai Lama made his way from the reception area, a news cameraman leaned forward. "Your Holiness, can I ask you something?" he blurted, then lowered his voice. "About my wife…" The Dalai Lama halted in his tracks, his retinue bumping into one another like a vaudeville troupe. He inclined his head toward the other man's until they nearly touched, placed a hand on his shoulder, and spoke softly with him for a while. The cameraman's voice rose and fell in agitation, but I couldn't make out the words. As they talked, the Dalai Lama's face seemed to subtly mirror the man's expression, as if taking on a share of his burden. And slowly the man's own face softened, resolving into a look of gratitude.

And so it went, throughout the day and into the evening. Mayor or teamster, cabbie or king, each person received the same keen, heartfelt regard. The Dalai Lama seemed to enter intimately into each person's world while remaining firmly grounded in his own. His quality of empathy, at once indiscriminate and specific, began to overwhelm me, not least because he made it seem so ordinary—ordinary kindness, ordinary consideration, taken to an extraordinary degree.

The Dalai Lama has often claimed he is a simple person. Though some find this a little coy, on one level it rings true. Isn't our image of holiness just a placeholder for what we all might be if our best moments were multiplied to an *n*th degree of constancy? The religious icons of compassion reach out to us in an apotheosis of recognizably human caring. The Chinese goddess Kwan Yin weeps as she extends her thousand-armed embrace to those who need succor. The Hindu deity Hanuman, depicted as half-ape, half-god (sound familiar?), cleaves open his chest to reveal his naked, undefended heart. The sacred heart of Jesus, Son of Man, is pierced with thorns, bleeds real blood. Vulnerability, these images say, is holy. It is our capacity to be profoundly moved by each other that makes us whole.

*I*N ONE STUDY OF EMPATHY, A PSYCHOLOGIST POSED A QUESTION to a precocious eight-year-old named Adam: "If you knew how someone else felt, would you be more likely to help them than if you didn't?"

"Oh, yes," Adam answered. "What you do is, you forget everything else that's in your head, and then you make your mind into their mind. Then you know how they're feeling, so you know how to help them.

"Some kids can't do that," he added, "because they think everybody's always thinking the same things."

Adam describes the kind of empathy that advances through the gates of compassion. In its most basic form, though, empathy is just our biologically based propensity to get under each other's skin. When I perceive your mood, a neuronal circuit flashes on. Your sadness or happiness evokes a corresponding feeling in me before I'm quite aware that it's happened. Studies have shown that just seeing another person's expression triggers, below the threshold of consciousness, the same facial muscles in the observer, which in turn stimulates the same inner feeling. A 2003 UCLA study revealed that when one person *deliberately* imitated another's smile, the emotional centers in his own brain lit up with happiness.

We are designed to be emotionally entangled. If you live in a bustling city, this sort of resonance occurs a dozen times a day. You hear a child lost in a crowd of shoppers, crying for her mommy, and your heart instantly goes out to her (along with a half dozen other people who are already dashing toward her to help). When a laughing couple passes by, their arms around each other's waists, you feel a scintilla of their joy. When a heated argument erupts on the street corner, your own adrenaline fractionally redlines.

Responses may vary, of course. One person may stride by a beggar with stony contempt, while another, stricken, puts a dollar in his cup. Someone might look at that pair of lovers and feel envy, or sorrow over a joy long departed, or annoyance at the lovey-dovey giddiness. But these are afterthoughts to a primal identification that has already occurred, as viscerally and immediately as stepping on a tack. Somewhere below the threshold of awareness, the mirror neurons have already launched into their oddly nondual theme song, *you in me, me in you.*

Of course, simply catching someone else's emotion doesn't necessarily lead to *caring* about them. Mengzi, a Confucian philosopher of the fourth century B.C., told of a king who looked out from his balcony and saw a man leading a piteously bellowing ox to be sacrificed. "Let it go!" the king shouted down. "I cannot bear its frightened appearance, like an innocent going to the place of death!" The man responded by asking how, then, he was to perform the sacred ritual. The king ordered that a sheep be sacrificed in the ox's stead.

Mengzi pointed out that the king possessed compassion's prerequisite: a responsive heart. "Superior people," says Mengzi, "are affected toward animals, so that seeing them alive, they cannot bear to see them die." On the other hand, Mengzi cautioned, the king's deed was still only an "artifice of humaneness": He had saved the animal that was suffering in front of him only to condemn an unknown one in its stead. It could be argued that the king had just acted to avert an upsetting spectacle, not out of any general concern for animal welfare. The story's translator remarks that this sort of reactive empathy can be "fragile and a bit capricious.... Confucian self-development lies in how we treat this spontaneous feeling of compassion: We must extend it more and more broadly, and we must act on it consistently."

Mere sentiment without moral action can be a dead end. We may weep at a performance of *Les Misérables* but spurn the panhandler outside the theater. Or perhaps we do hand him some money (because his misery gives us a twinge), but it's more akin to putting a coin in an expiring parking meter. We want to avoid the aversive stimulus of a guilt ticket. (To act out of guilt can be better than doing nothing, of course—just ask the man who's been given coins enough for a meal; or, for that matter, ask the ox. Some research even links "guilt-proneness" to the ability to take another's perspective, the basis of the moral sense.)

But the prime example of perspective-taking, even of compassion itself, is often held to be the Golden Rule, regarded in all religions as a benchmark of moral development. Sometimes it is couched as a preventive: "Do not do to others," says the Hindu *Mahābhārata,* "what would cause pain if done to you." Counsels Confucius: "What I do not wish men to do to me, I also wish not to do to them." Other times it is prescriptive, as in Jesus' formulation: "Therefore all things whatsoever ye would that men should do to you, do ye even so to them." (Mohammed says substantially the same thing: "None of you [truly] believes until he wishes for his brother what he wishes for himself.")

The Golden Rule is an ethical stanchion, a virtual eleventh commandment. But what is it really saying? It does acknowledge that others are subjective beings, just as I am, placing us all under the same big tent. But the central tent pole is, well...*me.* I start with what *I* would want, assuming that another would want the same thing. George Bernard Shaw challenged this with a trenchant quip: "Do *not* do unto others as they should do unto you. Their tastes may not be the same." If we really think about it, the Golden Rule is less like putting ourselves in another's shoes than imagining our own head transplanted onto their shoulders. Don't get me wrong: I'd rate it as a moral triumph and ample reason to hang up my selfish-guy spurs if I could really live by it. But I can't help but feel that empathy contains yet greater mysteries (perhaps a Platinum Rule: Do unto others as *they* would like to be done unto).

One day, running down the narrow hallway of my brother's apartment playing "monster" with my three-year-old nephew, I banged my toe on a table leg and, in a perfect diamond cutter blow, knocked the nail clean off. I stood there gaping, a little stunned as blood welled from the empty space. I would have thought Nicholas would be scared or repulsed: Young children often cry to see someone in pain, and seek to be consoled. But he just bent over to peer at it more closely. "Does it hurt?" he asked, looking up at me with concern. "Want me to get a Band-Aid?"

His precocious response (so says his doting uncle) was an example of that other-directed empathy that goes beyond mere contagion or resonance. Studies have shown that it even has a different physiology: It is associated with a decreased heart rate, while contagious distress causes an increase. It may literally be a healthier response. The two states also have differing facial expressions and varying degrees of skin conductance. Unlike contagious distress, other-directed empathy shows "somatic quieting...which often accompanies an individual's focusing attention on the external environment"—suggesting that it is a form of attention that reaches out to another's plight rather than inward, to one's own reactions to it.

Being able to feel our way into another's soul, to sense what is going on behind his social mask, is the passkey to kindness. A friend gave me a quote a few months ago, a one-liner attributed to the Jewish sage Philo of Alexandria, that I haven't been able to get out of my head: "Be kind, for everyone you meet is fighting a great battle." I've found, with a little practice, I can at least get this far.

"Sorry about the wait," the cashier apologizes. It *has* been a long time. She's been moving like molasses; the line at her register creeps forward by millimeters. According to the unwritten laws of retail, I'm entitled to a small display of petulance. Instead, I try to take her point of view. She's been on her feet all day. She's harried and underpaid. The job is repetitive, and impatient customers treat her like an appliance.

"Hey, it's okay," I tell her, looking back at the line. "There's only one of you and ten of us; we've got you surrounded." She smiles, shooting me a relieved look, and I feel good to have made someone's day easier. I've been lately trying to do this, a compassion miniaturist, as much as I can. I'm amazed it works almost every time.

I wouldn't say it's just a cheap trick, but I know it's not a very costly one, especially when compared with what some refer to as "radical empathy." Adam Smith, godfather of capitalism, a man whose name is forever linked to narrow self-interest, might seem an unlikely source of insight into the nobler regions of the human heart, but he came up with one of the better working definitions I've seen of, as it were, the emotional mechanics of high-level empathy. In *The Theory of Moral Sentiments*, he observed that true compassion is based on "an imaginary change of situations":

> When I condole with you for the loss of your only son, in order to enter into your grief I do not consider what I, a person of such a character and profession, should suffer, if I had a son, and if that son was unfortunately to die: but I consider what I should suffer if I was really you, and I not only change circumstances with you, but I

change persons and characters. My grief, therefore, is entirely upon your account, and not in the least upon my own.

This swift jackknife dive into another's pool of experience— some theorists refer to it as "alterity"—is an imaginative leap. Your tragedy may remind me of one of my own and make me weep; or your happy occasion may call to mind my similar one. But it is only when I become utterly alert to you *on your own terms,* open fully to your experience, that you know you are being seen, heard, and felt. This sort of empathy is enigmatic; it almost teleports us into another person's frame of reference. Or perhaps it could be thought of as a form of bi-location: Centered in my own heart, I'm also, through some spiritual legerdemain, centered in yours.

The notion of a reversal of place lies deep within the DNA of all spiritual traditions. Ninth-century Buddhist sage Shantideva urged all who wished to follow the path of compassion to partake in "this sacred mystery: to take the place of others, giving them his own." The saints wash the feet of the sinners, knowing themselves to be no greater than the least. The apocryphal tale of the Danish king who, in response to Nazi orders that all Jews wear a yellow star, donned one himself is emblematic of many Danes who were moved to risk (and sometimes lose) their own lives for their persecuted countrymen. In a more homely example, former senator Bob Graham of Florida used to take what he called a "workday" once a month, performing an ordinary job like bagging groceries or showing up incognito as a flight attendant to serve passengers their meals. It was good political theater but also a method of feeling his way into his constituents' hearts, minds, and lives.

Still, it is one thing to feel *for* someone else; it is another to, in some sense, *become* them. Is it possible to take this exchange too far—merging with another at the expense of your own authentic selfhood, or even the possibility of genuine relationship? Martin

Buber refused to use the word *empathy* because he objected to any connotation that the self could—or should—become lost in the experience of another. "A *great* relation exists only between real persons," he wrote. "One must be truly able to say *I* in order to know the mystery of the *Thou* in its whole truth."

Psychologists are particularly nervous about any social bond that smudges the ego's boundaries. After all, how many unhealthy relationships are based on a person with a fragile ego over-identifying with his or her partner's needs? In the helping professions, which attract people capable of deep sympathies, there is an expression for sacrificing oneself on the altar of the client's needs: *overcaring*. Some clinicians view what they term "affective resonance," when one person's heartstrings twang too closely in tune with another's, as an outright pathology.

Writer Alfie Kohn sums up the prevailing guideline among psychologists as to when deep empathy is even practicable: "One must feel sufficiently unthreatened and free, psychologically speaking, to relax a vigilant watch over (and attachment to) the self and to risk adopting someone else's perspective." He adds, as an afterthought, that it may also require "a certain generosity of spirit." Just so. But isn't generosity of spirit the jumping-off point for a meaningful life, not just a cliff's edge of psychic peril?

It's an imprecise science, if a science at all. If a person's ego boundaries are too thick, he or she may appear callous, obtuse, tone-deaf to others' feelings. On the other hand, there are those whose antennae are so sensitive they can't help being receptive to everyone else's broadcast; they may lose their own signal in the din.

The insensitive are a common enough social archetype—those folks who know just who they are and exactly what they want, bulling their way through life's china shops with little concern for incidental breakage. They're as often as not valorized as self-assertive go-getters with robust self-esteem. It's the hyper-empathic who are viewed as weirder and, in a strange way, less trustworthy. It's not only that their sensitivity can cause them to be invaded by *our* feelings; with their boundary-transgressing acuity, they may also invade *us*.

It's not so surprising that the Empath has become a standard sci-fi character, though usually more a figure of pathos than threat. In a famous Ray Bradbury story, a Martian wanders into a human colony on the Red Planet. One of the last survivors of a superempathic race, he is a shape-shifter. For one grieving family, he becomes the spitting image of their lost son; for another, he is their dead daughter resurrected; for a lonely woman, he is her runaway husband, returned home at last. The Martian says he is "imprisoned" by others' thoughts, captured by their strongest needs. When he tries to leave, he is surrounded by a crowd of clamoring Earthlings whose selfish desires for unqualified empathy turn him finally into a chimera, "melting wax shaping to their minds...his face dissolving to each demand...his face all faces, one eye blue, the other golden..." The story speaks volumes about our cultural anxiety that we may lose our very selfhood by being too open to others.

In an early *Star Trek* episode titled, fittingly, "The Empath," the crew of the *Enterprise* visits a distant stellar research station and discovers a mute young woman who has an eerie power. When she touches a wound on Captain Kirk's forehead, it miraculously appears on *her* forehead and then quickly heals. "Her nervous system is so sensitive, so highly responsive," says the somber sawbones Dr. McCoy, "that she can actually feel our emotional and physical reactions. They become part of her."

Here the Empath is a healer, albeit at a price to herself. Some might call it a bad case of overcaring. But she is also like the traditional shaman, who purports to suck illness from another's body into her own to heal it. I've interviewed medical doctors—those who are not just good technicians but, in a way that's hard to quantify, genuine healers—who describe this sensation of taking another's suffering into themselves. "It does hurt," one told me, "but I can't explain it; it's a good hurt—a *giving* hurt."

The figure of the Empath, at once healer and freak, stirs unease in our autonomy-obsessed culture. We long for deep connection and unconditional caring, yet the contempt one hears for "bleeding hearts" reflects ambivalence, even outright prejudice, toward the highly empathetic. Their attunement makes *us* vulnerable to *them*. Besides, they must have a chink in their character armor as wide as a barn door.* We get an impression of mutability, of chameleons who take on the emotional shading of any person they stand next to.

The joke is on us, though: Researchers have documented what they have dubbed the Chameleon Effect in just about everybody. Whether we know it or not, we're all a little like Bradbury's Martian, unconsciously mimicking each other's inflections, facial expressions, and gestures. (Not surprisingly, those who do this most readily also rate highest on the empathy scale.) Most of us, for example, feel an urge to yawn upon seeing another person do so. Psychologists have found that people who are particularly susceptible to this "contagious yawning" are also significantly

---

*Empathy can be used to gain power over others, an ability that shows up even in apes. Two chimps named Austin and Sherman were once kept together at the University of Georgia's Language Research Center. Austin, the subordinate male, figured out that Sherman was afraid of the dark. Austin used this insight to manipulate him: "[Austin] would go outside and make unusual noises to frighten Sherman, then rush in, looking back outside as if someone was out there. Sherman would become fearful and allow himself to be comforted by Austin." Austin, in other words, was a bit of a con man. Con men too are notoriously empathetic, using their ability to see into you to mold themselves to your fondest expectation or to suss out your secret fear—and then use it to clean out your bank account.

better at drawing inferences about others' mental states—in other words, they are more empathic. (If reading this just made you yawn: *bingo!*)

Is acute empathy neurotic or healthy, the ultimate spirituality or excessive codependency? All through the day, the mirror neurons sound their siren song—*you in me, me in you*—but in a single, near-autonomic flicker, we overrule them. We can't afford to respond to everyone, gushing compassion like a hydrant without any shutoff valve of judgment. Each of us tends to strike our own balance—partly from upbringing, or conscious decision, or life experience, but also from differences in temperament. We are not all made the same. Our empathic style may have something to do with where we naturally fall on that sliding scale between head and heart—a scale that turns out to be very wide indeed.

I'VE JUST MET SOMEONE WHO IS *ALL* HEART. CASSIE* AND I have known each other for only ten minutes, and this elfin-looking eight-year-old has already taken my hand, gazed up at me with her widely spaced eyes, and exclaimed affectionately, "My *good* friend!" Her playmate Laurel, a dark-haired little girl dressed in purple and pink, is just the same, as outgoing and simpatico as can be. So is her friend Regina, as well as young Josh. They even *look* the same, with their narrow faces, broad foreheads, pointed chins, and quick, wide smiles.

"Like brothers and sisters," Cassie's mom marvels, and, as it turns out, these children *are* genetic relations in a sense: Each one is missing a few crucial genes on the seventh chromosome, producing the rare disorder known as Williams syndrome. It includes distinctive facial features (hence the misnomer "elfin-face syndrome"), short stature, learning disabilities, and a slew of health

---

*All names have been changed.

problems (especially in the heart's aorta). But despite typically mild retardation, Williams kids often show pronounced musical abilities, deft verbal facility, and an extraordinary level of empathy. Laurel has easily memorized songs sung in Gaelic and Arabic. She can play exquisite Indian flute, executing all the subtle flutters of timbre without knowing how to read a note. She's sociable, quick, voluble. When I say, "See you later, alligator," she chimes in without hesitation, "After a while, crocodile." Yet I'd seen her minutes before unable to distinguish her right hand from her left.

What intrigues researchers is how these kids, deficient in so many ways, routinely score much higher than their peers in social skills—not only in remembering names and faces but in their pronounced empathic responses. All the parents tell me their kids are unusually sensitive to others' pain. When I put on my eyeglasses and accidentally pinch my finger in the metal hinge, Cassie's face is flooded with concern. She seems drawn to my injury like an iron filing to a magnet. "Are you okay?" she asks with great sympathy as she peers at the red welt. "Does it hurt?" Her mother, a hospice nurse, tells me of the time Cassie met one of her patients, an elderly dying man who "looked really scary—emaciated, jaundiced, tubes coming out of his nose. Cassie went right up to him, gave him a big hug, put her head on his shoulder, and said, 'Grandpa!' They became instant best friends. She insisted on visiting him every day until he passed away. 'My little sweetie,' he'd say, and light up like a Christmas tree."

To Williams syndrome children, *everyone's* a friend, a trait researchers call "hypersociability." As one mother puts it, not without exasperation, "No stranger-awareness whatsoever. I try to teach her what a stranger is, but the farthest I've gotten is she'll go up to someone and ask, 'Are you a stranger?' and then say, '*Now* we're friends!'"

We tell the kids that today we're going on a treasure hunt. *Treasure!* They all look at each other, disbelieving their luck. "Treasure!" they say, their eyes wide, their mouths little O's of delight, sunny little optimists on an impossibly sunny day. "Oh, *thank* you, Mommy!" says Laurel, and it comes from the bottom of her heart. They clearly are treasures to their parents. One parent contrasted her own chronic reticence with her daughter's social confidence. "Here I had this little girl with all these problems, and she'd walk into a room full of people, never shy, never self-conscious, and say, 'Hi, my name's Katey. What's your name?' I would think, *How did she do that?* She makes it look so easy. She taught me how to forget about myself."

I get the impression of little people with translucent membranes instead of skin—you can *see* their hearts pulsing. They exude affection. I watch Cassie march right up to a woman inching along on a walker and say with profound conviction, "I *love* your earrings." The woman basks in the glow of the best compliment she's heard all day. They chat, though Cassie's conversation is limited. She's fascinated by all things crystalline, and the diamonds in the woman's earrings are what she most wants to talk about.

Cassie beams at her. "My *good* friend."

I miss these kids the minute I leave; time spent in their company is utterly pleasant. It has given me a look at a form of human goodness, an innocence, both inspiring and tragic. I know there is anguish for the parents, even as they put on a brave face and tell me if they were forced to choose a disability for their child, this would be the one. Besides the terrible medical problems (Laurel's had two heart surgeries) and the great likelihood they will never function independently as adults (and often die young), the emotional roller coaster can be overwhelming. If the children find they can't soothe a playmate or if a baby gets upset in the market, they can become panicky and inconsolable.

"They have exaggerated emotional contagion," explains Susan Hepburn, a researcher who specializes in the disease. "They may instantly pick up on your emotion and say, 'You look frustrated today,' but they won't ask why or understand the context. Once they catch that someone's angry or sad, they're not sure how to proceed, how to figure out what they might say or do to help." She stops and gropes for the right way to put it. "They don't know how to *think* about feelings."

Then there are those who are their polar opposites: people with Asperger syndrome (AS), a less crippling form of autism characterized by a *lack of* empathic ability. People with AS often can only *think* about feelings. They tend to excel at logical, literal, systematic thought, yet are, in the coinage of Cambridge psychologist Simon Baron-Cohen, "mindblind," able only with extreme difficulty to discern other people's inner desires and intentions.

They must make their own reasoned analysis of the alien world of emotion to live in relationship with others, devising what an engineer might call workarounds for their empathy impairment. Writes one mother with Asperger's:

> Tone of voice, facial expression, body language—people give a dozen clues about their state of mind without uttering a word. Unfortunately, I do not always pick up on this...I therefore have great difficulty following a conversation, listening, being tactful, taking hints, making small talk, knowing when to use polite deception, and knowing what subjects are appropriate to talk about.

She describes not knowing how to emotionally bond with her children or intuit the meaning of one cry from another "unless it was an obviously alarmed cry." Instead she worked out a system to manage this most primal of empathic relationships, a set of rules to use when the babies were upset: first offering her breast, then checking their diaper, then rocking them in a process of elimination until they quieted down.

But she was a good parent, breastfeeding her children even though she took no pleasure in it, because, she reasoned, "I wanted to give them the best and nothing less." She questions whether her way is necessarily inferior. "Lack of empathy is not psychopathy, and it is possible to use reason instead. Sometimes it is better—how many things do parents do, not because it is wise or best but simply because that is the way 'everyone' does it?"

Her sentiments are echoed on a Web site called Aspergia, which contends that adults with AS possess a unique set of traits that may have been shared by Mozart and Darwin. (Bill Gates is often cited as a presumptive nominee for the AS Hall of Fame.)*

Maybe, they argue, they are just more rational, like Trekkie fave Mr. Spock. And who's to say that those they refer to as "neurotypicals" don't have their own set of deficits? "Wars are caused by people with strong emotions of affiliation," suggests someone on the site. Maybe, says another, there are reasons that evolution has conserved the AS gene. After all, far-flung Aspergia can count 20 million people worldwide, enough to populate their own Australia.

I met a citizen of the Aspergian diaspora. Sandra, a rotund and animated woman with a man's haircut—she likes to refer to herself as "a monk"—sat in the front row of a lecture about the

---

*Simon Baron-Cohen argues that, although classic autism is an incapacitating pathology, Asperger syndrome (not officially recognized until 1994) can extend right up to the borderline of normalcy. Indeed it may cross over the line. One study he performed with Cambridge students indicated that the engineers, mathematicians, physicists, and computer scientists among them had a greater number of AS-like traits—strong abilities in rule-based systems coupled with difficulty in empathizing—compared with their peers in the arts, humanities, and social sciences.

dwindling resources available to people with autism spectrum disorder (ASD), freely expressing her outrage. "It's a human rights issue!" she exclaimed when a particularly egregious funding cut was detailed. "How can we change this?" she asked loudly. "Absolutely!" she shouted with little self-consciousness whenever the speaker made a point she found on target. She is earnest to a fault, with an acute sense of justice, and not at all what I'd expected.

"Autism doesn't exist in a vacuum," she explains. "I'm influenced by Roman Catholicism, the Midwest, postindustrial society, and a degree in political science." She tells me she approaches her faith in the rational tradition of Saint Thomas Aquinas. "I know we all need each other in society," she says. "I know we need to give help, not just get it." She talks to me about the friends who come to her for help "with the vicissitudes of life," about the social skills group she runs for others with ASD. She reels off the highlights of her social network, waving her hand as if diagramming its key nodes on an invisible blackboard. "I have three godkids. I have twenty-four nieces and nephews, and I'm proud of every single one of them."

She knows she has certain deficiencies, but she reasons her way around them. "A professor taught me to read fiction by breaking it down into pieces of stories and characters. I need to chart the motivations. Things have to be explained in a logical manner. Like, *why* is that children's book hero called Captain Underpants?" (By contrast, I think of the Williams syndrome adult who said she loved fiction "because I can put myself in that book and be right in there with the characters and feel them go through these experiences.")

It could be said that Sandra is *all* cognitive empathy: It is *logical* that we are not separate; it is a logical imperative to serve one another. She is just one more example of the inborn drive for reciprocity and connection—for what Vietnamese Zen priest Thich Nhat Hanh has called "interbeing"—by which we define our humanity.

A drive and, to varying degrees, an unbidden imperative. Speaking of her Williams syndrome patients, Susan Hepburn says, "Their empathy makes them too vulnerable," and it's true. Even in normal people, one psychologist suggests, "the sense of self must be protected by an 'empathic wall' lest we be taken over by those around us." Williams kids are without walls entirely: no stone wall against neighbors or against strangers, those unmet friends; no castle wall against the enemy; no interior wall to brick in the heart. They have broken down my own categorical walls, as well: the ones that would define their condition as purely pathological rather than a poignant glimpse into our human capacities, that might deem them wrong and the rest of the world so right.

"I often have a feeling of wanting to just protect their naiveté," admits Susan Hepburn, "to somehow miraculously change the world into a place where you *could* safely like everybody and safely assume that everyone would also value you." She looks wistful.

Meeting these unusual people, I'm struck anew by how keen is our common desire to make contact. After all, we neurotypicals are not monochromatic. We each show up along a continuum from all heart to pure reason. We each have our own ways of reaching out to one another; we all burn with that ardent flame to, in E. M. Forster's words, "connect, only connect." But how much? How deeply? How far?

*T*HE GREAT MYSTICS SEE THE CONTINUUM AS A SINGLE CIRCLE, fusing the pure extremes of emotional and cognitive empathy into one blinding arc where the me-and-you distinction flares to transparency. This erasure of the border between I and thou is such a persistent perception that it can't be ignored.*

Saints of all religions have presented it as an apogee of compassion, one which they insist is attainable through inspiration, humility, and spiritual elbow grease. Said Meister Eckhart: "You need to love all persons as yourself, esteeming them and considering them alike. What happens to another, whether it be a joy or a sorrow, happens to you." Similarly, Shantideva recommends applying the thought "they are myself" habitually to every creature so that "one will come to care for them as much as one now cares for oneself."

We've all had, from time to time, an ineffable taste of nonseparateness, as with the lovers in a Pablo Neruda love poem where "There is no I or you / so intimate that your hand upon my chest is my hand / so intimate that when I fall asleep it is your eyes that close." But Shantideva puts forth the Buddhist notion that there *is* no self in the first place—that what we think to be the "I," the "me," is finally an illusory construct, a flowing process, not a thing. And if the self is unreal, so is all concept of "other," since the two terms have meaning only in relation to each other. To make a distinction between "you" and "me," he says, is as impossible as "to cut the sky in two with a knife." He promises that those who "cast aside the ordinary, trivial view of 'self'" are sure to gain "an attitude of wanting to protect others as oneself, and to protect all that belongs to them with the same care as if it were one's own."

I struggle to understand this rather rarified notion of selflessness. What if it's not a matter of my being generous to you

---

*The Latin root of *conscience* means "joint or mutual knowledge," the same root that underlies the word *consciousness*. Mirror neuron co-discoverer Vittorio Gallese goes so far as to suggest that the basis of consciousness might not be our vaunted "sense of self" but rather our "intersubjectivity," a sort of self-*and*-otherhood.

but more that you and I really are two hands of the same being? If I refuse you when you're in need, it's like the right hand refusing to remove a thorn from the left on the grounds that it's the *left* hand's problem.

You might try this exercise proposed by a Buddhist scholar to illustrate that the self/other dichotomy isn't all it's cracked up to be: *Put your right hand on the back of your left.* Try to feel the warmth and texture of the left hand's skin solely from the right hand's perspective, as if you've just placed your hand on your lover's. Feel how, from the right hand's point of view, the left hand becomes a fleshy object, an other.

Now try reversing it: Shift your subjective attention to your left hand. Feel the right hand's weight and warmth upon it. Without changing anything but your mind, the left hand now feels like "I" while the right feels more like "other"—when, in point of fact, both are "me."

It's hard to avoid experiencing both hands as your own. But even so, you may notice a peculiar flickering back and forth, like one of those Escher optical illusions of a staircase that appears to be going up and going down at the same time. Albert Einstein himself once referred to our sense of separateness as "a kind of optical delusion of consciousness"—a delusion that limits our caring because it "restricts us to our personal desires and to affection for a few persons nearest to us." To live in the world we'd really like to see, he continued, we must undertake a deliberate change in perspective: "Our task must be to free ourselves by widening our circle of compassion to embrace all creatures and the whole of nature."

I've known a few people who make it seem possible. I met Brother David Steindl-Rast years ago, when I was fresh out of the hospital for cancer surgery. I had gone to a conference but, in lingering postoperative trauma, found myself barely able to cope.

People spotted my distress and for the most part gave me a wide berth. Maybe it was the raw surgical scar across my neck, as if I'd been decapitated and had my head sewn back on, or maybe it was the shell-shocked look in my eyes; but even in a crowd, I felt terribly alone.

Brother David was coming down a path from the opposite direction, a gaunt man in a black-and-white habit who somehow exuded calm. Perhaps touched by something he saw in my face, he paused, sat down on a low rock wall, and gestured me over by patting a space next to him. We talked, or, actually, I talked. He encouraged me to unload the whole dump truck of my woes—his steady gaze told me he could take it. He was the first person who didn't flinch away.

He conveyed a few words of advice and comfort—something about an "unknown guidance system" that kicks in when you're really lost—but mostly he shared my pain without trying to do anything about it. When he quietly told me, without a speck of dogma, that I shouldn't assume that my suffering had no value, I never forgot it. I knew somehow that he had been there himself; that he had, in a sense, never left.

A tiny intervention, perhaps, but there doesn't seem to be much that's too small for him to notice or to care about. We've met again a number of times over the years, and I'm always reminded of his exquisite sensitivity to the living universe. Once, he described to me walking through a park and, seeing a board lying on the grass, being overcome by "how hard it was for the grass to breathe; it felt like I couldn't breathe." When he lifted off the board, he told me, "I heard the grass rejoicing."

You might think, *Oh, brother, spare me.* But he's not of the quaking aspen school of spirituality. His mysticism is infused with knowledge of the real world. I mentioned to him once how wrenching I'd found the beggars in India's Old Delhi, entire multigenerational families living on a single patch of sidewalk they'd claimed as their own. I couldn't imagine that the crumpled rupees I dropped in their hands could make a difference and had felt crushed by charity's impotence.

"I've seen those same people," he said softly. "It hurts the heart. Still we mustn't just regard them with pity but see what they have to teach us. They take care of each other every day as an extended family. They practice values many of us have lost. We should help, yes, but our compassion should be connected with gratefulness for what they offer *us*."

The thought took me aback. I'd been looking at them as if through a one-way mirror. In fact, we were each other's reflections. *No self, no other.* I was reminded of the way one Christian writer differentiated two forms of compassionate love: "Charity extends the privileges of insiders to outsiders; while *agape* erases the line between insiders and outsiders entirely."

Brother David tells me that he is inspired by the three Catholic rosaries known as "joyful," "sorrowful," and "glorious," which produce in him a "deep poetic stimulation of compassion." Contemplating Jesus' scourging, he feels a oneness with every beaten-down person in the world. It is not religious masochism, he says, pointing out that the earliest crosses were adorned not with Christ in agony but with jewels that symbolized "the triumph of suffering transmuted." When he meditates this way, he says he feels a fullness, a wholeness. There is no longer any part of life that can't be embraced.

Still, he says, "Sometimes, I have to protect myself. I can't take it all in."

I ask him how he deals with it. "Saint John's wor—," he says in a low tone that muffles the consonant.

"Saint John's word?" I ask, thinking of *Dark Night of the Soul,* that medieval masterwork of anguish redeemed.

"Saint John's *wort*," he corrects me, then laughs heartily. "But his word too."

The last time I saw Brother David, he mentioned a dream he'd had the previous night. "I dreamed I was eating a pear," he told me. "A wasp landed on it. I brushed it off, and it fell into my glass of water. The whole dream was about trying to fish it out." A few nights before that, he said, he'd dreamed of an ant struggling in the middle of a pond. He was trying to rescue it with a branch, but every time he came close, someone threw a stone in the water and the ensuing ripple washed it back out. Finally, the ant drowned, and he awoke feeling bereft. I thought of poet William Blake's comment on compassion: "He who would do Good to another must do it in Minute Particulars."

For in the end, empathy need not scale great spiritual pinnacles or be vetted with a psychological seal of approval. The minute particulars of relationship, in most cases, will do just fine. A friend once told me a story about his mother. On her first day in a new city, she had struck up a conversation at the train station with a woman making a stopover on a long journey and had unthinkingly handed her a sandwich she'd been saving for later. It was the beginning of a twenty-year friendship. After my friend's mother died, he found a packet of the women's correspondence. One thing had particularly struck him. "So many of the letters from this woman ended with the same words: 'I'll never forget that you fed me.'"

STREE

THE DE   OF LOVE

'We're all in the gutter,
only some of us are looking at the stars.

—Oscar Wilde

L AST SUMMER I SAW AN IMMENSELY FAT WOMAN—350 POUNDS at least—struggling to step onto a Manhattan bus. Wheezing with effort, perspiring through her floral print dress, she couldn't hoist her foot onto the platform. Her knee, encased in layers of flesh, wouldn't bend. The driver, with an exasperated sigh, bolted from his seat to try to shoehorn her through the door.

The passengers gaped and craned, their expressions ranging from embarrassment to scorn to a sort of horrified fascination. As schedules unraveled and tempers frayed, the irritation grew more audible. The thought flashed through my mind as it did through nearly everyone's: *How could anyone allow herself to get so obese?* Then I saw the expression on the woman's face: mortification. And my heart broke—for all her hard days and for all my hard thoughts.

Why was my first response not compassion but a series of assessments that went off like a string of mental firecrackers before

I even knew I'd lit the match? My judgment was so fused with my perception as to be inseparable: She became what I beheld. I was painfully aware of my mind—the mind itself—as a difference engine cranking out the petty distinctions that keep people apart. And I wished I could dismantle the whole stupid contraption once and for all.

So, I suppose I should have been glad when old Søren Kierkegaard showed up, clenching a monkey wrench in his ink-stained hand and hurling it unceremoniously into the churning gears. I knew him from college: religious philosopher, gloomy Dane, bit of a crank. He'd meant no more to me than any other Dead White Male of the Western Canon. But recently, on impulse, I'd rehefted one of his tomes and gained a new appreciation of this fiery eccentric who had shocked nineteenth-century society with his tirades against church hierarchy, sticking up for those "despised and rejected by men," proclaiming them nearest of all to God. As I discovered while reading his rhapsodic masterpiece, *Works of Love,* his pet peeve was smallness of heart. The chapter titles alone tell you what's on his mind (italics his): "You *Shall* Love," "You Shall Love *the Neighbor,*" and "*You* Shall Love the Neighbor."

Sir, yessir! I've taken to using WOL as a kind of oracle book, opening it every few days to random pages. Today's selection is titled "Our Duty to Love the People We See," and enough said. I find myself nodding when Søren cites "comparison" as "the most dangerous acquaintance love can make." It is, he says indignantly, his Nordic blood heating to a rolling boil, "a noxious shoot," a "cursed tree," a "withered shadow," a "swampy ground," and, lest we forget, "a hidden worm." I take his point. I'm sick of watching myself weigh in on this and inveigh against that, going over all humanity with a fine-toothed comb. I do it with my eyes closed. Let someone's accent be Upper Adenoid, New Jersey, or Marble-mouth, Georgia, and before I know it I've placed a subliminal red checkmark next to their name and referred them to the Credentials Committee.

I have a friend who's marginally even more exacting. Though I know she has a kind heart, it's often covered by a brittle tortoiseshell of judgment. She grew up poor—"pedigreed trailer trash," she likes to say, and like many who've come up the hard way she's put as much mileage as possible between herself and the dismal swamp of the past. She's even become a latter-day disciple of hypercapitalist Ayn Rand: By her reckoning, you're either roadmaster or roadkill. She works in public relations; has a prestigious address on her business card; is chic, svelte, and successful; and countenances no excuses for failure. But lately a downturn in the market has jumped up and bitten her. She's been going through a prolonged bout of unemployment. She's by no means out on the street, but it's shaken her up.

"The other day," she tells me, "I turned into the alley behind my apartment, and there was this bum going through my trash bin. I had all the thoughts I usually do—disdain, disgust, and, on top of that, irritation that I had to wait for him to get out of the way just so I could get into my parking space. I inched up behind him and was about to lean on my horn when he turned around. I saw his face, how ravaged this guy looked, suffering written all over him. And suddenly, I don't know, it was like breaking a spell. I felt this overwhelming sense of sympathy. I could just *feel* how ashamed he was, and then *I* felt ashamed, too. I rolled down the window and gave him a few dollars, and he almost cried, and I teared up, too. He was so grateful, it shocked me."

*F*AST-FORWARD A FEW WEEKS, AND SHE MIGHT HAVE DIScovered *me* swan-diving in her dumpster. For here I am, with a week's growth of beard, in my rattiest clothes, a toothbrush in my pocket, living on the streets of Denver. I hadn't planned to be here. This week I was scheduled to go to Cannes of all places, and thence to a farmhouse in glorious Provence, a dumb-luck invite only a dunce would turn down. But another invitation, this one from a group called the Zen Peacemaker Order to go on a "street retreat," had suddenly come up in the same calendar slot. "If you don't get on a plane to France," a friend said, "then *I* will."

But Søren, old Søren, in one of my necromantic readings, had nailed my Achilles' heel—snobbery—to the floor in one mercilessly deflating passage, mocking that person "who thinks he exists only for the distinguished, that he is to live only in the alliances of their circles, that he must not exist for other people, just as they must not exist for him." Of course, that's not *really* me. I live in a modest shack in the student badlands, drive a beater, have friends up and down the social ladder and across the zodiac; but still, when Søren skewers the elitist who tries to ensure he is "never among the more lowly"—who "will go about with closed eyes... when he moves around in the human throng"—I can't pretend I have no idea what he's talking about.

Because the point these days is to learn to *open* my eyes, along with that near-rusted lock on my heart, I knew what I had to do. The street retreat rules were simple enough: Hit the pavement unbathed and unshaven, without money or a change of clothes, joining for the better part of a week the ranks of those whom life had kicked to the curb.

The street retreats are the brainchild of Bernie Glassman, a man who has enshrined ignorance (which he calls "unknowing") as a central precept. A former aerospace engineer ordained as a Buddhist *roshi*, Bernie, who wears his beard in a modified Santa, had been looking for ways to integrate spiritual practice with compassionate social action. Sometime in the 1980s, he decided to spend a few months walking aimlessly around the inner-city neighborhood that abutted his meditation center, hanging out, talking with people, and listening to their problems. Out of this had grown, as naturally and prolifically as a zucchini patch, a sprawling multimillion-dollar social organization serving the rebuked and the scorned.

First there was the Greyston Bakery, which employed people just getting out of prison or off the street. The business grew, eventually snagging a contract to make brownies for Ben & Jerry's ice cream. But it soon came smack up against the endemic problems of the neighborhood. People missed work because of drug use. Batches of dough were ruined because employees lacked basic math skills to measure ingredients or reading skills to decipher labels on cans. But each problem had suggested, after trial and error, its own solution. The Greyston Mandala that emerged from Bernie's first street-scuffing walkabout now trains, employs, houses, and provides health services to hundreds of the formerly marginal as well as offers care and housing on the site of a former Catholic nunnery to people with AIDS.

When Bernie's fifty-fifth birthday rolled around, rather than rest on his laurels, he'd decided to spend a few days sitting homeless on the steps of the Capitol, figuring out what next to do with his life. During what turned out to be Washington, D.C.'s coldest, snowiest week in a half century, he dreamed up the multifaith Peacemaker Order, a spiritual path based on just "bearing witness" and seeing what happened.

"When we bear witness," he wrote, "when we become the situation—homelessness, poverty, illness, violence, death—then right action arises by itself. We don't have to worry about what to do. We don't have to figure out solutions ahead of time...It's as simple as giving a hand to someone who stumbles or picking up a child who has fallen on the floor."

Fine for Bernie, with his track record of weaving straw into gold. But if he hadn't recommended it, I'd be hard put to justify my week of taking to the streets in a bum costume.

*H*ERE I WAS IN DENVER!" EXULTED JACK KEROUAC IN 1947 after hitchhiking from New York. "I stumbled along with the most wicked grin of joy in the world, among the old bums and beat cowboys of Larimer Street." Kerouac managed to romanticize the down-and-out as the literarily up-and-coming, but those days are gone. His gritty cityscape—"smokestacks, smoke, rail yards, red-brick buildings, and the distant downtown gray stone buildings"—has given way to sports bars and brick pieds-à-terre. The old Denargo market where he once worked hauling watermelons is now the site of the million-dollar Jack Kerouac Lofts (which, says the sales brochure, "pay homage to a life of exuberant discovery, and offer a fitting home for those who are 'mad to live'"). Meanwhile the unfitting homeless, some of them the deinstitutionalized mad, are discovering a life less exuberant.

Denver has experienced a staggering 25 percent increase in homelessness. In a single year, hate crimes against the homeless population resulted in no fewer than nine beating deaths (with several *decapitations*). I feel glad I'll be traveling in a group of ten, ranging from students to doctors, led by a fifty-two-year-old streetwise Buddhist social activist and Peacemaker priest named Fleet Maull. Fleet's a big guy, and despite his soft features and benign expression he looks a little threatening. With his old bulky coat and lumbering gait, even the more belligerent street people tend to dodge him, as do the regular folks on their way to work.

We all gather to meditate each morning in a small park, an unkempt sliver of green down from the abandoned Sacred Heart School with its chipped Jesus statue and chiseled biblical inscription from Mark 10: "Suffer the little children to come unto me, and forbid them not." But it's forbidden to loiter, so we hit the ground walking, keeping on keeping on. After only a few days, the soles of my feet are already aching. *No wonder they shuffle,* I think, push-dragging the two anvils at the ends of my legs up and down the block. And now we too are on the ground, walking on it, sleeping on it. For them it's a life; for us, with any luck, it's an exercise in humility.

Humility comes from the Latin *humus,* meaning "earth, ground, soil"; it's the root of *human* and *humiliate* ("to lower the pride of"), as when we come down to earth with a crash, the ego one big purple bruise. I'd wanted to take this week to be a little less full of myself, to see if innate kindness would arise if I moved out and made some room for it. But what is arising is my innate irritability. I can be impatient, and homelessness involves lots of waiting: waiting for a soup kitchen to open, for your number to be called for a meal, for the rain or snow to let up, or for a cop to stop looking your way. It's a different map of the world: Which Starbucks has a security guard who'll let you use the bathroom? How long can you linger in this park before you're rousted?

My venerable friend Søren, in his tough-old-bird fashion, argued against harboring any delusions that "by loving some people, relatives and friends, you would be loving the neighbor..." No, he squawked, the real point is "to frighten you out of the beloved haunts of preferential love." Most of my new neighbors *are* haunted. Life has failed them, or they've failed it. A tall, stringy young man with lank, black-dyed hair tells me, "If you see Sherry, tell her Big John's back from Oklahoma." His eyes have the jittery glint of crank, each pupil sending out fitful sparkles. An alcoholic American Indian vet yanks open his shirt to show me his scars, the roundish puckers from shrapnel, the short, telegraphic dashes from ritual piercing at a Sun Dance.

An angry-looking man approaches me to demand that I give him a plastic fork, purpose unknown. When I demur, he stalks over to the dumpster and scrabbles through it unproductively.

"I'm sorry," I say.

"I'll just *bet* you are," he snarls, raising both middle fingers and staring at me with cold fury.

I can't say I'm pleased to meet him, but WWKD: What Would Kierkegaard Do? "Root out all equivocation and fastidiousness in loving them!" *Sir, yessir.*

The Buddhist sage Atisha recommended a prayer upon encountering those folks who mess with our minds: *When I see beings of a negative disposition, or those oppressed by negativity or pain, may I, as if finding a treasure, consider them precious.* It is good, Atisha said, when your comfy sweater of self-cherishing gets snagged on someone's rusty nail, unraveling as you try to pull away. Better, he said, not to pull away at all.

Every cerebral word of this homily is now running through my head as I step toward my new neighbor with a little nod of appreciation, hoping he hasn't stashed a ball-peen hammer in his trench coat. But he backs away, lip curled, then turns and runs, pursued by some host of invisibles. *At least,* I tell myself, *I've managed to become more curious about him than repulsed.* I don't know how these guys drove their lives into a ditch or how to winch them out. I just try to stay present to my heart's systole and diastole, sympathies opening, closing, opening, closing.

The homeless. Street people. In truth it's annoying they're out there, these deportees from ordinary life, huddled in doorways, sleeping curled up against the wall of a building, declaiming their private jeremiads. What gives them the right to intrude into our space (sometimes their smell, supernaturally potent, intrudes first), to interrupt our train of thought or flow of conversation, to make us feel that involuntary muscle spasm of conscience? Why *don't* they get a job, pay rent for a roof over their heads?

I fell in with a man named Fred who used to work in a livestock feedlot. "Rather feed 'em than kill 'em," he says mildly. He's a harmless-looking guy with a scraggle of graying beard, his soft face white as a daikon radish, wearing a cap embroidered with the Teamsters Union logo of two horses and a wheel. First his hours got cut, he tells me. Then the union bargained away his benefits. The plant closed down. He lost the house and then the wife. The kids grew estranged. The repo man grabbed the truck he'd counted on for sideline painting jobs. Fred seems understandably befuddled over his fate. How did he land here, anyway, snarfing down free church feeds and looking for day labor gigs as the months have spiraled into nearly two years now?

He used to sleep in the alleys, he says, but it got too dangerous. "This winter was rough, man. There were guys out there who'd slit your throat for your sleeping bag." He finally found what he calls a "campsite" somewhere in the city; he won't tell me where. "It's got three walls and an overhang, almost like a room," he tells me, house-proud. He knows that the building super is wise to him, but he takes care to clean up, neatly stowing his stuff. The other day the super even left him a broom, standing it up against the wall, tacitly acknowledging his tenancy.

Our own sitting room, when it's not a piece of pavement, is the bus terminal, aptly named for that percentage of its habitués who have arrived at their final destination and are going nowhere fast. We can sit until closing time, keeping warm. When a lady comes by panhandling for the two dollars more she needs for a ticket, I let her pass, thinking I'll use the little money I've cadged today to buy myself a corndog. Then, feeling remorseful, I run after her and give her whatever's in my pocket, three big ones, and she hugs me like I'd handed her a fistful of pearls.

Homelessness is a journey down the rabbit hole. The ordinary world vanishes. The roof over your head. The cash in your pocket. The food in your belly. Random acts of kindness become just that: sporadic, unaccountable, case studies for the *Journal of Irreproducible Results*. I'm amazed how fast my "real life" recedes. That night, as the terminal closes and the cold sets in, we trudge past a hotel where my girlfriend and I had stayed one New Year's, renting a suite with some friends, playing Scrabble and drinking champagne. I stop to peer in the window at the plush, cozy lobby, my breath making cloudy smudges.

We wander the dark streets of the Five Points ghetto incongruously close to downtown's glittering towers, but the only glitter here is from shards of broken whisky bottles we sweep aside before laying down our cardboard next to some concrete walls. I notice they're pockmarked with bullet holes. Apparently, our alcove is used for target practice by the local gangbangers, but it's the best squat we can find, with a generous overhang to keep out the weather.

"Do not judge your fellowman until you have rested in his place," said Hillel, and I *am* trying, if you can call this resting, lying supine on a deconstructed lettuce carton, frost forming on my sleeping bag, still fantasizing about southern France and fresh-grilled squid. I realize that this really *is* a meditation retreat, an active contemplation on the illusion of self-cherishing and worthier-than-others. Somehow, somewhere, the homeless fell down, and at this moment I'm no different. We all fall. We are all fallen. It suddenly seems like the boundary I'd put up against them is the same membrane that separates me from everyone—even from the dejected parts of myself I refuse to grant a home.

Still, I tell one of my fellow retreatants as we settle in, "I'm lying here thinking I really deserve better. I'm telling myself, 'I'm never going to do this again.'"

He laughed. "I'll bet every other bum in Denver tonight is thinking exactly the same thing."

The next morning we make our way down to the Holy Ghost Church, where you can get breakfast of a baloney and cheese sandwich with an *amuse-bouche* of mini-Snickers, plus all the hot bad coffee you can drink. I'm told that the line, snaking around the adjacent blue glass bank tower, is twice as long as last year. A church lady comes by offering wool hats hand-knit by members of the congregation.

These are the outposts of compassion, though too few and far between. We offer to help out at a Catholic Workers boardinghouse that puts up homeless families. We slap a new coat of paint on the fence and hunt down prehistoric dust bunnies behind the patched Naugahyde Barcalounger. In the parlor a zinc tub sits near the woodstove, catching raindrops through the leaky roof. The manager, a careworn soul with fine spiderwebs around her eyes and an apron of wrung-out blue, gives us tea and a place to sit for a while, occasionally shooting us an enormous smile.

Then I set out walking with Fleet. My toes are now blistered, and so are his, but he's more stoic about it, padding them with tissues. We drift over to the Jesus to the World mission, where a stocky, tough-talking preacher is shouting aphorisms at the lunch crowd.

"Stop telling yourself what you *can't* do, and you *may* start knowing what you *can* do!" he bellows. "If I'm halfway *in* the storm, then realistically I must be halfway *out* of it!" When he says, "The first word out of your mouth that curses your life is 'I,'" the Buddhist in me approves, though I'm nonplussed when he walks up to a man at the end of my table and practically shouts in his ear: "If you don't repent, God may need to *kill* you to get your attention!" The man continues his meal unperturbed, the fire and brimstone so much hot sauce and pickle relish.

The preacher dials it down a little, lowering his voice confid-ingly. "When I was in prison, a man planted the seed of the Lord in me, and—"

"What was you in the joint *for*?" a man yells out.

"Traffic violations," the preacher mumbles, momentarily off stride. "But that's not the point."

Fleet smiles faintly. Maybe it is; maybe it isn't. Fleet's got his own story. He knows all about the joint.

FLEET MAULL WAS A THIRTY-FIVE-YEAR-OLD GOLDEN BOY with a covey of beautiful girlfriends, a Tibetan guru, a yacht named *The Spice of Life,* and a penchant for thousand-dollar suits and lavish parties—all courtesy of a thriving cocaine-importing business—when he landed in the federal pen. Convicted under the drug kingpin laws, he plummeted from cloud nine to the concrete floor of a steel cage, sentenced to twenty-five years in the same Missouri prison where Robert Stroud, the Birdman of Alcatraz, spent his last days.

Fleet was surrounded by hard-case, thin-skinned gangbangers, where a man could be beaten with a padlock wrapped in a sock for a wrong sideways glance. *I don't belong here,* he thought. He'd grown up in a close-knit Catholic family with the upper-middle-class amenities: the gleaming cars, the exclusive education, the big house with the sweeping lawn on a hushed, elegant street. After dropping out of college, he'd worked awhile for his father's com-pany, but he soon grew bored. Following the spinning compass needle of 1970s hippie hearsay, he'd wound up in a Peruvian vil-lage in the shadow of Machu Picchu. Later, on a visit to Bolivia to renew his visa, he'd scored a kilo of coke. At first it had been almost a whim, a lark. Soon his one-off drug deals to pay the upkeep on his Peruvian paradise burgeoned into the freewheeling smuggling operation that led to his bigtime bust.

Landing in prison catalyzed a remarkable transformation. "The minute the cell door shut," he tells me, "I had this profound experience of really, really deep regret and remorse. I began to come out of the drug and alcohol haze. I realized what I'd done to family and friends, to myself. It caused a kind of conversion experience, just this 180-degree turn. And I developed a profound desire to erase any kind of harmful things I'd done in my life and find a way to be of some benefit."

Thrown into a cramped unit, with 175 men sardined together on a floor built for fifty, he chose an upper bunk where there was enough headroom to sit cross-legged on a folded blanket and meditate. He remembers asking a prisoner to turn down the radio and getting a venomous response: "Who the *fuck* do you think you are? This is *jail*. Your world don't revolve around *you* anymore." Fleet had been a dilettantish student of Buddhism before; now he became a locked-down monk, meditating in a broom closet amid the racket of fights, blaring TVs, and raucous games of slap-down dominoes. Years later, when good behavior earned him a private cell, he'd awaken every morning at 3 a.m. to meditate some more.

He'd also begun to realize that he was no one special. It hit him, he says, when he broke down crying one day while talking on a pay phone to his former girlfriend. "I was wailing that I was no better than the rest of these people in here, waiting for her to contradict me. But she just said, 'Well, honey, *of course* you're not.' Being thrown into this hell realm, not being able to separate myself from the environment, actually pulled me out of myself for the first time."

What affected him most was the yard. Springfield is a high-security prison hospital with 300 mentally ill, 600 desperately sick, and 300 nominally healthy inmates to run the place. He'd watch the emaciated men dying of cancer and AIDS, the paraplegics and the quads, castaways from the rest of the prison system, marooned all together, and each alone, on this gray concrete archipelago.

The AIDS epidemic was accelerating, and its prisoner-patients had been isolated in the mental health wing in a secure unit for their own protection. Sometimes they were sent out to community hospitals to die shackled to their beds; most were fading away alone in the prison ward, facing the con's ultimate defeat: a death behind bars. Fleet, who had been delegated to run a film projector in the unit, smuggled in magazines, getting to know the men. Eventually he teamed up with a paraplegic prisoner to create a visitation program. It slowly grew into a full medical hospice, the first inmate-staffed program in a U.S. high-security prison.

It became a school for compassion, with once-violent cons caring for men who'd arrived at life's most helpless and vulnerable juncture. In a place where the strong routinely preyed on the weak, it was astonishing, Fleet tells me, to see hardened killers washing their patients' wasted bodies and changing their soiled bedclothes. Prisoner staff and prisoner patients talked and sat in silence, wept and prayed together, went through the long dying together up to the uncanny moment when the body's husk was quietly abandoned. If the dying patient was a Christian, then Fleet, a former altar boy, would recite the Lord's Prayer.

Four years later, in 1991, his National Prison Hospice Association became an officially recognized organization. By the time he'd completed fourteen years behind bars and mounted a successful appeal to get released, the model he'd helped create had spread through the federal prison system. "The hospice gives both guards and inmates permission to care," Fleet says. "It restores their humanity. They begin to feel, 'We're a community. We don't just let our guys die with nobody taking care of them.'" A prison chaplain at Springfield said that the greatest transformations he had seen in his career were among the inmate volunteers.

Fleet himself remains a little impenetrable. Long years of circumspection and regimentation have left a mark. There are glimpses of the person he was before, the arrogant, macho dude who stepped on and over people in pursuit of selfish pleasure. But I get the feeling that that person has been melted down, tempered, refined and recast; there's not a lot of the base metal left.

THE SAINT FRANCIS CENTER IS THE BEST FEED IN TOWN: HOT soup with chunks of real roast beef floating in it, salad with tangy dressing and piles of fresh tomato slices, hard-boiled eggs, real fruit—even a few strawberries and, the pièce de résistance, pumpkin pie. No sermons, all succor. It would have made the saint laugh to see the poor so honored in his name, remembering his days as a rake who loved to put out a big spread for all his friends.

Before Saint Francis became, as it were, a holy bum, he was Giovanni Bernardone, a high-flying young bachelor in a city known then as the Babylon of Italy. A rich kid pursuing the troubadour tradition of wine, women, and song, he was said to have lived "riotously," often playing the role of *rex convivi*—the host who underwrote the revels and the banquets.

But one day, out riding in a handsome new outfit, he saw a beggar and, his biographer says, "touched with compassion, changed clothes with him." Trading places with society's poorest and most beaten down seems to have liberated Francis from all judgment. He describes in his last testament how painful it had been to see lepers until he lived in their midst, but "when I left them, that which had seemed to me bitter had become sweet and easy."

The famous Saint Francis prayer is a paean to this confounding spiritual intention to turn exactly what we wish most to receive into that which we resolve to give: "O, Divine Master, grant that I may not so much seek to be consoled as to console; to be understood as to understand; to be loved as to love...."

Francis and his disciples, "careless of the day," wandering from place to place, sleeping where they fell, were essentially homeless beggars. So were the Buddha and his followers, making the rounds with their wooden begging bowls. But the thought of doing what the Zen Peacemaker Order refers to as "begging practice" horrifies me. Sure, I'd done that high-class begging known as fundraising, my palm outstretched for checks written out to high-minded projects, but I'd always felt it was worth the other person's while; there were good deeds to show for it. Here on the street, I have nothing to offer. I'm a walking bundle of needs, and it galls me.

Besides, it isn't easy to get those needs met. Faces turn to stone at a plea for food money. Eyes flicker sideways, ahead to the middle distance, to the ground, anywhere but the empty space where I'm standing. The Confucians of the Sung Dynasty compared not feeling compassion for a stranger to not feeling your own foot has caught fire, and many of us have gone numb. (I think of an acquaintance of mine, an internationally known designer of leafy town squares in the New Urbanist style. "Of course," he once said to me ruefully, "the more open space, the bigger the quotient of 'bummage.'")

Bummage I am. I supplicate downtown pedestrians, dauntingly busy on their way from here to there, clutching purses and shopping bags and cell phones and lovers' waists. My panhandling talents are nil. Each rejection thuds like a body blow. I can see the little comic strip thought balloon spring from people's brows— *Get a job; I work!* It occurs to me to just forget it. Though we've agreed that during the week we'd each scrape up $3.50 for the bus fare home, throwing any extra into the kitty for the homeless shelter, I think, *Why put myself through it? I'll send a check when I get home.*

But I'm hungry *now.* I'm also starting to realize that there's more to "begging practice" than meets the eye. Roshi Bernie

Glassman has explained it with disarming simplicity: "When we don't ask, we don't let others give. When we fear rejection, we don't let generosity arise." I realize that the street, much like a meditation cushion, has put my issues on parade, and the begging routine's got them goose-stepping smartly past the reviewing stand. There's the Humiliation Battalion. The Fear of Rejection Brigade. The Undeserving Auxiliary. And of course, the Judgment Detachment, for I find I'm even judging my potential donors: Are *they* good enough to give *me* a dollar?

My profound reluctance to ask passersby for help feels not unlike my aversion to calling friends when I'm needful in other ways, those times when I'm feeling sad, lost, lonely. I prize autonomy; I'm overproud of it. I don't *want* to owe people for my well-being. Or just maybe I don't want to owe them my love. I wondered suddenly if I wasn't rejecting gratitude itself, that spiritual 3-in-1 oil said to open the creakiest gate of the heart. Aren't we all indebted to parents, teachers, friends, and loved ones for our very existence?

Dear Søren Kierkegaard thought even this was a crock. Sure, he said, we *think* a person who is loved owes a debt of gratitude to the one who loves him. There is an expectation that it should be repaid in kind, on installment, "reminiscent," he says sarcastically, "of an actual bookkeeping arrangement." Instead he turns the whole thing on its head: "No, the one who loves runs into debt; in feeling himself gripped by love, he feels this as being in an infinite debt. Amazing!"

It is his most radical proposition: We owe those who elicit love from us for allowing us to be filled with the stuff. We owe a debt to those who suffer because they draw forth our tenderness. (Do I think that by avoiding others' suffering I can hoard my stash of good feelings and not get bummed out? The helper's high phenomenon suggests the opposite: It's giving that turns on the juice, taps us into the infinite current.) Giving and taking start to seem less like zero-sum transactions than some universal love-circuitry, where what goes around not only comes around but comes back redoubled.

Still, "How would you like to enter into Kierkegaard's infinite debt of love?" is not going to win Year's Best Panhandling Line. I ask a stylish young guy—fawn-colored coat with a *No War: Not in Our Name* button, a canvas messenger bag in muted gray—if he can spare a little change for food. He calls out chidingly over his shoulder, "I don't give *on the street.*" Fair enough. But the bank building's LED thermometer reads 25 degrees, and the sun still hasn't gone down. I haven't had dinner. Sleeping on the street is a frigid proposition, and body heat requires calories. Then I realize I'm judging him and everyone else, defeating the whole purpose of the exercise. I make a point to mentally bless all comers and goers.

I approach a bearded guy in a fringed suede jacket. He declines, but a few minutes later, hearing me unsuccessfully petition a half dozen more people, he comes over and hands me two dollars, cautioning sotto voce, "Don't tell anyone I gave it to you," as if worried I'd alert a gang of accomplices.

I've now streamlined my pitch: "I'm sleeping on the street tonight. I'm hungry. I wonder if you could help me out at all?" Most people's eyes still slam down like steel shutters over a storefront at closing time, but then a man who's just passed me with a curt *no* pivots abruptly and walks back with a green bill. "On second thought, I can." And I see in that moment how much more effort it takes to resist the raw tug of one another.

I strike out another twenty or thirty times before a crisp-looking gent crosses my palm with silver. "Thanks so much, it's chilly out tonight," I mumble, surprised after so many averted gazes. "It *is* cold," he says sympathetically, in three words restoring my faith.

Such little ups and downs are a roller coaster out here. There's scant insulation from the shock of existence. Still, I'm able to feel, palpably, because it hovers constantly above my head, that the same sun shines on each of us, paupers or potentates, saints or souses. Beauty itself is available gratis, something I forget when I'm rushing along like the business guy in *The Little Prince*, "concerned with matters of consequence."

With nothing better to do and nowhere else to go, I can stand stock-still and gaze in wonder at a blue sky streaked with salmon clouds reflected in the windows of an office building. I awoke one morning to see we'd camped beneath a tree crowned with one leftover copper leaf burnished bright by dawn. I heard birds chirping mightily over the traffic and smelled in the cold air the tang of impending spring.

"The gifts of the street," Fleet likes to call them. But of those gifts, Jesus was best of all. He came into our lives unbidden, heralded by an aroma of whisky and unwashed clothes. He'd approached us one day in the park like a shy deer, sidling up to the edge of our meditation circle, a youngish man in an oversized checked wool shirt worn *vato*-style. He'd dropped to a crouch, made an odd little genuflection, sat down, and introduced himself in short Spanish phrases: *Jesus. Jesus Martinez.*

He was from Chihuahua state, he said, having paid a *coyote* a few years ago to smuggle him across the border.

"*Trabajo?*" we asked. "Any work?"

"*No tengo.*"

Jesus carries a black plastic garbage bag that serves as his allpurpose valise and storage locker. He'd worked as a gardener for a while, for a brother who was a contractor, but says he's been living on the streets a long time now, he claims by choice. "The sky is my roof," he says. "The grass is my floor."

He's got a misdemeanor rap for public drunkenness and a restraining order from his ex-wife ("I got mad and pushed her," he says, looking abashed) that keeps him from seeing his daughter. He's an illegal and is worried about deportation. He decides he'll just hang out with us for a while.

One of our group, Tim, a religious studies major from Maine, has forgotten to bring along a sleeping bag. The night has turned freezing, with the next day threatening snow. We hunker down, curled up together in a dog pile, but Tim goes to sleep shivering and anxious. The next morning he wakes up warm. Some anonymous Good Samaritan has gently draped a sleeping bag over him while he slept. It's Jesus' bag, though he'd vanished in the night like an apparition. He had given away the single most valuable thing he owned, becoming in that instant another of love's debtors.

Jesus shows up again a few days later. Now he's talking to us more. Odd gems spill from his mouth. "Nobody has a heart with separate batteries—they all have the same source," he announces, adding that to convey the thoughts that fill his head using his poor English is "like trying to put an elephant through the eye of a needle."

"Why don't you work?" someone asks.

"Work is always fighting, fighting. People fight for money. I'm a lover, not a fighter. I love life, not money." He claims he wants to attend seminary someday, maybe become a priest, and who's to say? Maybe Jesus is spending time as a self-styled Franciscan, careless of the day—or as one of those that Islam calls the *Malāmiyya*, those who "draw blame," courting contempt by living like beggars to preserve their purity of heart. I don't want to romanticize him, but it's clear his story's not over yet.

As for us, we'll soon be going home. And on our last day, in our last circle, suddenly Jesus says in eloquently simple English, "I've been watching you, not saying much, but I think you are true people. I feel you are with me, and I am with you. Because I was with all of you for these days, I didn't drink at all. Not once. So you have been good for me." He says it with no discernible flattery but with a village courtliness almost quaint in its sincerity. "I wish you all a long life. I hope all of us will never die. I wish all of you to be happy."

Okay, I think, waiting for the hustle to kick in. *What does he really want?* To my surprise, he asks for nothing—no money, no clothes, no place to stay. When one of our group, a doctor named Charlie, offers his beautiful hand-knit woolen gloves, a secret concession to luxury he'd smuggled along, Jesus refuses. He is persuaded only after Charlie unobtrusively dons Jesus' own filthy and torn gloves, making it an exchange. Jesus wants no charity. Compassion, he's clearly saying, is more than a gesture from the intact to the damaged.

And he's right: Sometimes, even in charity, the most open hand remains at arm's length. The great Hasidic sage Reb Nachman was in the habit of using whatever money he had to pay off the creditors of people who had fallen on hard times. He'd saved many a man and woman from the fate of debtor's prison. But one day he ran out of money, was dunned for what he owed, and, when he couldn't pay, was thrown into prison himself.

"Why, O God?" he implored from the darkness of his cell.

And God answered, with a touch of irony: "So you could *really* know how much good you've done." It is a story about giver and receiver made one, in an exchange of places, in the bearing of witness, in God's own infinite debt.

God knows I'm no Reb Nachman. Back home again I'm delighted to be sleeping in my own bed. Bathed, shaved, dressed, and fed, I take a stroll on the mall with a friend. He looks at me askance as I press a dollar bill into a panhandler's palm and then, seeing how browbeaten the man looks, peel off another two and chat with him for a while.

I'm trying to become insufferably virtuous, I tell my friend. How am I doing? Pretty good, he allows; you're getting on my nerves.

Soon I'm giving money to the people with cardboard signs who stake out corners on trafficked streets, remembering when I was stranded once on the highway, having to scare up a ride with a magic-markered plea. One guy comes up to the window to recite his story as my car idles at a light. He's a former truck driver with a neck injury, he says, saving up for surgery. He seems so sincere I believe him, though I'm not sure that really matters: I know he has his reasons. I hand him a bill and drive off. Then, feeling suddenly touched, I circle the block and cut recklessly through two lanes of traffic to give him another. "For your medical fund," I yell, practically hurling a tenner at him to beat the light. "God bless you, you and your family," he yells after me; and yes, I think, how Dickensian: oh, *kind* sir. But I also mentally thank him for helping me sink deeper into that debt that swallows all others and makes them small—small and of no consequence.

I won't claim I've changed that much—not in a week or two, not in a few months. But I do feel as if my inner pockets have been turned inside out, shaking loose some small change in my life. I've developed a soft spot. I can't help but notice the people at the margins, the invisible ones, the ones who used to be the extras in my movie. I know the feeling: *you in me, me in you.* It makes me an easy touch. The money I give out starts to mount up, 20, 30, 40 bucks a month, unburdening my wallet, filling the heart's purse; but somehow, this is better than okay.

The Good Eye

Whenever catching sight of others
Look on them with an open, loving heart.

—Patrul Rinpoche

*T*HE GREAT NINETEENTH-CENTURY JEWISH MYSTIC LEVI Yitzchok, the Rabbi of Berditchev, was known throughout Europe as the Master of the Good Eye. It was said that he could see nothing of people's sins, only their virtues. He'd roust the local drunk from his stupor on High Holy Days, seat him at the head of the table, and respectfully ask for his wisdom. He'd *noodge* a man who'd publicly flouted the Sabbath by praising him as the only one in the village who wasn't a hypocrite. He extended his caring to all, whether powerful or impoverished, scholarly or simple, righteous or reprobate.

The rabbi's inspiration was a Talmud passage that calls for everyone to be weighed "on the scales of merit" (*zechut,* from the Hebrew *zach* or "purity"). The meaning of *zechut,* explains one scholar, is "to intentionally focus on what is most pure in each person—to see their highest and holiest potential." It is a reminder that compassion is not just a gift but a path. The Good Eye is a shift of perception, a transformative art that takes some practice.

My friend Rhonda, a nurse by trade and by calling, is something of a *zechut* artist. When she is warm to you (and she is to most everybody), you feel like a rare edition of yourself. I've followed her on rounds, watching the crankiest patients brighten at her approach, seeing even the most needle-phobic relax and smile, as if her IV were an act of bestowal. She's another of those people who coaxes your petals open. Rhonda learned at the feet of a great teacher—her grandmother, Margaret, also a nurse.

One night Grandma Margaret was summoned to the obstetrics ward of her Arizona hospital. A Down syndrome child had just been born, unpredicted in those pre-amniocentesis days, and the distraught mother was threatening to kill herself rather than keep the baby. When Margaret saw the child, she made an impossible leap of faith. "I'll take that baby home," she announced, "and I'll love her." True to her word, she raised a foster daughter who bloomed into a high-functioning young adult. "I didn't see any defects," she told Rhonda. "I saw a blueprint for perfection." Grandma Margaret once confided her greatest secret: "When I look at people, I see only the best part of them."

I used to think that people who regarded everyone benignly were a mite simple or oblivious or just plain lax—until I tried it myself. Then I realized that they made it only *look* easy. Even the *Berditchever Rebbe,* revered as a man who could strike a rock and bring forth a stream, was continually honing his intentions. "Until I remove the thread of hatred from my heart," he said of his daily meditations, "I am, in my own eyes, as if I did not exist."

He was a man who didn't take the Good Eye for granted. He believed in tending the heart, watering its roots, pulling ego's fibrous, prickly weeds by hand. The distinction between our ordinary eye and the Good Eye is, as is the one between ordinary sight and *in*sight, a quotient of conscious cultivation. It is the gist of the scriptural predicament *You have eyes, but you see not.* We have the necessary parts, but as the label on the shipping carton says, "Some assembly may be required." Luckily, all spiritual traditions concur that it doesn't take a lightning bolt on the road to Damascus or a blast of enlightenment under the bodhi tree. The soul is educable.

Life offers up its own daily catechism, even if it's just seeing people in a little better light. Why not just resolve to give everyone the benefit of the doubt? "If we treat people as if they were what they ought to be," said the poet Goethe, almost nailing it, "we help them become what they are capable of becoming." Or, more to the point: Treat them as they already *are*, if we but had the Good Eye to see it.

Once, at a conference, I noticed a man striding toward me, his face alight. He seemed really happy to see me. When he got closer, he pushed his glasses up to the bridge of his nose, peered at my face, looked down at my nametag, and took a step back.

"I'm so sorry," he said, embarrassed. "You looked just like a friend I haven't seen for years. You even have the same first name..." He trailed off; the effusive warmth seeped away. I told him it was fine. His Good Eye had enveloped me in a gaze of anticipatory delight that made me feel golden. We wound up having lunch. He told me about his research (which coincidentally dovetailed with my own); he talked about the happiness and the sorrows of raising a young daughter with multiple sclerosis (for everyone is fighting a great battle). We still stay in touch.

Maybe we should all take off our glasses and hope for more cases of mistaken identity. For that matter, it might be *un*mistaken. Why *not* welcome everyone as some long-lost cousin, sprung from our African mother, bumping into each other again after a fifty-thousand-year separation. *Wonderful to see you after all this time—you look great!*

A friend of mine, a psychologist, works at Arkansas' infamous Tucker Max Prison. She's well aware that most people look at her prisoner clients and see only dregs—"ugly toothless hulks," as she puts it—but she claims she can see only "radiant bulbs with these big lampshades blocking the light. I know they're supposed to be 'untreatable psychopaths,' but I feel like, *Oh, take that fright-mask off!*" She's remarkably successful. Around her, tough nuts crack open; even wary, death-row guards have been known to cry.

"It's like there's this horribly thick suit of armor," she explains, trying to make me see it through her eyes, "and I know someone's trapped inside, so how do we get them out?" I ask her why she even bothers. "The joy!" she says, as if it's the most obvious thing in the world. "Just the joy of being with people when they show up as they really are."

If we can't see who people really are, say possessors of the Good Eye, it's just our ordinary eye playing tricks on us, focusing on differences and defects, blind to deeper connection. If we mistake each other for strangers, it's just blurry vision. The Good Eye is the corrective to Einstein's "optical delusion of consciousness." As with the rearview mirror that cautions "Objects may be closer than they appear," we might be much closer than we think.

Sixteenth-century Tibetan meditation master Wang-ch'ug Dorje recommended a practice he called "the Activity of Being in Crowds." Walking through a throng, he said, is a "good opportunity to check your progress and examine the delusions, attachments, and aversions that arise." A bustling mall is an especially good place to check my Good Eye for jaundice. With everything winking merrily, beckoning with come-ons for instant gratification, I go into a sort of trance. The mind itself gets into the spirit of things, hawking its tawdrier wares; my finicky responses to the goods on display merge with my reactions to the people I pass—little covetous twinges, subtle flickers of attitude, petty judgments on how people walk, talk, dress, and chew gum. Here a surge of superiority; there a deflating thought of inadequacy. Here a lurch of desire for a sleek, well turned-out woman; there a picador's lance of envy at her undeserving boyfriend in the slobby polo shirt.

The Koran describes envy as a veil that beclouds the eye of the heart. It's one of Saint Augustine's seven deadly sins (which I interpret as "biggest obstacles to selfless love"). Envy turns other people into sources of resentment: *If I had what you have, I would be happy.* It tints everyone in bilious shades of green. It's a zero-sum game. Envy's only hope is that the other person will be diminished, as if that would free up proportionately more for itself. (It extends all the way to that uniquely German coinage, *schadenfreude,* gloating over another's misfortune, the Good Eye turned into the Evil Eye itself.)

But just as there are emotional toxins, there are also antidotes and remedies—what the apothecaries of yore called "specifics." In Buddhism the supreme medicine for envy is said to be *mudita,* or "sympathetic joy," which calls on us to feel happy about another's success. Easy enough when it comes to rejoicing for those we really care about: Every parent *kvells* over his or her kid's triumphs; a teacher exults when her favorite student aces the math exam. But to expand this feeling from a narrow circle to a wider arena is like pulling wisdom teeth.

I once witnessed an exchange between a Tibetan lama and a questioner on this subject. "Rinpoche," inquired a pleasant middle-aged man in a checked sport shirt, "my son is a linebacker for his high school football team. I find myself rooting for him to cream the opposing quarterback. Is there anything wrong with that?"

"Of course not," the lama replied. "You love your son, and you want his happiness, and he's happy when he beats the other team. This is only natural."

There was an audible sigh of relief in the room. The spiritual path may be challenging, but it's not *unreasonable.*

The man smiled. "Thank you, Rinpoche," he said, making a brisk, reverent folding gesture with his hands.

The lama laughed sharply. "I was only *joking!* Actually, this is not at all the right attitude. In fact," he said, glancing at the man mischievously, "a good practice for you would be to *root for the other team.* See *them* winning, see *them* happy, see *their* parents overjoyed. That is more the *bodhisattva* way."

I have a wildly successful acquaintance who's in my field. I've seen him on magazine covers, a smug, airbrushed grin on his face. I've been training myself, as an antidote to a fulminating case of green-eye, that whenever I feel that little twitch of envy, I wish for *more* bluebirds of happiness to come sit on his eaves. "Don't you mean," asks a cynical friend, "come *shit on his sleeves?*" But the fact is, my good wishes provide an unexpected sense of relief. It's an unknotting, expansive feeling, as if what's his and what's mine suddenly, metaphysically, belong to both of us and to neither. (I recently came across a line from Yoko Ono: "Transform [jealousy] to admiration / And what you admire / Will become part of your life.")

Try it for yourself. Root for the other team. Visualize someone who makes *you* envious. Think of them in all their irritating splendor, enjoying the perks and accolades *you* no doubt deserve. Then wish sincerely that they get even *more* goodies.

Isn't this the mortal sin of "low self-esteem"? Well, not exactly; it's more like a metaphysical jujitsu. In rooting for someone else's happiness, we tune to a different wavelength. We feel more beneficent, less deprived, more capable of giving. The focus on another person's satisfaction becomes a lodestone that paradoxically draws us closer to our own. (And isn't most envy just our own potential disowned?) Seeing the world through another's eyes (*you in me, me in you*) makes one feel there's at least twice as much to go around;

not more money or fame or square footage but the foundation of the whole pursuit: love.

It could be argued that this approach might work in a monastery or on a mountaintop, but not in real life, where the game is tooth-and-nail and rooting for your own team is what keeps the opposition from eating you alive. I recently saw a quote from megamogul and master of the Squinty Eye, Donald Trump, extolling the benefits of pure paranoia: "People you think are your friends in business will take your money, your wife, your pets... Life's a vicious place. No different than a jungle." Yet there are people who swim in the piranha-infested corporate waters for whom the Good Eye has not only been good karma but good business.

*A*T THE INCANDESCENT TURN OF THE CENTURY, WHEN EVERY tech stock was a fireworks display and bubbles popped only in champagne flutes, Ricardo Levy's star shone bright over Silicon Valley. The son of a Jewish father who had fled Nazi Germany to settle in Ecuador, Ricardo was CEO of a bricks-and-mortar company selling real goods amid the valley's vaporware vendors. In the 1970s his startup had been an entrepreneurial shot in the dark, but Ricardo had parlayed a newly minted doctorate, a knack for discovery, and a drive to excel into what he calls "a nonstop adventure of continuous transformation." Soon his company was racking up a half billion dollars in annual sales.

His product was literally transformative: The company designed and produced essential industrial catalysts. Ricardo can discourse happily about them for hours, sounding more like an alchemist than a chemical engineer—how they enable magical conversions of materials, serving as facilitators (or, as he calls them, "midwives") for disparate substances to join together and give birth to something new. Business was good, and, as a bonus, the company did some good in the world. Ricardo felt proud to have patented a process that produced more energy with minimal pollution, a happy union of the bottom line and his environmental concerns

But by 2000 he found himself stretched to the breaking point. Through a series of acquisitions, his company had turned from a midsized shop into a lurching industrial titan. "I was trained as a researcher to discover things," he says, "not to manage thousands of people." He decided he needed guidance.

There is no shortage of advice for the entrepreneurially perplexed. Stacks of business bibles reveal how to turn companies into lean, mean, no-fixed-limit cash machines; armies of consultants feed CEOs' obsessive drive to play king of the mountain. But Ricardo was after something else. "I'd always been a seeker of depth, not height," he says in his lightly accented English. "I'd seen enough to be suspicious of the shadow side of power. I knew some of those Enron guys."

He turned to an old friend, Andre Delbecq, a legendary management consultant who also taught at a Jesuit college. Andre had recently gone on his own quest, taking a sabbatical at the height of the Silicon Valley's giddy ascendance to pore over the world's spiritual teachings, seeking "that paradox of perfect humility and perfect hope" that he believed was the hallmark of true leadership. After returning from sailing the Turkish coast, Andre invited Ricardo and a select group of CEOs to hear a presentation of his findings, promising them a management course that would change their lives as well as their business practices.

It was certainly unorthodox. If most executive training is a regimen of psychological power-lifting and ego steroids, Andre replaced yes-I-can with not-so-fast and no-you-don't: Don't be enslaved by your own ambitions; don't think only of the bottom line; don't, for a while, think at all—especially about yourself. He scoured the world's religious practices, in the end deciding to teach his students the Buddhist meditation of tonglen—an imaginative exercise that calls for breathing in others' suffering and breathing out lovingkindness. "There was no other discipline I'd found," he told me, "that enabled people to immediately grasp openness and humility for themselves." Ricardo found the practice edifying, even elating.

Andre gave his students assignments that plunged them into places they feared, having them spend time with Alzheimer's patients, prisoners, or the homeless in what he called "I-Thou encounters, just listening to and learning from, not judging anyone's value or worthiness."

Andre had the executives tell one another their personal stories, asking if anyone in their own family was struggling with disease, drugs, or mental illness or had found themselves on the wrong side of the law. The Titanium Men of Silicon Valley were astonished to discover that their most formidable colleagues and competitors were grappling with the same mortal complement of weal and woe. Andre became a sort of heart-coach, urging them to widen their sympathies by considering how each of their employees faced similar difficulties. He assured them that if they entered their workplace with what he called "compassionate presence," they'd discover the hidden life of their company.

To put that vulnerability into practice in the business world, where dog really does eat dog and big fish swallow little fish and pick their teeth with the bones, had seemed like folly. But Ricardo tackled it with his usual full-on commitment. At the time, the fate of his entire company balanced on a single excruciating choice point. He had been negotiating to take over a large pharmaceutical company when discussions had turned hostile, finally reaching a bitter impasse. He put the talks on mental pause. "I decided I had to try to feel empathy for all parties, including the other side, the adversary. I needed an inner answer, not a spreadsheet answer."

He had a realization that shocked him: "I saw it would be better for *them* to take *us* over.

"This would be traumatic for me because I'd be disassembling the business I'd built over decades. But when I put myself aside and considered everyone else involved—our shareholders and employees, the *other* company's shareholders and employees—I knew it was right." The decision was pure intuition, he says. People inside and outside the organization thought he'd gone crazy. In 2000 his company's financial bellwethers were surreally bright; every indicator pointed due north. But three months after the deal closed, the tech economy went south, and as Ricardo says dryly, "It turned out in retrospect the direction I chose had been to everyone's benefit."

Ricardo found that his practice led him to more-generous policies for his employees. He backed benefits packages that cut into his profits because it seemed to him the right thing to do only to find that it also made the company stronger. Tonglen was, he realized, the spiritual equivalent of the catalysis at the very heart of his business. "You take in suffering, transform it to positive energy, and then offer that out into the world."

I HAPPENED TO BE PRESENT ONE OF THE FIRST TIMES TIBETAN meditation master Chögyam Trungpa sprang this bizarre-sounding practice on an unsuspecting Western audience. One student of yoga had raised his hand and asked, with some bewilderment, why it wouldn't be better to imagine breathing in love and light and breathing out all negative impurities. Ricardo, the creator of environmentally benign industrial processes, would have appreciated Trungpa's unhesitating reply: "Well, then you'd just be like a polluting factory, taking in all these good resources and spewing out your gray cloud on everyone else."

The practice *is* decidedly counterintuitive. Sometimes when I begin tonglen meditation, I feel a wild surge of resistance, a fear of (there is no other way to put this) contamination. The unhappiness of others feels contagious: I don't want to inhale their cooties. But when it "works," the practice is so rewarding that I'm ready to throw myself in again. To stop dodging people's misery and discord, to discover that I can give of myself with each breath and not feel depleted (in fact, to feel oddly nourished) is a revelation. When I can stay with it, I notice I don't feel so guarded; my borders seem more porous. I'm less inclined to hold people at arms' length.

I admit to sometimes finding tonglen a challenge that I don't have the spiritual chutzpah to meet. But at best I find the technique radically simple and simply radical: an imaginative leap into otherness. There's a through-the-looking-glass moment, an almost audible *pop,* as I seem to find myself looking at the world through different eyes. It enhances what some psychologists refer to as "intersubjectivity"—a shared space of experience. If our usual ego-identity is maintained by keeping the good and estimable stuff in here and the yucky stuff out there, tonglen dissolves some of the rigidity of selfhood.

When my mind has some downtime that I'd normally fill by gossiping idly to myself, I try to remember to do tonglen. It's my mental screensaver. On the highway the other day, a college kid whizzed past at one and a half times the speed limit in a silver Hummer, honking wildly, blaring hip-hop from every window of his gas-hog, giving me the finger for good measure. I could feel my temper about to flare like a bottle rocket, my accelerator foot begin to twitch. Instead, I zeroed in on the back of his fast-receding head, breathing in his rage and frustration (which surely wasn't personal). I could almost feel his emotional claustrophobia, his agitated need for speed. I remembered being nineteen, riding the testosterone express.

What amazed me was that I didn't feel anger but some actual sympathy for the guy—along with a whoosh of inner freedom. Normally, when I feel hurt or affronted, my emotional choices seem to narrow. I can either absorb the blow and feel wretched or deflect it back to the other person (or later on some hapless bystander): It's like a choice between suicide or murder. With tonglen, I get to choose life.

Shambhala Mountain Center, an ink-brush painting of scrub pine hills, chattering magpies, and skittish prairie dogs near the Colorado-Wyoming border, has for decades been my place of retreat. It is dominated by the astonishing Great Stupa of Dharmakaya, a ten-story shrine whose gold-leaf spire suggests some unregulated spiritual broadcasting tower. Chögyam Trungpa, whose relics it houses, would have found it wondrous and maybe a bit absurd: an ornate memorial to his teachings about the simplicity of the present moment; a soaring monument to the enlightenment that's right under your nose.

On a recent visit, making my way down the hill after meditating before the stupa's gargantuan, faintly smiling Buddha statue, I fell in stride with an athletic-looking woman in khaki shorts, hurrying down the path. When I mentioned my writing topic, she slowed down to talk. She had a story, she said—a simple one about meditation and compassion.

"I first started to meditate when my boyfriend dumped me," she said as I huffed along beside her in the thin mountain air. "I needed to sort through all the bad feelings, but I was afraid that I'd look inside and find out one thing: that I basically sucked. Gradually, though, I found it didn't matter if I thought I was horrible or if I thought I was great: I could drop my whole story and just breathe. It was a chance not only to explore myself but to get *over* myself. Meditation became this tool to not react in my usual way."

She was a ski bum, she told me, the "rabble-rouser and hell-raiser" in a family of perfectionists. Her older sister was the one with the high-powered, big-city job and the fantastic two-career marriage, the one who would come to her house and "just criticize everything about me right down to the stinky sponges in the sink. She'd drive me crazy until *wham!* I'd get combative and we'd have some huge, screaming fight."

During one of her sister's visits, they set out on a scenic drive. "Well, soon it was the usual: 'You're driving too fast! There's a beer can on the floor; the car is filthy!' And I noticed my habitual response coming up inside: *Who the hell are you to tell me how to live? Back off!* But this time the words didn't come out of my mouth. For once I was able to just notice her, notice my own feelings, and breathe.

"When I didn't react, it made her even madder. She upped the ante. There was this onslaught of everything she could throw at me: '*I* make all the money in the family; it's me who'd have to scrape you up if anything bad ever happened to you,' *blah, blah, blah*. But even though I heard her anger and anxiety, I was able to slow down; and instead of getting defensive and lashing out, I just asked her, 'Are you okay, Carol?' And I meant it. I wanted to know.

"Well, she was so caught off guard, she didn't even have a retort. Instead she started to blurt out everything about the screwed-up place her life had come to—how she was going to leave her husband, how she'd be alone in the city, how she was afraid she'd never have children—and then she just broke down sobbing! And all the snotty comebacks I'd stored up just evaporated. I could feel the whole burden of my personality, her personality, our history, fall away, and like some beautiful plant springing up out of nowhere, there was just compassion."

Her story, like Ricardo's, confirmed for me a spiritual insight— call it, To Find Your Heart, Lose Your Head—that's as close to a universal principle as you can extract from the mystical traditions. The ego is really a sort of trance state from which it is possible to awaken. And beneath its incessant inner commentary, behind the persuasive story lines and the beliefs that spawn them, beyond the passions that give those beliefs their emotional clout, there is a wellspring of pure compassion.

The great Hasidic rabbi known as the Maggid told his disciples that the best way to realize the love at the heart of the Torah is to "cease to be aware of yourselves. You must be nothing but an ear which hears what the universe of the word is constantly saying within you. The moment you start hearing what you yourself are saying, you must stop." The Buddha, in a radical act of reflection, suggested we disbelieve our thought process entirely.

Easier said than done, of course. If you want a little aperçu on that subject, try sitting stock-still for a while on a cushion or a chair; just sit there, observing the old inhale and exhale, trying not to get carried away by those broken-record thoughts yakking in the background; just sit, dangling from a rope of breath above the morass of your charming personality, and you will soon be at one with a hundredfold generations of meditators who have dis-covered self-delusion's ripeness.

In seeking what Buddhism calls Big Mind, I confess I some-times look inward and find new vistas of smallness. But my practice, such as it is, hasn't been all eddies and doldrums. Sometimes I can forsake the drone of internal gossip, opt for the unadorned Now. Then I find myself gazing into a void where, moments before, the bustling manufacturing hub of selfhood had been on track to fulfill its daily quota. I get acquainted with my mental habits—tics, really. I start finding my neuroses less dramatic than tedious; enough to tell them, when I'm really not in the mood for entertain-ing, to just buzz off.

Once, at a seminar, I heard a Westernized lama say that a meditator's state of mind should be like that of a hotel doorman. A doorman lets the guests in, but he doesn't follow them up to their rooms. He lets them out, but he doesn't walk into the street with them to their next appointment. He greets them all, then lets them go on about their business. Meditation is, in its initial stages, simply accustoming oneself to letting thoughts come and go without grasping at their sleeves or putting up a velvet rope to keep them out.

Similarly, Sufi teachings specify that a certain impartiality is required to mount the "thrones of compassion." It is said one must remove the veil of *wahm* ("opinion" or "conjecture"). "The real heart," said the Islamic sage known as the Prince of the Illumined, "is that heart which is neither on the right nor on the left, neither above nor below, neither far nor near"—that is, beyond ordinary cognition and its incessant parsing of differences.*

No one would claim it's not tricky business. Such work, the alchemists used to say, is *opus contra naturum*—work against our natural tendencies—here the mind's impulse to classify this person as near, that one as far; this one a beloved, that one a rival. Various traditions call for cultivating detachment from the potent cues presented by the outer world (or, for that matter, the inner one): Do you feel distaste when you see a particular person coming toward you on the street? If so, regard that distaste as a thing apart, disconnected from its object, generated in your own heart and mind. By the same token, don't just swoon over the feeling that reflexively arises when someone flashes her most attractive smile.

---

*A friend told me of visiting the Dalai Lama in India and asking him for a succinct definition of compassion. She prefaced her question by describing how heart-stricken she'd felt when, earlier that day, she'd seen a man in the street beating a mangy stray dog with a stick. "Compassion," the Dalai Lama told her, "is when you feel as sorry for the man as you do for the dog."

Both are (in this practice, at least) obstacles, obscurations; they get in the way of a lovingkindness beyond mere personal preference

It's not unlike the Christian practice of "discernment," which a theologian once described to me as "learning to see in a way that is consonant with God's way of seeing. As long as there's ego-attachment," she said, "we're seeing other people in a fun-house mirror. As long as our eyes are clouded by longing, needing other people to be this way or that for us, there's no such thing as compassion." I'd always admired Christianity's emphasis on doing good, but here was a practice of *seeing* good that resembled Eastern-style meditation. I had always wondered about the relationship between this inner Christianity and more churchly forms of worship. If I wanted to get a real insight, I was told, I should talk to Father Thomas Keating, the monk who had almost single-handedly revived the contemplative method of realizing God's illimitable love.

*T*O GET TO FATHER KEATING'S MONASTERY, YOU MUST PASS, as all pilgrims must do, through a vale of temptation, in this case the Gulch of Glitz known as Aspen. I manage to ignore all its allurements (save a real New York–style Reuben with meltingly tender pastrami), heading out past the private airport where sleek personal jets take off and land with a purling roar.

All's quiet a few miles down a dirt road at Saint Benedict's Monastery, its soaring, carved wood architecture at once a psalm to the earth and a paean to whatever lies beyond. Father Keating emerges to greet me. An eighty-one-year-old man in a plaid wool shirt, watchcap plunked on his bald head, he could be an ancient mariner home from the sea or some ex-stevedore hired as keeper of the bell tower. For him, God's love calls for workmanlike practice.

"Jesus had a formula," he tells me as we sit practically knee to knee in his cramped office. "In the Sermon on the Mount, Jesus says, 'Pray to your Father, your Abba, your Daddy, in *secret*.' Go into your inner room at the center of your being. Close the door, not just to the external noise and distraction but to the inner dialogue too."

Keating speaks in lovely, loping, run-on sentences. When I close my eye, his deep, creaky voice conjures some old cricket sachem, sawing a rhythmic evensong on long bowstring legs. "You have to silence the emotional programs that sustain who you think you are," he says, "allow the ego's self-reflective apparatus to fade out, put aside that false self based on childhood emotions—the reaching out for happiness, security, approval, affection, esteem, all those exaggerated needs we impose on others—and just do nothing.

"But not *just* nothing. Rather nothing of our *own* but everything of what God proposes we do. God prefers this kind of love—not what you're willing to do but what you're willing to *receive*. Our lack of confidence in his great love is the only problem." Although this isn't a particularly funny remark, he smiles with such gentle irony that I can't help but burst out laughing, feeling some perfusion of high seriousness and puckish joy.

"We say that when you enter prayer, *nothing* is worth thinking about," he says, peering out through his enormous round glasses, "whether it's a sense perception, memory, plan, concept, or image. It doesn't mean no thoughts but to disregard them. They're placed in the 'cloud of forgetting,' which contains the ultimate knowledge of what is but which is unknown to the intellect."

I suggest that it must be hard for someone who is so clearly an intellectual to relinquish all thought and center himself in the heart. Father Keating smiles. "All you need is a willingness to suffer and a willingness to love." All the rest of it, he stresses, is the false self and its gnat cloud of petty thinking that obscures love's ultimate Source. So far as he's concerned, organized religion has too often swarmed with the gnats instead of soared with the angels.

"Such a shame what we've done to the Mystery," he murmurs with a sigh, "with all our naive loyalties!"

The history of religion is not an uninterrupted purview of the Good Eye. Alongside its numberless good deeds are uncounted (and unaccountably) bad ones. It's tragicomic to hear, at the dawn of the twenty-first century, imams promising Paradise to infidel-slayers, pastors invoking a Prince of Peace who sounds more like Rambo, rabbis sanctifying biblical land-grabs, Buddhist priests blessing military juntas. (I recently heard a cleric, who surely spoke for sectarians everywhere, decree from the pulpit, "Every-one is created by God, but not everyone is a *child* of God.") A good organizational consultant would counsel the world's major faiths to reexamine their original mission statements: The core business of Jesus Inc. or Allah Ltd. or Moses Corp. or Buddha LLC is surely not to sell tickets to heaven or peddle get-out-of-hell-free cards but to distribute every kernel of wisdom from their ancient store-houses that might help us love one another.

We *are* slowly emerging from millennia of holy know-it-alls beaning each other with their Infallible Books, passing judgment with their Divine Laws, and trying to enforce competing copy-rights on Ultimate Truth. The God of our times is no longer some Big Eye in the Sky but the Good Eye itself. He is turning into what Friedrich Nietzsche, who preferred deities of blood and thunder, once sneeringly called a "changed god...Now he counsels 'peace of soul,' hate-no-more, forbearance, even 'love' of friend and enemy... Now he is merely the good god."

I'll take him. So will, it seems, a lot of other people. In churches, synagogues, temples, and mosques around the world, there has been a quiet revival of the inner traditions for transforming the heart. Just as the formula for baking a loaf of bread is similar across cultures, the same techniques for compassion seem to crop up everywhere: loosen the bonds of discursive thought, extend the circle of caring, cease armoring against suffering, wish for others the same happiness you wish for yourself.

"Religious stories are training," a rabbi once told me, "not just rulebooks." At their best the practices we call spiritual are tried-and-true ways to unplug from the ego's matrix and awaken from delusory life, to shut the biased and nearsighted Squinty Eye and open the Good Eye wide. The Little Prince said it as well as anybody: "It is only with the heart that one can see rightly."

Such seeing, however, may require deliberately redirecting the gaze. Awhile back I decided to unplug my television. I wanted to clear my head of mass culture with its endless parade of imaginary characters who not only clutter the mind but, I began to think, subtly sidetrack the heart. In my TV's old corner, I've created a small shrine, an experimental compassion lab. Arrayed among the candles, incense, and homemade icons are photos of friends and loved ones, little endorphin triggers, jump-starts for the heart. There's also a photo of Juan, the seven-year-old Salvadoran I've started sponsoring through an international aid agency. This little boy, in his faded Spiderman T-shirt and dirty blue pants, has become part of my orbit of caring, a link to the larger human family. I've also included some pictures of people I really don't like. I try to breathe in their suffering and breathe out my goodness. I remind myself I don't need to reserve a stash of happiness for my exclusive use. Like digital data, infinitely replicable because it has no substance or extrinsic cost, I can afford to give it away, even to those whom I deem undeserving. There's more where that came from.

To all this, you might well say, "So what?" Don't just sit there, *do* something. The world is on fire, or it's drowning. Too many people are tragically dying, too many lucklessly born. And it's true: The Good Eye should guide the Good Hand, set the Good Feet in motion. But I believe that old existentialist Albert Camus had it right: "We all carry within us our places of exile, our crimes, our ravages. Our task is not to unleash them on the world; it is to transform them in ourselves and others." Inner transformation doesn't supplant outward action but nourishes it. I project less on others of my own need for redemption. Do-gooding becomes more alloyed with be-gooding. The Good Eye is not merely a gaze but a creative force, like the penetrating sunlight that quickens a buried seed.

Am I getting anywhere? Is there anywhere *to* get? These days I can feel unexpectedly pierced by something I hear, something I see, some stray thread of feeling I might have overlooked. I've placed a few eye drops in the Good Eye. I'll sometimes feel a soft explosion of warmth or ache in my chest and think that it's my heart shaking off its torpor. I hear it murmuring; maybe someday it will shout.

Heart Science, Heart's Mystery

1 will take the stony heart out...
and give them a heart of flesh.

—Ezekiel

Man will become better when you show him what he is like.

—Anton Chekhov

"WHAT IS THE HEART, BUT A SPRING?" ASKED SEVENTEENTH-century materialist Thomas Hobbes. He wasn't waxing poetic about upwelling waters of gladness or a season of tender buds but making a case for the heart as a gearworks—a mechanism that, however marvelously constructed by that intelligence he called the "Artificer," was as devoid of sensibility as a clock.

This view has held sway for centuries, though it's deeply at odds with our felt experience. When psychologist Carl Jung, on one of his perennial quests, visited Chief Mountain Lake of the Taos Pueblo, the tribal elder told him he judged the whites to be quite mad.

"They say they think with their heads," the chief said.

"Of course," said Jung. "What do *you* think with?"

Mountain Lake pointed to his heart: "We think *here*."

I've always taken this idea—the wisdom of the heart and all—to be a metaphor albeit a charming one. But in cultures the world over, it takes on a peculiarly literal cast. Among the Sufis, the physical heart is a container for *al-aql,* the intellect, and *al-fouad,* a second, "sensitive" heart that can see into the hearts of others. Aristotle claimed that the heart was responsible for "the power of perception and the soul's ability to nourish itself." In the Eastern Orthodox tradition, the heart not only is a human being's emotional core but is identified with the mind. Similarly, the Japanese have two heart words: *shinzu,* the physical organ, and *kokoro,* "the mind of the heart."

Does the heart have a mind of its own? Neuroscience has long known that the two hemispheres of the *brain* think somewhat independently—the right side being, in a sense, more heartful, specializing in emotional and intuitive functions, and the left leaning more toward rationality and logic. The idea of heartfulness as an independent form of cognition was illustrated, albeit inadvertently, in a widely reported 1986 experiment. A test group of college students was shown a documentary about Mother Teresa. Immediately afterward, their saliva revealed increased levels of S-IgA, an immune system–boosting hormone. The conclusion reached in the popular press: Compassion makes you feel good *and* it's good for you.

But the media reports overlooked a strange fact: Most of the students said they'd found the film depressing. After seeing it, they reported a *decrease* in feelings of love and friendliness and an *increase* in "overall negative mood." They found the plight of the poorest of the poor, the sick and the dying of Calcutta's slums, deeply dispiriting. Mother Teresa's rigid religiosity made some uncomfortable. The surprise was this: Both the students who had negative reactions *and* those who had positive ones showed the same immune system boost.

What's going on here? The experimenters surmised that while conscious judgments were taking place in the left brain, the right brain was responding to the emotional thrust of the film—images of altruism and compassion—and translating them into physiological responses. The left brain was put off by the film, but the right brain was turned on. It was as if the students were literally of two minds, and when push came to shove, the heartful mind had the final say.

The heart itself may be smarter than we think. It not only receives impulses from the brain but *sends* information to it via the vagus nerve. The heart generates its own hormones and releases them into the body. It even broadcasts its own electromagnetic field thousands of times more powerful than the brain's. And though scientists once thought the heartbeat was as monotonous as a metronome, its rhythm under resting conditions shows odd irregularities that, when carefully analyzed, seem to correlate with specific emotions.

This latter claim remains controversial, but according to scientists working at the Institute of HeartMath, that organ pulsating in your chest cavity really does know a thing or two. The institute, whose scientific board includes Joe Kamiya, the father of modern biofeedback research, along with an impressive array of cognitive biologists, cardiologists, brain physiologists, and biomedical engineers, claims to have the data to prove it. They have set out not just to study the heart but, as one researcher told me, "to maximize the heart's influence on the brain" (or, as another put it, admitting it sounded like "squishy" science: "to illumine the mind with the heart's knowing").

*T*HIS ALL SOUNDED GOOD TO ME, SO WHEN I WAS INVITED TO interview a few of the scientists at HeartMath's sprawling, 160-acre campus in northern California, I leaped at the chance. But first I'd been penciled in for some hang time with the organization's enigmatic founder, "Doc" Childre.

I was prepped for the meeting by a mutual friend, who described Doc as an eccentric genius who once claimed to have lived a year without food, like some supernatural Taoist hermit. Those days were over. He now liked a good smoke and a cold beer, and, as a man of the South, he favored his barbequed short ribs slow roasted.

I was told that Doc liked to meet people at night, and I was led by flashlight to a barn, where I was directed to climb a ladder to a loft, its beams decked with strings of white Christmas lights. I found Doc sitting in an old club chair. With his gray beard, faded plaid shirt, and a bandana wrapped around his head, he looked like Willie Nelson. He poured me a cup of warm whisky and one for himself, fired up a nonfilter, and popped the top off a tall frosty one.

"If you can't have your cake and eat it, too," he pronounces with a croaking laugh, "why'd they bake the damn cake?"

Truth to tell, I don't remember much of our conversation. As the evening took its course, my notes are in a progressively shakier hand. I remember sitting there companionably with the reclusive guru of HeartMath in his Bat Cave, finding him immensely likable as he talked elliptically about "domains of higher-frequency emotions," the "heart's nervous system," the "access codes to holographic dimensions," and "bringing the heart to the street."

I do remember one koan delivered by the flare of a lighter held to the tip of his cigarette: "Love's not enough," he said, the flame underlighting his bewhiskered face. *"It's the care that puts it in the real!*" It wasn't exactly technical, but Doc's ideas, backed by some hard research, have been showing up in such august publications as the *American Journal of Cardiology*.

Cardiologists had for years been studying subtle, beat-to-beat irregularities in heart rhythm called heart-rate variability (HRV), mostly as a diagnostic tool to measure nervous system aging and emotional stress. But Doc had added a key insight. Different HRV patterns seemed to correlate with specific emotional states, in particular those that psychologists call the "qualia," such as compassion, love, and forgiveness.

Measuring inner states with instrumentation is nothing new. Electroencephalograms (EEGs) have shown that alpha and theta rhythms in the brain are associated with the calming effects of meditation and yoga (known generally as the "relaxation response"). But HeartMath's research added a new wrinkle. Measures of heart-rate variability show that the patterns generated by altruism and compassion are distinctly different from relaxed meditative states. Researchers claim that states of mind (or, better, states of heart) that have more to do with caring about others than with seeking inner peace actually have greater health-promoting effects on the immune system and the autonomic nervous system. "Love and caring," says HeartMath researcher Rollin McCraty, "drive the entire bodily system to oscillate at its resonant frequency," a purported state of harmony between brain and body that he says he can scientifically measure.

McCraty, a wiry biophysiologist with a thatch of reddish hair, takes me on a whirlwind tour of his biophysics lab, pointing out his spectrometers and cell-culturing rooms; his supersensitive, shielded confocal microscope for directly observing DNA; his towers of tall, silvery, sixty-channel processing units and assorted boxes whose blinking amber diodes and ebony and brass knobs are straight out of Jules Verne. All told, he can measure damn near anything having to do with the heart. Using a technology called spectral analysis, McCraty has shown that positive feelings create orderly "coherent" frequency patterns in the heart's electromagnetic (EM) signal that correspond to coherent rhythms of heart-rate variability. Not only that, he says, but the heart's EM field signal affects the brain's own electrical rhythms; and not only *that*, but one person's coherent heart frequency can affect another person's EEG and—well, you get the drift.

McCraty, a confirmed cardiophile, can riff with authority all day long and deep into the gloaming on the heart's incredible powers. He cites evidence that some sensory information is routed to the heart *before* it arrives in the brain. The heart, he says, sends far more messages to the brain via its ascending (afferent) nerve pathways than the brain sends down the heart's mail chute through its descending (efferent) ones.

"Emotion," he says succinctly, "is faster than thought."

This model—let's call it The Heart Is Quicker Than the Mind—seems to be showing up everywhere. Primate researcher Frans de Waal's perception-action model suggests that in both apes and humans, emotions—including the empathic instinct—trigger a physical response *before any conscious decision has been reached.* Psychologist Jonathan Haidt has put forward a similar heart-over-head hypothesis (which he calls the social intuitionalist model). Haidt believes we first have an "emotionally tinged intuition," followed by intellectual justifications for what, in effect, the heart's already decided. When Thomas Carlyle noted a few centuries ago, "It is the heart that always sees, before the head can see," he may not have been far off.

The heart is now known to influence the brain via everything from neurotransmitters to pressure waves. It sends signals to the brain that activate or inhibit the cortex itself, giving the heart a neural vote (and maybe a veto) on cognitive functions as well as its own back-channel influence on emotional centers like the amygdala. Nor does it always have to go through the brain's bureaucracy because—did I mention?—the heart turns out to have its *own* brain of sorts, some forty thousand neurons and support cells arranged in an intricate architecture resembling that of the cortex. Research indicates that this heart-brain can learn, remember, and sense. The heart-brain even secretes its own dopamine, a component in the pleasure circuits that strongly influence our behaviors, suggesting our heart may play us like a violin. It is also known that the heart generates its own supply of oxytocin, the so-called cuddle chemical, which, though it has a half-life in the bloodstream of only seconds, can create a lifelong imprint. Could it be that the heart strikes up love's music and the brain, that happy fool, dances to its tune? More often than you think, your heart really is the boss of you.

Using only the inner science of contemplation, mystics and meditators throughout the ages have made the same discovery. When fourteenth-century monk Saint Gregory Palamas wrote, "Our heart is the place of the rational faculty," he wasn't just speaking of the heart-as-metaphor but, according to one contemporary Greek Orthodox archbishop, "this spiritual heart located in the bodily heart as in an organ." The Hindu Upanishads describe a "self-luminous Being who dwells within the lotus of the heart, surrounded by the senses and the sense-organs, who is the Light of Intelligence"—an image strikingly like that of a cognizing brain ringed by its perceptual organs.

The relatively new field of neurocardiology has discovered that the heart *does* have its own sensory organs: Some of the heart's nerve ganglia receive information directly from the skin (giving new meaning to the phrase *you touched my heart*). There are forty nerves from the heart to the muscles governing subtle facial expression. What is inscribed on the heart may indeed be written all over your face. (It may also explain why changing your facial expression can also change your mood.)

To get an idea how far all this diverges from the original (and still influential) insights of the early psychophysiologists, consider that Walter Canon, the father of psychosomatic medicine, once claimed that a severed head, if kept alive, would have a full range of emotion and cognition. Cyberneticists talk about downloading the software of the human personality into indestructible robot brains and bodies in some postmodern version of the Tin Man. The ancient Egyptians knew better. Though they removed the other major organs (including the brain) during the process of mummification, they left the heart, which they considered the seat of the soul, intelligence, and emotion to ensure that resurrection would be worth all the trouble.

Doc Childre realized that the heart doesn't exert its uplifting influence on body, mind, and spirit entirely on autopilot; it's helped by conscious intention. He and his researchers discovered that, just as holding your hands in front of an imaginary campfire causes your palms to measurably heat up, so visualizing the heart glowing with warmth produces a distinct physiological effect— in this case, one that seems to correlate with feelings of calm and lovingkindness. Simply giving the heart your full attention seems to produce physiological patterns that correlate with compassion itself. HeartMath researchers have noted that these "coherent" patterns of heart-rate variability are associated with positive effects on autonomic nervous system balance, cardiovascular efficiency, and reduced secretion of the stress hormone cortisol. Other tests have revealed that coherent HRV patterns produce greater increases in cognitive functioning than even the relaxation response, giving the expression *putting your heart into it* new scientific heft.

Researcher Rollin McCraty offers to give me a practical demonstration. He sits me down in front of a biofeedback-equipped computer that displays changes in heart-rate variability as dynamic graphics in a video game. "It's the opposite of games that encourage aggression," he explains as he fits my finger into a pulse sensor that will pick up my HRV readout. Rather, he says, the point of this game is to train players to generate the physiological states associated with love, care, and compassion. When my heartbeat hits the magic love frequency, the barren black-and-white landscape on the screen will bloom into a colorful flower garden.

As I sit before the screen, doing my best to germinate some love seeds (*uh-oh:* compassion performance anxiety), I manage to entice a few sprigs to poke up from the digital dirt. McCraty taps the keyboard, and another screen appears, this one of three bar graphs representing low, medium, and high HRV coherence. I try simply meditating, but, to my surprise, this mostly produces readings in the low end, with a little blip of activity in the center column.

"Now try focusing in your heart," McCraty suggests. "Think of someone you love."

I imagine my daughter's face and am amazed to see the medium graph rise like a soufflé and spill over into the high range. "That's great," he says encouragingly. I decide to try my hand, or at least my finger, at another game in which coherent HRV readings are synched to the movement of a colorful hot-air balloon. Putting a little love in my heart, I quickly attain liftoff and am soon wafting over a bucolic landscape on a self-generated breeze of affection. But then my focus drifts. My balloon nearly shears the roof off a farmhouse before clunking to the ground.

I take off the sensor and hand it to McCraty. He takes a deep breath, inserts his trigger finger, and does everything but crack his knuckles. Soon enough his balloon is up, up, and away, sailing blithely over every obstacle—stone walls, houses, treetops, mountain ranges—and into nothing but blue skies.

When he sends me back with a home-version kit for practice, I hook it up right away to my computer. After playing around with it only a few times a week, I actually start getting better; at least, my readings increase. So does a feeling in my chest I can only call the warm fuzzies. Yes, there's something a little absurd about sitting in the glowing cathode twilight, entrusting my heart to the gondola of a digital blimp—I mean, *get a life*. But I find to my surprise that as I walk through the day, even this little bit of practice really does make me feel different. What I might call head-centered consciousness seems to look out at the world from a narrow turret, surveying the terrain, evaluating, while this heart awareness has a more tender, inclusive gaze.

Of course, this hardly requires a machine, and as the novelty fades I'm disinclined to cuddle up with my computer on a daily basis. Besides, does the heart really need formal training? We know we've mastered the basics. We're *supposed* to love our kin; we're *designed* for it. Why make an extra effort to feel it for neighbors and strangers? Why tamper with human nature?

But the activation of the heart through deliberate practice is a venerable tradition. Until awakened through concentration and prayer, said the early Christian patriarch Saint Markarios of Egypt, the heart's greatest potentials lie dormant. For the uncultivated, he wrote in the *Philokalia,* "The heart is a tomb, and there our thoughts and intellect are buried." But with attention and intention, mystics claim, it can be transformed: We can learn to see with the heart, think with the heart, live through the heart. *The*

Way of a Pilgrim, a nineteenth-century work revered in the Eastern Orthodox Church for reviving the meditative tradition of the Desert Fathers, describes a practice called the Prayer of the Heart. The book's author promises that by reciting the words "Lord Jesus Christ, have mercy on me, a sinner," many thousands of times, the prayer will become "self-active," eventually synchronizing with the heartbeat itself, producing a flow of constant compassion.

The Pilgrim claims he was taught by an old cleric in an isolated monastery, who instructed him in practices that contemplatives of any Eastern tradition would recognize: visualization ("forming a mental picture of His constant presence"), mantra ("a constant interior Prayer of Jesus"), clearing the mind of thoughts, and focusing on the heart. "Sit down alone and in silence," he was told. "Lower your head, shut your eyes, breathe out gently, and imagine yourself looking into your own heart. Carry your mind, your thoughts, from your head to your heart." The Pilgrim was urged to repeat the prayer frequently, matching each recitation with his outbreath. Taking a job as a gardener, he practiced the "self-acting spiritual prayer" thousands of times a day until finally he attained his goal: "to reach the realm of the heart."

Fans of author J. D. Salinger will remember *The Way of a Pilgrim* as the dog-eared tract clutched by Franny Glass when, home in pieces from a disastrous college love affair, she sprawls on the family couch, lips moving in breathless, unceasing prayer, determined to install in her soul some final principle of mercy. Franny is the author's lampoon of a religious fanatic. The whole notion of repetitive religious practice struck Salinger, as it does many of us, as so much medieval mumbo-jumbo.

The consensus among the world's spiritual traditions has always been the opposite. Some Tibetan Buddhist practices call for a hundred thousand or a million repetitions of prayers and

visualizations. To remove the "locks" upon the heart, some mystical schools of Islam call for chanting over and over again one of the
ninety-nine Beautiful Divine Names of God. Such customs make
us free spirits uneasy: Isn't this just so much holy brainwashing?
But the contemplative traditions claim that we are already brainwashed by habitual thinking, and each day is a new trip to the
Laundromat. After all, aren't many of our whirling thoughts just
repetitive mantras to our own minor gods and personal demons,
incessant prayers for success and true romance, variants on "I'm
not good enough" or "I'm too sexy for my shirt"?

Changing this inner drone calls for training in new cognitive
habits, though we're more likely to exercise for well-cut abs than for
a well-tempered heart. It takes effort to detach from the cavalcade
of small thoughts and vain imaginings, the rehashing of slights
and plotting of triumphs, the cataloging of merits and demerits
that constitute our self-centeredness workout tape. I know that I've
already done enough spadework via countless such thoughts to
dig myself into a ditch of churlish habitude.

Why not, then, visualize myself as a loving *bodhisattva*
dispensing boons with a thousand arms rather than as a grab-it-
all-with-both-hands mogul? Why not call to mind examples of
human kindness rather than fill my head with the daily news and
its forlorn proofs of human folly? In either case, I am forming a
picture of the world that influences how I feel and what I do.

A change of heart is rarely a one-shot deal. As seventeenth-
century French philosopher Blaise Pascal observed, "The strength
of a man's virtue should not be measured by his special exertions,
but by his habitual acts." Science is now validating this observation
and more: for the word *virtue* substitute the term *neuroplasticity*—
the recently discovered ability of the brain to alter its very structure
through mental training—and Pascal was right on the mark.

*L*ONDON'S BOXY BLACK CABS, WITH THEIR ROOM-SIZED interiors and foldout jump seats, are, compared with American yellow cabs, marvels of comfort and convenience. But that's not the only difference. A New York taxi driver can learn enough about his city's rectilinear grid to get his hack license in a few days (though that plastic-encased mug shot may mean only that you know where you're going better than he does). A London cabbie, by contrast, must spend years acquiring what is reverently called "the Knowledge" before he or she is certified. On a trip to London, my driver explained how, to pass the stringent licensing test, he had biked through the city's twisting, medieval byways month after month, memorizing every corner and cobblestone. "I've got this town's whole bloody street map, down to the last lamppost, etched right here," he said with a finger tap to his forehead.

His claim may not be exaggerated. Researchers at the University College of London discovered that the longer the cabbies had been at their jobs, the larger was an area of the brain—the right rear hippocampus—crucial to storing mental maps of the environment. There had been, they concluded, a "redistribution of gray matter" based on intensive learning and prolonged mental habit. The study added to a growing body of evidence that what we habitually think and feel actually resculpts neural tissue. "If you do something, anything, even play Ping-Pong, for twenty years, eight hours a day, there's going to be something in your brain that's different from someone who didn't do that," notes Harvard neuroscientist Stephen Kosslyn. "It's just got to be."

What about compassion? There's a saving grace when compared with Ping-Pong: We're prewired for it. Empathy is integral to the human operating system, and building on its substrates can result in surprising demonstrations of human potential.

In recent experiments at the University of Wisconsin, a European-born Buddhist monk named Matthieu Ricard was placed inside a functional magnetic resonance imaging (fMRI) machine, which shows, in real-time and crystalline detail, the brain's dynamic processes. Inserted into a beige tube with racketing, whirling monster magnets, Ricard turned to a meditation he described as follows: "Let there be only compassion and love in the mind for all beings—friends and loved ones, strangers and enemies alike. It's compassion with no agenda, that excludes no one. You generate this quality of loving, and let it soak the mind."

As he did this practice, his brain showed a dramatic increase of activity in the left middle frontal gyrus, an area associated with joy and enthusiasm. In another series of tests at the University of California, Ricard proved to be adept (two standard deviations above the norm, a scientifically unprecedented variance) at perceiving split-second changes in the facial muscles' expression of emotion, an ability strongly correlated with empathy. Most telling, when he was shown a film clip of severe burn victims having dead skin painfully stripped from their bodies—a sequence used in psychology labs to reliably trigger the instinct of disgust—he reported instead a sense of "caring and concern, mixed with a not unpleasant strong, poignant sadness."

Tibetan Buddhists believe that compassion can become second nature for anyone who practices diligently enough. At the University of Wisconsin lab, a tape of a woman's bloodcurdling scream was unexpectedly sprung on another monk in the midst of his compassion meditation. Rather than eliciting the predicted negative emotional reaction, his scan showed an unexpected activation in the left prefrontal area of the brain, a region associated with *positive* emotion. A warm response to others' suffering had become so ingrained as to be automatic.

At a 2003 conference at the Massachusetts Institute of Technology (MIT), neuroscientist Richard Davidson, who oversaw the groundbreaking Wisconsin experiments, presented the results of a series of follow-up studies. Davidson, who spent time in Asia studying meditation when he was younger and retains the air of an enthusiastic grad student, flashed a PowerPoint slide of a bell curve rising like a red mountain out of a flat landscape. It was a graph, he explained, charting 150 people's normal brain state. For the great majority, the brain tended to purr along in some Goldilocks zone between left prefrontal (positive emotion) and right prefrontal (negative emotion) activity.

But there was one tiny data point at the far edge of the chart, a solitary pilgrim wending his way from the looming red peak of statistical normalcy toward parts unknown. That point was Matthieu Ricard, who had been scanned while practicing deep compassion meditation. His reading was literally beyond the curve in the area of positive emotion—the most extreme such result ever documented.

At the MIT meeting, where Davidson shared the stage with the Dalai Lama, he quoted the Tibetan leader's contention that "the wiring in our brain is not static, not irrevocably fixed. Our brains are adaptable." Davidson seemed nonplussed when his statement was met with a spontaneous outburst of applause mixed with actual cheers from an audience of usually sedate neuroscientists. It was as if he had promulgated a declaration of human independence—which in a sense he had.

The meeting was epochal in one respect: It was the first formal exchange between cutting-edge Western brain science and traditional Eastern mind science. It was if two hemispheres of knowledge were sending forth the neural tendrils of some new corpus callosum. Davidson points out that psychology has spent nearly its entire history studying negative emotions, positing that fear, sex, and aggression were baselines for human functioning.

Meditators, on the other hand, have been learning for millennia how to deliberately elicit positive emotions. In Tibet, while the world had blustered through the age of steam, thrown the switch on electricity, and unleashed the atom, Buddhist monks had sat calmly by the flickering light of millions of yak-butter lamps, doing essential R&D on the energies of consciousness itself. The results, now documented in the lab, prove in the words of psychologist Jerome Kagan, "Joy and serenity are not slavishly tied to our physiology. We are not programmed neurons over which we have no control. We are collaborators in the generation of our thoughts and emotions."

The person who sets out to develop what the Dalai Lama calls the Good Heart is trying to encourage certain propensities and override others. No one would suggest it's easy. I sometimes wonder if contemplation is, for human beings, as fundamentally new a way of cognizing as the bonobo Kanzi's leap into symbolic understanding. He's on the very brink of thought, while our project may be to see *through* thought itself, thus earning our full name: *Homo sapiens sapiens,* the creature that is aware of being aware.

But the monks insist that their state of mind (and heart) isn't dependent on any superhuman evolutionary leaps. It's more like the old joke: "How do I get to Carnegie Hall?" "Practice, practice, practice." They have, comments one scientist, "mastered a metacognitive skill of noticing a reaction and being able to channel it." It's been estimated that to acquire the mastery that actually alters the brain—to become a chess expert or a good violinist or, presumably, a journeyman *bodhisattva*—takes some ten thousand hours of practice. But there's still plenty of room for us amateurs. Every little bit of metacognition helps.

I've met Matthieu Ricard on a number of occasions. He does not emanate palpable sunrays; rainbows don't sparkle in his eyes.

An impression of roly-polyness reveals on closer look a man who, at nearly sixty, has the barrel-chested stolidity of a wrestler. As a graduate student at Paris's Pasteur Institute, he made original discoveries in genetics. At age twenty Ricard saw a film about Tibet and was transfixed. He traveled to India, met a famous teacher in Tibet's "wandering yogi" tradition, and spent summers studying in India while he completed his biology doctorate. Powerfully drawn to the spiritual life, he finally left France, took monastic vows, and continued an intensive discipleship, doing long retreats and becoming a translator for the Dalai Lama.

Ricard is affable and direct, though I wouldn't call him inordinately warm. He's too down-to-earth to come off as a mystic. When I tell him ten thousand hours sounds like a bit much, he mentions several new studies in which groups of people will be taught compassion techniques while their progress is monitored. "My rough prediction," he says, "is that you'll see a sharp upward curve, maybe the most dramatic change, in the first six months." He chuckles dryly. "On the other hand, meditation's not the seven-day cure for self-centeredness—more like seven years!"

When I ask if he thinks some people are predisposed, perhaps even genetically so, to be kinder, he cites a recent animal experiment. Baby rats from a genetic line that had been bred for fifteen generations to be "superanxious" were placed with mothers bred to be overcaring. "If these babies spend just ten days with the overcaring mothers," he says, "their superanxious genes don't get 'expressed.' The pups grow up normal. That's amazing, fabulous— just think what potential we humans must have! Even if 50 percent of our character is genetic, the other 50 percent is plastic. Personally, I believe even a higher percentage can be altered. You're not just stuck with what you are. Nothing's graven in stone. Learning can radically change you."

I press him on this: Isn't it just harder for some people to learn to be kind, while others seem to have a positive talent? "Yeah, yeah, *oui*, of course," he says, sounding a little impatient. "Look, *I'm* not instinctually compassionate in my nature. None of us is born with full knowledge. Take love: Most everybody can love in the normal sense. Your family loves you; you love your family. A friend treats you well; you feel affection. If he's mean to you, maybe you don't. Well, what about a total stranger or even an enemy who treats me badly? Can I have genuine love and compassion for them? I think the world really needs that kind of learning. We spend all these years getting regular schooling or job training. If just a little of this mind training came into mainstream education, it would be a big, big, *big* contribution."*

He elaborated on this theme on a panel at the MIT conference. "In the West we think freedom means that every thought that arises in my mind, I'm going to do it. So we are the slave of every thought." Citing anger, compassion's fiery nemesis, he remarked: "The point

---

*I spoke with Dr. Lobsang Rapgay, a former Tibetan Buddhist monk and a professor of psychiatry at the University of California, Los Angeles, as he was completing a study on moral reasoning and compassionate action among Tibetan monks, using his psych grad students as a control group. "It's hard to figure out if some of these lamas are actually making the leap from studying and meditating on compassion to actually doing it," he told me. "They will do their practices, be kind to a stranger on a pilgrimage, throw a fish back into a lake, and so forth. But when I posed survey questions like, 'If you were asked to take five days away from whatever you're doing to help a sick friend, would you?' the grad students mostly said sure, while some of the lamas said they would keep on with their practices. The grad students often scored higher on the empathy, sympathy, and love scales." When I told this to Matthieu Ricard, he made clear he was a strong partisan of the traditional meditative disciplines. "Maybe at first, it's like you're just laying down the plumbing and the electrical wiring in a building, so you're not putting a roof over anyone's head. But when the building is finished, it's like having a hospital instead of trying to heal people one by one on the street. It's more powerful to train to be a better person before just rushing out to help the poor. If you get rid of self-importance," says Ricard, who has quietly built dozens of clinics and schools in Tibet, "then you can be genuinely helpful to everyone, no strings attached."

is to learn not to jump into that chain reaction but instead just let the feeling be, look at it—what *is* that? Why should it multiply that way? It is like stopping a forest fire at the first spark."

I once observed a group of violent offenders in an anger management class. One woman, who had been convicted of second-degree battery, talked about her struggle against her automatic responses. She described the "pictures I get in my head when my boyfriend is late getting home—that he must be cheating, so by the time he comes back, even if he's innocent, I'm really mad at him." She was touchingly insightful about "where my anger takes me," noting that when these images appeared in her mind, "my breathing speeds up, I clench my fists, start talking to myself, getting angrier, imagining how I'm gonna mess him up." Now, after therapy and training, she finds there are times she can interrupt the cycle by picturing she is saying to her anger, "You're *not* going to take me there," enduring "the uncomfortable feeling I get when I *don't* do something, 'cause it's in my comfort zone to violently act out." Hers was a poignant variant of what each of us struggles with in our own way: applying the gift of free will toward becoming a better person.

"Freedom is the freedom to not be carried away by an emotion," one of the MIT neuroscientists remarked. But then he added, "It's also cultivating the ability to love."

In the Buddhist system, this cultivation of beneficial patterns of heart and mind is known as the accumulation of merit. Though sometimes viewed as simply doing good deeds or performing prayers to accrue "good karma," merit is more than just a stockpile—it is a living principle. The flow of thoughts, images, and feelings that form our consciousness is said to be a "mind-stream." Whatever we drop into it tends to keep circulating, whether a rusting beer can or a lotus petal. The idea is to place more positive intentions and loving thoughts into the stream while refraining from tossing in any more junk, thus purifying the waters and restoring what Buddhists consider the mind's natural ecology of benevolence.

Whatever our religious persuasion, practice, or lack thereof, the nonnegotiable terms of life seem to be much as Gandhi described:

> *Your beliefs become your thoughts.*
> *Your thoughts become your words.*
> *Your words become your actions.*
> *Your actions become your habits.*
> *Your habits become your values.*
> *Your values become your destiny.*

*A*FTER GYALWA KARMAPA XVI, LEADER OF THE KARGYU Order of Tibetan Buddhism, died of stomach cancer in a white room full of beeping machinery in a hospital in Zion, Illinois, his monks propped him up in meditation posture and refused to let the body be moved. Though he was clinically dead, there was apparently some unfinished business. As doctor after doctor confirmed by palpating the holy man's chest cavity, the Karmapa's heart remained persistently, inexplicably warm.

"The monks called me in about twelve hours after he died," an attending physician, Dr. Ranulfo Sanchez, told me when I investigated this wild-sounding story. "The body was cold, but the area over his heart was still normal body temperature. It was really very strange. I can't explain it. None of us could." Though medical personnel were dumbfounded, the monks showed no surprise. It was a sign, they said, of the great lama's indestructible compassion. After three days the Karmapa's heart grew cold, and the body, now a shell, was removed for his funeral in Sikkim.

I met the Karmapa a few times. What I remember most is his warmth, like the radiant heat of a woodstove, his laugh (*jolly* really is the only word), and his wide smile. And there was something else, some unmistakable emanation that made you feel just great—encouraged about your possibilities, affirmed in the rightness of your existence (and, for that matter, everyone else's). I once watched him bless a crowd of several thousand people, one by one, touching their foreheads with his heavy ritual *dorje* and, when his arm tired, lightly tapping them with his empty Coke can, gazing at each who passed with equal delight. I was reminded of a line from William Shakespeare: "My crown is in my heart, not on my head."

I once spent a night sleeping on a couch in the living room of a ski chalet his students had rented for him during a visit to Wyoming. I awakened at 5 a.m. to the sound of his chanting. Peeking in on him as he leafed patiently through folio sheets of prayers reminded me of watching my Orthodox Jewish grandfather recite his morning *Sh'ma*. Here was the Karmapa, believed by his followers to be a supreme *bodhisattva* of compassion—a man who according to tradition had already been on the job for sixteen lifetimes—still practicing, practicing, always practicing.

His posthumous heart trick is beyond explanation. But I can't help but feel that that last bloom of warmth was a gift, one final summoning of attention—some small proof of a power as deathless as the poets have always claimed. I heard in it some final communiqué, in the vernacular of the flesh: *At the end of our upward striving, all things come to rest in the heart.*

THE GIVEAWAY

Whatever joy there is in this world
All comes from desiring others to be happy
And whatever suffering there is in this world
All comes from desiring myself to be happy.

—Shantideva

*H*AROLD MINTZ IS A BIG, SWEET GALOOT. HE INSISTS ON picking me up at the train station so I don't get entangled in the color-coded sailor's knot of the Washington, D.C., subway grid. When I slide into the front seat of his car, he gives me a broad smile and punches my arm, like I'm the buddy he was out shooting hoops with last weekend. He's a large-boned man, six foot five; with his walrus moustache and thin gold earring, he could be a hip off-duty fireman, the kind who'd tell you a knock-knock joke while resuscitating you from smoke inhalation. When his wife calls on the cell phone ("Yep, got him, honey!"), his ringer trills a few upbeat bars of "Zippity Doo Dah."

The forty-six-year-old sales VP is as gregarious as a golden retriever and just as convinced the world means him well. He knows why I'm here: a field trip to observe, in its native habitat, the rare *Altruistus americanus*. I've got the wrong guy, Harold says as we pull up to his tidy brick Georgian.

"Well," I point out, "that *was* you who gave away your kidney to a total stranger." He shrugs, smiles a little.

Harold's is one of those stories that sound to skeptical ears like tabloid fare—vaguely freakish, possibly pathological, completely unlikely. Here is a man who donated his kidney to someone he didn't know from Adam or Eve.

Evolution, master of redundancy, has seen to it you really need only one kidney, but if both of them go, you're toast. Fifty thousand Americans in renal failure are now awaiting kidney transplants. Only twelve thousand per year will receive them, some from relatives, but mostly from cadavers. (Nephrologists refer to the poor-quality kidneys they're forced to use in the shortage as "crumbs.") Several thousand patients die each year, waiting. A healthy, transplantable kidney could scarcely be more precious. A few years ago, somebody offered one on eBay. It turned out to be a hoax, but before the company shut it down (human innard peddling being illegal), the bidding had reached $5.7 million.

The idea of making a bodily sacrifice on another's behalf, with its undertones of myth and martyrdom, is unsettling and not a little awe-inspiring. The first live organ donor of record, the god Prometheus, gave up his liver to bring humanity the gift of fire. There's Christ's oblation on the Cross and the offering of his flesh as love's ransom. And there is the *Jatakamala,* a treasury of the Buddha's deeds of compassionate sacrifice, Asian children's fables that make the Grimm Brothers' tales look as tame as Teletubbies. In one story, the Buddha plucks out his own eyes and gives them to a blind man. ("To the virtuous," says the text, "no suffering exists but that of others.") Fifth-century itinerant monk Faxian describes a great gilded stupa in the ancient kingdom of Taxila (Chinese for "the severed head"), commemorating the Buddha's gift of, yes, his *head* to a man who, presumably, had lost his own.

But Harold Mintz insists he's got his head securely screwed onto his shoulders. He shows me his psychiatric evaluation, a donor prerequisite, as proof. "The docs said I'm as sane as anyone. And I'm definitely no saint. The best part of this story is that I'm completely normal."

"Okay, then, why'd you do it?" I ask again.

"Dominoes," he says. Seems his dad was an architect, and as a child Harold loved to imitate him by creating elaborate setups of dominoes. When he could no longer stand the suspense, he'd give one of his just-this-side-of-Vegas creations a nudge and watch enthralled as gravity set off a clacking chain reaction.

"It was beautiful," he says. "When that happens in real life, we call it fate." And it does happen, Harold insists, sure as you're born. As he sees it, his donation was scarcely of his own doing but rather a case of one thing leading to another by the push of some greater index finger.

One domino, he says, was his father's death from cancer at age fifty-six. Harold had felt a sheer helplessness that "ripped my heart to pieces, seeing this linebacker-sized man just shrink away. I remember looking at his glasses on the nightstand after he died, sobbing my eyes out, wishing I could have done something, anything." A few years later, at the mall on Valentine's Day, Harold passed an elderly couple sitting at a fold-up table with a hand-lettered sign that read, "Help Us Save Our Child." "I was there to buy some pants, not hear some bring-me-down story," he says, "but when I saw people whipping past them without even looking, I had to double back." The couple was searching for a matching bone marrow donor for their leukemic daughter, and Harold agreed to be tested. To his intense disappointment, a near-match turned out to be a hairsbreadth miss.

Not long after that, another domino fell. Flying cross-country, Harold saw an in-flight movie about a high school football player who had donated a kidney to save his sick grandmother. Harold had felt so moved he'd jotted down the 800-number at the end of the rolling credits. (As he tells me this, it rings a bell: I'd seen this film—one of those based-on-a-true-story heartstring-tuggers—somewhere before.) Soon after, Harold happened on an article about a white schoolteacher in North Carolina who had given a kidney to a black student using a relatively painless new laparoscopic procedure.

It was a revelation. "You can give away your spare and save a life? And your race doesn't even matter? How great is *that*?" Impulsively, Harold resolved to become a donor. Then click-clack, another domino fell: He found out that one of the few anonymous donor programs in the country was in a nearby town. He signed up, went through a battery of psych tests, and after passing the medical screening was elated to get a go-ahead. His wife was less enthusiastic. "But by the time I finished explaining to her that it's *ER* for real—that I could be part of this medical miracle that saves someone's wife or mom—she was bawling her eyes out."

Ethiopian refugee Gennet Belay, wife to Tsegaye, mom to Meseret and Abiy, had been on dialysis three times a week for more than a decade, enduring more than operations to keep her alive, her name going nowhere on the endless list of would-be kidney recipients. To Gennet, an accountant, her life felt like a wall clock set at five minutes to midnight. But two weeks before Christmas that year, she found herself being wheeled into an operating room in Falls Church, Virginia, while Harold was trundled into an OR near his home in Georgetown. With the reggae music Harold had chosen thumping softly in the background, surgeons made a few slits below his navel, threaded in a small video camera, inserted their retrieval instruments, and gingerly jockeyed out his kidney.

When Harold awoke from the anesthesia, he was awestruck to hear a nurse say, "Your kidney's inside someone else, peeing up a storm!" Two months later, at a banquet arranged in their honor by the transplant consortium, the two oddly intimate strangers were introduced for the first time. Their families have since become friendly, having dinners together, talking often on the phone, and exchanging holiday cards and birthday presents.

"It's a fairy tale," Harold says, "a tearjerker with a happy ending, just like that movie." I suddenly remember where I'd seen the film, and it gives me a slightly eerie sensation. My friend Anna wrote it, I tell Harold. I'd watched it in her living room. A half hour later, in one of those rare strokes of cosmic bureaucratic efficiency, my cell phone rings and Anna's name shows in the little window. Just calling to say hi, she says. "Someone wants to talk to you," I tell her, handing the phone to Harold.

"Did you ever think your movie'd actually save a life?" he yells. I can't hear her end of the conversation, but by his *There you go!*'s and *Is that cool or what?*'s, I know she must be gratified. We all feel unexpectedly swept up in a vortex of shared elation.

"Dominoes!" Harold exclaims triumphantly after we hang up, and indeed, under his umbrella of goodwill, I can't help feeling that Anna's call has revealed a piece of that pattern Hindus call Indra's Net: the universe as an infinite web of jewels, each one reflecting all the others. Still, I tell him, I don't entirely understand why he did it.

"Anyone, if they'd experienced the same things I had, would've done the same," he says flatly. If only *I'd* known his father, run into the leukemia lady at the mall, seen Anna's film; well, it would likely have been me on that gurney.

But that's just the point, I tell him. It *wasn't*. I've seen what he's seen. My sister had leukemia, my marrow was tested, and it wasn't a match. They tried my brother; it didn't work. She died. We all wept for years. I've seen the same tearjerker movie, watched the disease-of-the-month telethons. But Domino F, in my setup, is still inches too far from Domino G; when it falls, it just falls flat.

He shakes his head. He's not buying it. This is a guy who called up his four best friends before his operation and suggested that they *all* go in and donate their kidneys. "It'll be fun," he told them. "We'll wake up in the hospital together and eat strawberry ice cream." He still seems perplexed that each found a plausible-sounding reason to beg off.

I will give my kidney away eventually—both of them, having signed that driver's license consent form committing them and other choice parts to needy others—someday. Just not now. "Look, I admit not everyone's going to be a living donor," Harold says. "Not everyone's going to run into a burning building either. But if you came across someone in real serious trouble, wouldn't you want to help?" He starts ticking off hypotheticals in a practiced rhythm. "What if you could give up an organ to save your child? No question, right?"

"Sure," I say.

"Okay, imagine I fall down right here on the floor in front of you. I'm writhing in pain"—he flops down on the carpet for effect—"sudden renal failure. Your kidney's a good match; you can save me. Wouldn't you do it?"

I look at him lying there, miming a helpless creature with its legs in the air. He's making a piteous expression—*"wouldn't you?"*—with his scrunched eyebrows. I laugh, think about it for a minute, then realize, "Okay, I would." I feel like I'm taking a pledge. It's exhilarating and vertiginous.

"Good," he says, sitting up. "So, what if it was your assistant, the girl who called me—Dana?"

Dana's a lovely person, smart, funny, dedicated. But what if my daughter needs my kidney someday? He reminds me that in this exercise, Dana needs it *now*.

"Maybe," I allow cautiously, "if there was no one else closer to her."

"What if it was your neighbor?"

I don't say anything, mentally temporizing.

"The next-door lady who once clipped your hedges for you?" he prompts. "Took care of your mail when you went on vacation?" Harold's in sales mode, and in his line of work he's what's known as a closer. My kidney wakes up and squirms.

"Maybe, maybe not," I say, sounding, to my ears, a little petulant.

"Okay, then what about someone four blocks away, some deserving person who—" I hold up my hand, telling him I'll take a rain check. I really *don't* know. He gives me one of his genial arm-socks. "Good answer. I like that. It's honest."

What Harold has described is the basic instruction manual for all compassion do-it-yourselfers, aspiring *bodhisattvas,* and saints *manqué.* Step one: Recruit the heart by thinking of those you love the most, tapping a reservoir of deep concern. Step two: Let it flow, extending until it reaches neighbors, strangers, even enemies. Step three: Repeat. Never stop.

But after years of spotty meditation practice, I still struggle. Why does it come so naturally to Harold?

Some might accuse him—and have—of grandstanding, of getting more bang for his own ego, as he well knows. He sent me an e-mail, teasing and maybe just a little anxious about what I might write: "Hi! Just checking on how that 'people who do good things but aren't *really* as good as other people might think they are' thing is going?" And it's true: I'm still trying to wrap my mind around what he did and why.

The motives of people who seem exceptionally unselfish or downright self-sacrificing have been debated for centuries. "The humblest man alive," wrote Bernard Mandeville, a satirical

eighteenth-century Dutch philosopher, "must confess that the
reward of a virtuous action...consists in a certain pleasure he pro-
cures to himself by contemplating his own worth." Or is it a case
of low self-worth? Exhibit A might be someone like Joseph Cornell, the avant-garde artist whose cunning shadow boxes are in
museum collections the world over. Cornell lived his entire adulthood with his mother and his disabled younger brother, Robert,
who had cerebral palsy. A recent biographer wrote:

> The sacrifices that Joseph made on Robert's behalf were certainly
> valiant, yet the self he inhabited was so diminished he could not
> afford to think of his deeds in such generous terms. The truth is
> that his mother made him feel that his own needs were unimport-
> ant beside Robert's—that he should be ashamed of having needs in
> the first place...

Harold seems to have no problem taking care of his own needs.
He just likes to take care of other people's too. The good news, it
occurs to me, is that though there's some x-factor I can't put my
finger on, maybe Harold differs from most of us only by degree.
He's uncomfortable with the word *compassion,* he says. "It makes
it sound like I'm not just like everyone, but I am." I've noticed
how many people who do good are embarrassed to be tagged as
do-gooders. They're more in the mold of what Hispanic tradition
calls the *santas sombras*—the hidden saints—who quietly go about
their good works and may turn out to be that neighbor who, come
to think of it, has always been a little on the superfriendly side.

S TEVE AMAN LET HIMSELF GET WRITTEN UP IN THE PAPER ONCE,
but he's not sure he liked the sensation of seeing his name in
print. He too donated a kidney to a stranger but tells me, "I turned
down *Good Morning, America* and all the rest of them. That isn't
what this was about."

Steve lives far from Harold's manicured D.C. exurbs in a fly-speck town by the Erie Canal, a place where the granite quarry sits next to the local graveyard that's slowly filling with its products, and the bright light on the main drag is Judy's Coiffure and Krafts. It's no poverty pocket—there's a gentleman farm here and there, and Steve's got a swatch of acreage—but it's the boonies.

Steve's place has a funky, laid-back ambience. There's a stuffed buffalo head above the CardioMax exercycle and below it a prostrate dog so inert I first take him for a cast-off throw rug. A faux-crocheted "East, West, Home Is Best" hangs on the wall. As we settle down to talk, I note the telltale kindly guy gestures. He sees me washing my eyeglasses and hands me a paper towel; when he makes tea, he puts a small ice cube in my cup so it won't be too hot. Compared with Harold's brash bonhomie, Steve is more self-contained, interior. He wears a hearing aid with a little antenna sprouting from it and glasses as big as shop goggles—your high school chem teacher (which isn't far off: he's a former chemical technician for Kodak). If Harold's a garden-club tulip, Steve's a modest jack-in-the-pulpit whose late-blooming path of generosity was more roundabout, if no less certain.

Steve wasn't a particularly generous soul when he was younger, he says. He was a severe introvert. "I would've been happy taking my wife and kid to the woods and being a recluse." He remembers always feeling inwardly like an idealist—"a dreamer," as he puts it—but never felt it possible to be one in the world. Though he'd been "ecologically minded" ever since reading Rachel Carson's *Silent Spring*, he toiled for more than a decade in the Kodak lab with "all those nasty carcinogens." He kept his head down, an employee-of-the-month type, toeing the company line, punching the clock.

Except that he had become an alcoholic. His Alcoholics Anonymous (AA) sponsor introduced him to a self-help group called

Lifespring, where, he says simply, "you learn to love yourself and accept others." The courses gave him what he calls an "aha experience." The core of it, he said, was "dealing with the fear of not having enough." It led him to realize that "whatever I had *was* enough. I was sufficient just as I am. And that made me see that I don't need to hang on so tight—that I have things I can give."

Sometimes all that is needed is a channel, some pipeline for pent-up goodness, a wire for love's current. Steve started giving blood at the local Red Cross. "I had never thought that people could get gratification from donation with nothing in return," he says. At some point, he says, "I decided I didn't have to be afraid of what would happen to me if I didn't follow the regular path." He left his job and began working full-time at a tree nursery, finding that he had "green in my veins." He did some volunteer work for environmental groups. He bought a parcel of land "to preserve it for the next generations.

"It wasn't that I was so selfish before," he says, "but I hadn't explored too many ways to share." Now Steve would do something to help out and discover he got back more than he gave. That felt so good that he'd try giving some more. The feedback loop grew into a virtuous circle. Tortoise step by step, he experienced a gradual "unfolding of gifts," and, in an echo of Harold, he says, "the dominoes began to fall."

Steve's wife, Mary, a medical technician, had become interested in her part-Mohawk heritage, and together they began to explore American Indian philosophy, attending the ceremonial Sun Dance. Steve was floored by the dancers' sacrifice as they pierced their skin with slivers of bone attached by leather thongs to a Maypole-like post. "It takes real generosity of spirit to undergo that pain and discomfort, dancing for four days with no food or water, offering your flesh for the sake of the people." His biggest inspiration came

from a practice of many tribes called the Giveaway. "If you have
something you don't use," he explains, "you put it someplace where
others can take it if they need it." Steve says his lifesaving deed was
just that—a giveaway. As he sees it, he had an extra kidney and
figured he'd drop it off in the community free box.

One day he saw an item in a Rochester paper about a man
who had put out a desperate public plea for a kidney. Steve had
been longing to take another step, "to do something important for
someone really in need." This looked like an answered prayer. He
zapped an e-mail to the man, who turned out to be a former TV
broadcaster whose wait for a donor transplant had lasted nineteen
years, most of them touch-and-go. A few months later, they met
for lunch. "I think he had to make sure I didn't want anything from
him," Steve says. "But it really wouldn't have mattered who he was."
They turned out to be a perfect match.

I ask to see his scars, and he pulls down his shorts to show me
a thin scalpel line above his groin. It gives me a twinge to look,
but he swears the operation, using a minimally invasive extraction
method, was mostly painless. He knows people see him as heroic
but says, "I didn't do anything above and beyond." He has a motto
that in anyone else's mouth would sound like stilted white-guy
Indian-speak: "To be a hollow bone, grateful to be used for Spirit."
He says it without sanctimony, but is Steve just too self-effacing,
too grateful to be *used*? In an indigenous culture, he would be
prized for his humility; a shrink might diagnose him as a case of
fuzzy boundaries.

*I*N THE EARLY 1960S, WHEN "HARVESTING" A KIDNEY MEANT
slicing a foot-long incision across a patient's back, occasionally snapping a rib, a New York hospital sent out a public appeal
for donors. They netted nine people willing to undergo the pro-

cedure on a stranger's behalf. According to one monograph, all reported "positive emotional benefits, with no regrets or psychological complications after donation." But the project was abruptly terminated because, the report said, doctors "remained suspicious of these donors' psychological status and motivation." The decision reflected more than medical ethics. It was a snap referendum among medical professionals on whether extraordinary acts of compassion were compatible with mental health. How many people were really capable of such high-end selflessness? There had to be something wrong with them. The pilot project was shut down, and no further reports were heard for forty years.

Then, in 1999, an organ procurement nurse named Joyce Roush happened to be in the audience when a Johns Hopkins surgeon described the new, less traumatic kidney extraction method. She felt so inspired she volunteered on the spot. "It was an instantaneous decision," she says, "and one I never had second thoughts about." She was matched to a thirteen-year-old boy from Maryland. When the media trumpeted the successful laparoscopic surgery, the hospital was astonished to be deluged with dozens of people clamoring to offer their kidneys, too.

It ignited a tiny (just several hundred, so far) but growing trend, one so new it's still searching for the right sobriquet. Some use the studiously neutral term *nondirected live donation;* others, the arms-spread-wide *benevolent donation,* the religiously tinged *Good Samaritan live donation,* or the mysterioso-sounding *altruistic stranger donation.* The labels describe with varying nuance those who perform a feat so spiritually swashbuckling that one newspaper dubbed it "the ultimate gift of human kindness."

In surveys conducted around the world, between 1 and 5 out of every 10 people say they would willingly donate a kidney while they were still alive. Who *are* these people? What motivates them?

How many would really step up to the plate and knock one out of the park, and how many are just taking practice swings out of some wishful moral virtuosity? (As one study dryly notes: "Reported intentions are not necessarily highly correlated with actual behaviors.")

I once saw a sign, a little professional homily, at a nurse's station: "Sympathy sees and says, I'm sorry. Compassion feels and whispers, I'll help." What are the x-factors that distinguish the altruistic from the merely sympathetic? The answer might contain a golden key to human nature itself.

"He's a giver," a friend once remarked about a mutual acquaintance. I'd never heard anyone parse people that way. In my intellectual New York Jewish family, it was the march of human folly, not the roll call of charity's armies, that was fodder for dinner table repartee. The crowd I ran with were self-anointed urban smarties: People got points for being bright, talented, funny, attractive, socially deft, and nice, in approximately that order. I've wondered if the super-good-deed-doers aren't different from most people in some crucial respect. Are their dominoes preset to fall in a kindlier pattern? Does some combination of genes and upbringing give their generosity a hair-trigger threshold?

As I was skimming a foot-high stack of papers I'd collected on kidney donors, one snagged my eye: "Lunatics or Saints?" was its no-nonsense subtitle. The principal author was Canadian researcher Antonia (Toni) Henderson, a vivacious, animal-loving psychologist who, when I called her, had just returned from taking her Rhodesian ridgeback to a "tracking class" for search-and-rescue training.

Over a period of years, Toni has been doing her own tracking, interviewing would-be donors by the dozens. I tell her what a blast I'm having with the people she calls "living anonymous donors"

(LADs for short). "Me, too!" she says. "I started interviewing them with all these cautions and caveats, but they just boggled me!" I know what she means. Spending time with the givers is part of my strategy to jump-start the heart, hooking my cables to their 12-volt Diehards, inducing my own to turn over.

Toni has spearheaded a series of studies as part of an ambitious effort to create the world's first large-scale kidney donation program with standardized practices and protocols. "It's been a hard sell," she says in a tone of diplomatic understatement. The first funders she approached were big pharmaceutical companies. She says: "They thought anonymous donations were ridiculous: What kind of person would want to do such a thing? To be fair, this isn't your usual Hippocratic Do No Harm. You're proposing to take an optimally healthy person and physically compromise them. There has to be at least a clear psychological benefit. A father-to-child transplant, that's a no-brainer. But when someone says, 'I want to give my kidney to a *stranger*,' the surgeon has no idea why. I'm not sure I do, either; I mean, *explain* these people to me!"

Maybe it's a tautology, I suggest: If there's really such a thing as a true-blue altruist, they do selfless deeds because that's just what altruists do, just as finches trill and sockeyes thrash upstream. The fact is, no one really knows. Though there are now some sixty hospitals in the United States willing to accept volunteer donors, there is still no precise agreement on what really motivates these people.

The hairsplitting is not just an academic exercise. A medical system in an organ shortage crisis that mistakes, say, a person with pathologically low self-esteem for a Good Samaritan risks exploiting a weak spot in someone's psyche just to fill a quota. A few transplants that began as happy stories have wound up as cautionary tales: In one reported case, a donor harassed his kidney's new host, who finally had to get a restraining order.

In her initial study, Toni made a first culling by simply waiting to see who among the ninety people who had first called to
offer their organs were committed enough to slog through the
paperwork. Confronted with endless questionnaires and lengthy
interviews, half dropped out, sorting in a stroke the genuinely
motivated from the merely well intentioned. Those that remained
were eventually divided into two groups: one assessed as having
the right stuff (LADs) and the other designated as non-LADs.
Interestingly, there were some similarities in both groups: 24 percent of the LADs said they "cannot bear another's suffering," as did
14 percent of the non-LADs. But the question of whether they had
a consistent history of altruism (doing community work, giving
blood, donating bone marrow, and the like) turned out to be the
clincher. Nearly half the LADs answered in the affirmative compared with none of the non-LADs.

Living anonymous donors, in other words, walk the talk: They
do philanthropy, deliver Meals on Wheels, volunteer in homeless
shelters, and perform that steady stream of good works that invisibly keeps society running. Quotidian stuff, some of it, but that
was the point: Whether by temperament or force of habit, they had
developed an everyday practice of actively caring.

But are they just self-sacrificing neurotics? Victims of a martyrdom complex, atoning for some nameless guilt? In Toni's study
the LADs scored no differently on the "neuroticism" scale than
the average population. "I'm trained to detect pathology," she says,
"but these folks are psychologically healthy. In fact, I was surprised
by how many of them clumped on what I'd call the 'saintly side' of
the spectrum. They really *are* motivated to make the world a nicer
place." I became aware that Toni and I were giggling conspirato-
rially, like two people in on a delightful, mildly illicit caper: Just
thinking about the LADs had given us a contact high.

Toni then decided to embark on a larger-scale study, asking one thousand randomly selected adults in Vancouver whether they'd be willing to donate a kidney to family members, friends, or strangers. Once again most never bothered to complete the screening process. Of the 250 who did, only 50 stuck it through to the follow-up. Of those, 16 were adjudged to be committed LADs.

It might be thought of as a down-and-dirty census of the seriously kind. If we were to idly wonder what portion of humanity (in western Canada, at least) are dyed-in-the-wool givers, the answer would seem to be 1.5 percent. One person out of seventy—one person, say, on your typical suburban square block—who would go beyond neighborly greetings and friendly favors and even laudable charity to put their body on the line for you. In trying to create a gold standard for kidney donors, Toni has inadvertently created something even more interesting: a frequency analysis and quick-sketch portrait of the contemporary altruist.

Some of the features that jumped out were unsurprising. Respondents scored high on the category Toni dubbed "tender-minded." ("If I can do something for someone else to alleviate their suffering," one said, "why wouldn't I?") But they were tough-minded too: prone to "question authority and to entertain new ethical, social, and political ideas." They had an "insatiable intellectual curiosity and...a willingness to think outside the box." They were, in other words, iconoclasts, not looking over their shoulders for consensus before plowing ahead, independent enough to step out of the crowd and do what many people—including friends and family—deemed outrageously stupid.

In my own less scientific observations of the LADs I've met, I've noticed a certain willingness to work without a net. Steve Aman talks about the times he's "stepped into the unknown," plunging into radical life-changes on pure faith. Harold Mintz is an avid skydiver and a bungee-jumper. Comparing notes with other donors, Harold concluded, "We're risk-takers" (a skeptic might say risk-seekers). His bungee-jumping credo could be a metaphor for how givers tend to function in the world: "You have to get your body to leave the safety of the platform and launch into thin air." But his risks are also calculated—he prefers bungee jumping because "you know you'll get yanked back before you go *splat* on the pavement."

I got an impression of people who live in the here-and-now. "I don't do what-ifs," says Harold. "I make decisions based on today. If someone needs my kidney now, they should have it. If I need a kidney down the line, someone will step forward later for me." Nurse Joyce Roush, when asked if she's worried a family member might someday need the organ she's given away, echoes Harold with uncanny precision: "I've never lived my life by what-if. If that what-if happens, there will be an answer then."

Toni's study also noted "a highly integrated spiritual belief system, though not necessarily based in an organized religion." If Harold could be said to have a religious philosophy, it's probably the Great Domino Theory, some belief in a Force that works with surehanded certainty in human affairs yet welcomes all the help it can get. Steve told me, "The heart is the Creator part that lives in each of us. I believe in it, even when my head tells me a different story." Even those with traditional religious beliefs held to a just-do-it brand of faith: "If I had ten kidneys," said a Methodist pastor in Alabama, "I'd give away nine of them. I never felt like it was courageous. I just knew it was right. I don't know how a Christian could *not* do this."

Despite what might sound like transcendental leanings, they were not like Voltaire's Candide, bumbling through life with utopian naiveté, lambs among the wolves. Rather, I observed a strong streak of pragmatism and tenacity, an instinctive knowledge that a helping hand requires a certain strength of grip. As he pursued each step leading to his donation, Harold says he "pushed hard, as if there was a marathon runner in front of me. I was going to do whatever it took, no matter what." Steve wasn't shy about playing hardball when one hospital balked at the unusual procedure, letting them know he'd take his case and his kidney elsewhere. Joyce Roush, the pioneering donor, shouldered her way through obstacles (including her husband's initial opposition) to become a figurehead and a tireless proselytizer for the lifesaving procedure. They reminded me of a Ralph Waldo Emerson quote I keep on my bulletin board: "Truth is handsomer than the affectation of love. Your goodness must have some edge to it, else it is none."

In spite of their generally clear-eyed assessment of reality, "trust" was also a remarkably high-scoring measure among the LADs. According to Toni's study, "They believe that others are not maliciously intentioned and will treat them with honesty and benevolence." It struck me that it was not that they wanted to make the world a nicer place; they think it already is. They live in the sort of parallel universe where Harold might genuinely believe all his friends would jump at the chance to go into surgery with him and have a post-op ice-cream party. Joyce Roush too assumes people are, well…more like her: "I had this mental image that once they knew it was available, lots and lots of people would line up to do this," she says with a laugh. "Like when Elton John tickets go on sale in Fort Wayne."

I get the impression that trust is the strong center pole—trust in others, in the future, in a higher power, in fate, in the heart— trust in a universe so provident they can afford to give things away rather than cling to what they have. I started with an image of them as natural-born saints or else as moral alpiners, strivers huffing and puffing toward the shining white summit of Mount Virtue. But they're relaxed about it all. They find the summit in their own backyards. As they would have it, their neighbors (and that includes you) are good; the *world* is good, its ugly spots no more than blemishes on a fresh-picked apple, little affecting its savor. They live in the world as if it *is* the benevolent place we might wish it were. Their attitude is contagious.

PETE DUBROWITZ, THE MAN NOW PLAYING HOST TO STEVE Aman's kidney, answers the door in the frayed jeans and stained work shirt of a serious weekend gardener. He guides me back to a postage-stamp yard engulfed by a riotous raised-bed cornucopia. A dozen varieties of peppers dangle from their stalks, gleaming like red, green, and yellow Chinese lanterns.

Pete looks older than fifty-three; with his thin, sandy hair and hawk's eyes, he has the mug of a second-card pugilist, a stand-up guy who refused to take a dive and has been put through the wringer. He recites in his still-mellifluous newscaster's baritone a litany of the failed operations, the endless dialysis, all the miserable death-cheating crises: "I flatlined twice. I had to throw the priest out of the room in the middle of last rites."

Pete's quest for a living donor was a last-ditch gambit. Even his terse newspaper ad was a stripped-to-the-basics last hurrah: "Wanted: Your Spare Kidney," followed by his e-mail address. The less-is-more ploy generated a flurry of local publicity, and responses ran the gamut. "One guy said I could have his kidney for twenty-five grand. Another wanted visitation rights! Another one said, 'Hey, it'll be fantastic. We can go to church together *every single day.*'" Pete winnowed the roster down to six. Steve was number two.

"Steve was just so unassuming," he says. "He had no agenda. It was basically, 'I have a spare part; if you can use it, you can have it.' After the immune-factor screenings, my doc asked, 'Where did you *find* this guy?' The chances of a match like this are one in 10 million." Steve and Pete had even gone to the same high school. (Donors all seem to have these crazy-odds stories. Harold told me he and Gennet had unknowingly once lived in the same condo complex.)

"The enormity of what Steve did—I mean, who *does* this?" Pete marvels. Certainly not him. He freely admits he had been what's known in the business as a media whore: "The stuff I used to do was lowest common denominator—just grab viewers fast, cheap, and easy. I could've gone to any city and slapped together a half-hour local news show: eight minutes of commercials, six minutes of national, then a minute and a half for a local murder-suicide or some building burning down. It's like rubbernecking at an accident; people can't look away.

"Okay," Pete says, changing the subject, "so I went after my third kidney transplant. The neighbors were saying, 'Why does he deserve three? Just because he's the TV guy?'" His eyes narrow. "To which I say, 'Screw you, I'm not counting!'" He catches himself and softens. His life, he says, took a radical turn after the operation; Steve's act of compassion knocked him for a loop. Pete tried hard to stand pat but found he couldn't keep grubbing along as a Class-A cynic with Steve's giveaway pulsing inside him.

His new life lease is more like a new incarnation. He's gone from a jaded media hard-ass to the director of the city's Big Brothers, Big Sisters program. When he talks about it, the down-market news palooka vanishes. His face looks transformed, lit up: "I've had the five most rewarding years of my life. I've taken the health I've been given and helped kids—we've just doubled our numbers! Before, I couldn't look at myself in the mirror. My TV station had this spinning blue Earth logo, but what damn good was it doing for anyone? Now, in my little piece of the world, I change lives every day. I tell Steve all the time, his part's playing its part in all this.

"Steve and I," Pete says, "we're pushing to create a blind-pool national registry of living donors." He pats his lower back, giving his blood brother's kidney a proprietary attaboy. "I gotta tell you: *This* is the gift that keeps on giving."

THE ALTRUIST

If there is any kindness I can show,
or any good thing I can do to any fellow being,
let me do it now, and not defer or neglect it,
as I shall not pass this way again.

—William Penn

I F THERE'S A FACET OF HUMAN NATURE THAT, WHEN YOU HOLD it up to the light, shines bright enough to blind you, it's altruism. A selfless deed, witnessed up close, is like a lamp blazing up from darkness before your pupils can adjust. We're a little bedazzled by people who don't seem to be out for themselves, who do good unto others without stopping to consider if others will do good unto them. We each know ourselves to be capable of selflessness. We'll lay aside our needs—even our lives—for our nearest and dearest. But beyond the charmed circle, we tend to parcel love out, weighing who deserves what (while placing a subtle thumb on the scale of *What's in it for me?*). Altruists seem to have inscribed in their very bones the great writ of all faiths: Love the stranger. They don't give themselves just to family and very best friends but to pretty much anyone who asks, sometimes till it hurts.

To give without gain goes against the basic instinct of self-interest—an instinct with a several-billion-year pedigree.

Biologists get into high dudgeon just thinking about it. Evolution, asserts biologist George Williams, "can honestly be described as a process for maximizing short-sighted selfishness." Looking out for number one is the motive force rippling up the phyla from paramecium to paraprofessional. Most evolutionary biologists concur that there can *be* no such thing as selfless altruism. What seems like a generous deed is just a strategy to get others to help *you* (a principle, called return-benefit, that has been observed even in vampire bats). The theory holds that most self-sacrificing behavior in nature, including human nature, can be attributed to "kin-directed altruism." When a parent gives up comfort, food, or life itself for his child, that feeling of selfless love is based on a compelling instinct to preserve the carriers of his genes.

Biologists support this stance with observations that the amount of caregiving bestowed by one animal on another often correlates with eerie precision to the percentage of the giver's genes that the beneficiary carries. Though evidence is spottier in humans, one oft-cited study of twin children revealed that identical siblings, who share all their genes, cooperated and helped each other more than fraternal twins, who share only half. Any seemingly altruistic action, it is claimed, must be driven by this desire to enhance one's own survival or that of one's genetic "conspecifics." Darwin went so far as to write that any trait not based on genetic fitness but solely "for the good of another would annihilate my theory, for such could not have been produced through natural selection."

The altruistic kidney donors—the LADs—seem to exist as if to confound theory. They do not set out to benefit themselves (in fact, there is some detriment); their recipients are not kin or even friends who could give return-benefit but unknown persons often not even in their communities. Altruism has become a hot-button issue because it poses a central mystery. Writes Frans de Waal: "We are facing the profound paradox, that genetic self-advancement at the expense of others (which is the basic thrust of evolution) has given rise to remarkable capacities for caring and sympathy." That paradox has lodged like a chicken bone in the throats of some theorists: They can't completely swallow it, but they can't quite cough it up. As science tries to get to the bottom of human nature, altruism presents a parallel challenge to scale the heights.*

When I was researching the kidney donors, I did an informal poll among my friends: Do you know someone who, no matter how rough the going got, would act for your welfare even at the expense of their own? One woman described her two-step test for compassion: "First, would they risk hiding me from the Nazis in their attic? Second, if we all had to hide out together and there was only one candy bar to live on, would they share it with me?" When I asked who among her friends made the cut, she could only name one, then added, "I know he'd want to share the candy, but his *wife* would talk him out of it!"

She's not alone in applying tough standards. Social psychologists too use a tight mesh to separate "pure" altruism from helping behaviors that, examined more closely, are as subtly contingent on getting as giving. The filter is exceedingly fine. Psychologists suggest we may help others to alleviate the shame or guilt we'd feel if

---

*Evolutionary biologist Richard Dawkins, who has been called by critics a "fundamentalist" and an "ultra-Darwinist," is these days doing a little public chin-scratching: "The easy altruism is kinship altruism, reciprocal altruism," he told the host of a London radio show. "But I think there's a harder problem still—what you might call real altruism, altruism which couldn't conceivably ever have been thought of as hoping for reciprocation, giving money to charity in secret and insisting that your name is not publicized. Even giving blood for which you get precious little reward—that kind of giving." He hastened to add: "But we've got to [explain] it in a Darwinian way because we are Darwinian products. We've got to make the best of our Darwinian explanation, and that's sort of the best shot I can do at the moment."

we *didn't* help; or we may do a good deed not for outward recognition but inward self-esteem; or an altruistic-seeming deed may help us avoid public censure for appearing to be mean-spirited (this one comes with the convoluted theoretical moniker "self-interested refusal to be spiteful").

Some researchers claim to have sieved out one gold-standard group that helped others even when they themselves had everything to lose and nothing to gain: Gentile citizens of Nazi-occupied Europe who rescued persecuted Jews. Here were people who really did hide people in their attics, risking their own lives and those of their loved ones to save total strangers from annihilation. There was not even, as with some kidney donors, a possible payback of community acclaim for their deeds. The only recognition they could expect was betrayal to the SS by a craven neighbor.

This line of research was begun by Samuel Oliner, an investigator with unique qualifications. As a Jewish boy in Poland during World War II, he was sheltered by a Catholic peasant woman after his parents and every inhabitant of Poland's Bobowa ghetto were machine-gunned into a mass grave. Emigrating to America after the war, he became a college professor specializing in Holocaust studies. He began his pioneering focus on what he called the sociology of compassion after a German student came to him in tears, asking to drop his class because she couldn't bear her feelings of guilt. Assuring her that she was not to blame for the "cancer of the Third Reich," he resolved to search out those who had shown compassion even in the face of Nazism's insidious, metastatic growth.

Oliner and his wife, Pearl, studied both rescuers and a control group of bystanders who had failed to act, interviewing some eight hundred people in seven countries. They found that rescuers had a particular characteristic: They were unusually empathetic. Take Stanislaus, a man from a poor Polish Catholic family who had saved dozens of Jews, teaching himself bricklaying so he could build false walls and hidden entryways to conceal them around Warsaw, secreting them even in his own house, feeding them from his and his mother's own meager ration. Asked why, he answered: "When someone comes and says, 'I escaped from the camp,' what is the alternative? One alternative is to push him out and close the door. The other is to pull him into the house and say, 'Sit down, relax, wash up. You will be as hungry as we are because we have only this bread.'"

"What distinguished rescuers from nonrescuers," the Oliners wrote, "was their tendency to be moved by pain. Sadness and helplessness aroused their empathy. More frequently than others, rescuers were likely to say, 'I can't feel good if others around me feel sad,' 'Seeing people cry upsets me,' 'I get very upset when I see an animal in pain.'"

I thought of Toni Henderson's LADs, who were found to have "an extraordinary empathy, such that they could understand a stranger's suffering, and felt compelled to do what they could to ameliorate it." Were they really the same sort of people? The rescuers' stakes were infinitely higher of course and, not surprisingly, few in Europe chose the risk: It is estimated that out of the continent's 700 million people only about half a million were active rescuers, saving some 1 million Jews. But LADs and rescuers alike claimed they performed their altruistic deeds because it seemed to them, beyond any risk-benefit calculus or even moral deliberation, the only thing they *could* do.

S O, OKAY: YOU'RE JOGGING AROUND THE PARK AND OUT OF THE corner of your eye you see a child fall into the duck pond. Without thinking you leap in, grasp her by the collar, and paddle safely back to shore. You're a hero. Are you an altruist? Those who are adept at teasing out the nuances of why we do such things might say: *Well...sort of.* You might not ordinarily be particularly

selfless, but in the immediacy of the moment you react to save the
day. And as they say, that ain't just chopped liver.

But social scientists set the bar for "true" altruism (if such a
chimera exists) yet higher. One criterion is an *ongoing* pattern of
good deeds. Kidney donor Harold Mintz, for example, had given
blood in high school and then gone on to organize entire blood
drives. He had sought for years to find a way to act on his deep
sympathy for people with incurable illnesses. But even here, a pur-
ist could quibble about whether Harold was strictly selfless. He
certainly makes no bones about the personal satisfaction his do-
gooding has given him. "Hey, when you gave blood, they let you
out of fifth period, and the cheerleaders made brownies for you!"
He enjoys the attention from being what he calls "a poster boy" for
kidney donation. The psych report Harold showed me reads, "He
has insight into the narcissistic rewards of his altruism." A psychologist might pounce on him as living proof of the principle that
"psychological egoism" (sociologists call it "rational selfishness")
underlies even the most generous gesture. And there is that matter
of the selfish gene's dear love of kin: Biologists would claim that
when Harold speaks in schools and churches, and garners glowing
PR write-ups, he enhances his and his family's "biological fitness"
by gaining allies and status. Though this doesn't sully the magna-
nimity of his act, it creates some theoretical ambiguities.

Sociologist Kristen Renwick Monroe was well aware of these
arguments when she set out in the Oliners' footsteps to study
Holocaust rescuers. If Samuel Oliner is the grand old man of
altruism studies, Monroe is the field's spitfire. Once, after listening to a group of skeptical biologists and economists insist that
all altruism was disguised selfishness, she burst out that they were
"trying to stuff a fat lady in a corset—you get her all laced up and
she looks great, but it distorts the underlying reality. Saying altruism is just kin selection or group selection or reciprocal altruism is

just an attempt to smuggle in self-interest and say theirs isn't really altruism at all."

Auguste Comte, the eccentric nineteenth-century French visionary who coined the word *altruism* (literally, "other-ism"), didn't deny there were self-serving motives for generous behavior, but he believed these existed side by side with an instinct to live unselfishly for others. The emotional part of the brain, he proposed, harbored the altruistic drives* that coexisted with egoistic ones. Comte, a utopian who wrote tracts on the moral evolution of humanity—an old etching shows a man with a noble brow and a yearning gaze, one eye glimmering with a tear—went on to establish the field of sociology and to found the philosophy of positivism. But his views on altruism were soon eclipsed by the Darwinian revolution. Ever since, the concept of altruism has been a sort of scientific pariah: odd man out in modern sociology (which assumes people are self-interested "rational actors"); sob sister of psychology (which tends to focus on ego-integrity); invisible man in economic theory (to ensure the best work from our fellows, wrote Adam Smith, "we address ourselves not to their humanity, but to their self-love").

With the work of the Oliners, Monroe, and others, the subject is being rehabilitated, part of a debate about whether humankind is at least as cooperative as it is competitive. The question is a vital one. Among the underpinnings of any society are its assumptions about human nature. If we consider it a scientific fact that we are fundamentally egoistic, our educational system will teach children to be self-assertive individualists, relegating kindness to

---

*The debate over whether it is thought or feeling that generates our moral sensibility may never be resolved. But it is sure to take on new life as brain scans are used with increasing sophistication to map cognitive functions. A recent study using fMRI scans may have vindicated Comte: It showed that while subjects confronted with a technical problem used the brain's higher cognitive centers to solve it, a moral dilemma lit up the emotional areas of the brain.

a secondary value.* Our business culture will enshrine maximal
self-interest, with any small gestures toward the common good
pegged to larger trade-offs. A theory can become a society's self-
fulfilling prophecy.

Monroe wanted to find a way to challenge accepted theory,
teasing out a thread of "pure" altruism from more-normative social
behaviors. She decided to compare a group of Holocaust rescuers with two other groups: entrepreneurs and philanthropists. The
entrepreneurs, the "rational actors" of the social sciences, turned
out to have a charitable streak, but it did not generally extend
beyond their immediate kin. The other group, philanthropists, was
generous in conventional terms but cautious not to give away so
much that they couldn't pass on the great bulk of their wealth to
succeeding generations. Both entrepreneurs and philanthropists
imposed subtle and not-so-subtle obligations on their recipients,
their behavior generally conforming to predicted kinship and
return-benefit considerations.

But Holocaust rescuers were another story. They offered what
Monroe calls "dramatic refutation of the kin selection hypothesis." As Monroe explains: "Every single rescuer knew they were
endangering their family members through their attempts to help
Jews. Under the Nazi policy of kith and kin, the rescuers' relatives,
including even their youngest children, could be killed because of
their actions. This meant...those who shared the rescuers' genes
could be killed because of the rescuers' actions. The Nazis thus
attempted to use biology to deter rescuers, but did not succeed."

---

*I recently witnessed an illustration in microcosm: Deirdre, my friends' six-year-
old daughter, wanted to give an adored playmate the greatest birthday present she
could imagine. As she scoured her room, her eye fell on her own "bestest" Barbie
doll. "Help me wrap it," she told her mother, who was appalled. "We can't let her
just give away her favorite toy," she told her husband. "She has to learn to value
her own possessions, respect what makes *her* happy. Besides, she'll just cry for it
back tomorrow." Husband and wife disagreed, but Barbie stayed.

Altruistic kidney donors too seemed to flout natural law by privileging a desperate stranger above their own kin. And as in Charles Dickens's savage caricature of the charitable Mrs. Jellyby in *Bleak House* (who gave money to starving children while her own went hungry), they sometimes incurred social mockery and even hostility.

In 2003 a professor of Renaissance literature and Pennsylvania real estate mogul named Zell Kravinsky decided to give away one of his kidneys, specifying only that the recipient be an African-American woman. He was turned down by two hospitals before Philadelphia's Albert Einstein Medical Center agreed to perform the procedure. ("I had to convince them I was doing it," he says, "because it is logically and morally compelling to save someone's life if you can.") He emerged from a successful operation to discover that the path of altruism is not always smooth.

Zell's wife, a psychiatrist, threatened to divorce him, especially when it emerged that he was also giving away most of the family fortune to endow hospitals. People he'd known for years turned a cold shoulder. The *New York Times* was moved to editorialize: "His brand of altruism borders on obsession, perhaps even a sort of benign madness." When Zell remarked on a talk show that he could, in theory, conceive of donating even his *other* kidney if it were the only way to heal, say, someone who was creating a cancer cure that would save millions of lives, the conservative host seemed on the verge of bashing him with a chair: What about his wife and kids, to say nothing of his *own* life?

Zell recognizes that his views are a little extreme. In our conversations he struck me as a stringently (and not exactly joyously) idealistic man whose deeds have caused considerable family turmoil. He wrote me: "I've just now come from a tearful session with my oldest son, who feels passionately that those very acts reflect my lack of compassion for him. The issue is complex, more so in his mind than in mine; my zealotry simplifies everything but leaves a complicated trail of tears that runs all the way from the hospital to my doorstep."

In a response to one online critic, Zell wrote: "I would go through fire for my kids, literally, and I would do the same for yours. If we can only agree that *all* our kids are, equally, of a preciousness beyond speech's capacity to declare it, then maybe no kids will get hurt, or feel diminished. Perhaps I'll feel a bit underdeveloped until the eyes of other men's children provoke the same stir in my heart as my own children's faces."

Here may be the crux of why some people are put off by kidney donors: What kind of person would put a stranger on a par with his own family? Harold Mintz told me, "One friend from Ireland was really upset with me. He said, 'Your wife or daughter might need that kidney someday!' Joyce Roush admitted that her own family did not immediately climb onboard her decision. "Honestly," she said, "my husband just about threw up." Zell Kravinsky's mother told a newspaper reporter: "You can give money; you can give service. Body parts are quite another thing. You give them to family members, and even that's a great sacrifice."

It's a perennial question about the amplitude of compassion and the carrying capacity of the heart: Do we have only a fixed quota of loving to allocate between family and the world at large, so that if one receives more, the other gets less?

Conversely, does altruism leave less room for ordinary affection? I have a friend who has dozens of people in her life whom she seems to love unconditionally, bailing them out of crises, taking their late-night phone calls, loaning them money, incurring their eternal gratitude (which she brushes off as unnecessary).

"Do you love me? Really love me?" her husband asked her the other day.

"Of course, I *really* love you," she replied, puzzled. "Why do you keep asking?"

"Because you *really* love *everybody*," he said, his feelings spilling out. "It doesn't make me feel special!"

According to at least one study, such feelings might sometimes be valid. In a study of UCLA students, researcher Belinda Campos found that a factor she called "love of humanity" had relatively little overlap with romantic love, with family love, or even with friendship. These data could be read in different ways. It *could* mean that the tight bonds of romance, family, or friendship simply crowd out concern for those outside the charmed circle. It could mean that humanitarians do indeed have less left over for their intimates.

Sociologist Kristen Renwick Monroe calls the "pure" altruists she studied "John Donne's people," after the poet's declamation that "no man is an island, entire of itself; every man is a piece of the continent, a part of the main." Perhaps Donne's perception of an interconnected humanity provides some more final insight into what makes altruists tick. Monroe believes that the key to the Holocaust rescuers' activities is their unshakable sentiment that "all human beings belong to one...family...forming such a central core of their identity that it left them no choice in their behavior toward others."

I heard it again and again in conversations with kidney donors. "Humanity's a family thing," Harold said. "My brother, my boss, someone a town or a country away—it's the same." Steve Aman confided he was preparing for a Mohawk ceremony called "making relatives" to tie a ritual family knot with a man he'd met at a Sun Dance. "Young guy, had a tough life, about to get a heart-valve replacement. I want him to know I'm really there for him." A West Virginia postman donated a kidney to a man on his rural route he saw only once a month, explaining to his astonished wife that the people on his mail route "are like family to me." Maybe altruists don't so radically refute the kinship hypothesis, after all. Everybody shares the same genome. We *are* all kin. They may just be the ones who know it bone-deep.

S TILL, MANY FIND ALTRUISTS SUSPECT. UNDER WHICH CATegory of too good to be true should these people be filed away? When I bring up altruism in conversation, I hear particular distress at the notion that there could be people who are congenitally kinder. It's one thing to acknowledge, say, musical prodigies but quite another to speak of kindness virtuosos. We tend to view compassion as neither a talent nor a skill but a quality of the moral sphere, where we are all, in principle, equally endowed.

Indeed the analogy between inborn talent and compassion is too facile. There are too many cases like Ebenezer Scrooge, an apparently unendowed wretch who lived his life "self-contained and solitary as an oyster," only to wind up a joyous, selfless dispenser of boons. In the moral sphere, we are all remarkably capacious for the very reason given by Confucian philosopher Mengzi: "All men have a mind which cannot bear to see the suffering of others." (A more accurate translation from the Chinese is "heart-mind," as in the Buddhist notion of *bodhicitta,* the heartmind of compassion.)

Studies of Holocaust rescuers and LADs reveal people who believe they are no better or worse than anyone else. And though Toni Henderson's volunteer donors scored high on the scale of "humanitarian values," most were not grand crusaders, seeming to dwell more in the realm of private deeds and personal conviction. Still, there is no use pretending their viewpoint wasn't unusual (if it weren't, there would be tens of thousands more kidney transplants and millions more Holocaust survivors). Monroe observes that rescuers' kindnesses were unusual in that they were not constrained by "personalistic or empathic ties to family, gender, and religious, national, or ethnic groups," nor even by ordinary emotional affinities: "Women were not more likely to help other women," she writes. "Children and babies were not particularly cherished because they were more innocent."

If anything, the decision to risk themselves for others was curiously impersonal.

Monroe had this dialogue with one of the rescuers:

Q: Would you help somebody you don't like?
A: Absolutely.
Q: Would you help a person that you thought was terrible?
A: If something happened to that person, certainly. If I can help somebody, I will be happy to do it.*

This attitude is similar to the Buddhist concept of "boundless impartiality," described in one text as "giving up hatred for enemies *and* infatuation with friends." It resembles, too, Saint Thomas Aquinas's *caritas,* which extends even to enemies because, in his reasoning, if one loves God and God loves all, then one must love everyone God loves. Harold Mintz pretty much summed up the *Summa Theologica* when he remarked, "Even if my kidney had wound up inside a total jerk, it'd still be cool."

---

*Monroe claims that not even empathy was necessary for those she calls "pure" altruists. She quotes from another interview:

Q: Was empathy part of your rescue activities?
A: Meaning what?
Q: Feeling that "this could be me."
A: No, never even thought of it.
Q: You didn't think of that at the time?
A: [*Shakes her head no*]
Q: Did you feel sorry for the people? Pity?
A: I don't know. I didn't feel anything to be honest.

It sounds almost *too* cool: Where is love's passionate, exclusive attachment to specific persons? But love of humanity, abstract to most of us, seems for the altruist to be as palpable as that "real love" that we (and our genes) so wildly applaud. "There are such helpers in the world," said the poet Rumi, "who rush to save / anyone who cries out / Like Mercy itself / they run toward the screaming." Is it possible that what most of us feel as a stirring (which we heed with such fidelity as we can muster) is experienced by some as an irresistible instinct?

In 1902 biologist Peter Kropotkin speculated about the instinctual basis of compassion. A former Russian anarchist who'd escaped the clutches of the czar's prison when his friends organized a daring daylight jailbreak, he had observed the symbiotic behavior among different animal species living in the frozen Siberian steppes. Citing Darwin's little-noted ruminations on the enhanced survival conferred by cooperation, Kropotkin argued that more crucial than the "law of mutual struggle" was "mutual aid." He puzzled over the helping impulse in humans, concluding that love and sympathy were too narrow a reading of the "moral feeling" (which he described as an "unconscious recognition...of the close dependency of everyone's happiness upon the happiness of all"). Kropotkin explained: "It is not love of my neighbor—whom I often do not know at all—which induces me to seize a pail of water and to rush towards his house when I see it on fire; it is a far wider, even though more vague feeling or instinct of human solidarity and sociability which moves me."

*W*HERE DOES THIS TENDERNESS COME FROM?" ASKED RUS-sian poet Marina Tsvetayeva. How do we account for altruism? Is it a special gift, like a green thumb or perfect pitch? A perspective picked up from one parent or a gene cadged from another? The product of religious epiphany or of life's on-the-job training? Is it taught (through pedagogy) or caught (through emotional contagion)?

Biologists speculate that evolution selects for some, but not too many, highly selfless individuals in a given species grouping. (Too many, the thinking goes, and they'd *all* become prey.) The least disruptive scenario as to how altruism may have evolved is that although, as one scientist puts it, "self-sacrifice is counterbiological" for any given individual, generosity among members of an animal colony (or a kinship-based clan) who share genes would lead to more *overall* genetic success. (As Darwin himself put it: "Those communities which included the greatest number of the most sympathetic members would flourish best.")

There is evidence that along with genes predisposing people to temperamental traits like shyness or risk-taking, there are also "altruism genes." Maybe *these* are the people who spend their lives succoring the sick, feeding the hungry, clothing the naked, comforting the abandoned, making peace between enemies.* As one Holocaust rescuer told Monroe: "Life is possible because a certain number of people are not selfish and believe in sharing with others." She added, "If there is not love and sacrifice, no concept of others, then maybe life would be possible in some ways, but it would be a terrible tragedy."

Most social theories hold that altruists are the product of moral example, the power of which has been demonstrated even

---

*In 2005 a team of Israeli scientists reported in the journal *Molecular Psychiatry* that they had found a gene variant on chromosome 11 in people who scored highly on a Selflessness Scale questionnaire. The gene appears to boost receptors for the neurotransmitter dopamine, which produces positive feelings. In 2007 another study—this one based on choices that players made in a game designed to elicit either generous or selfish behavior—found strong correlations between generosity and variations in the gene known as AVPR1a. The gene promotes the release in the brain of a hormone, vasopressin, that is implicated in social bonding.

in the lab. In one experiment children watched an adult play a miniature bowling game and win tokens that could be exchanged for toys, then give half of her winnings to poor children. A second group saw the adult win the tokens but use them all for herself. Observed later at play through a one-way mirror, the children who had witnessed generosity behaved more generously than the other group. The impact of this single "exposure" to kind behavior was noted in their play even four months later. Experiments have also revealed that children who are shown TV programs with positive messages about helping others exhibit more "prosocial" behavior.

Early cultural influences are formative. Hopi children are taught at an early age that nothing is more important than having a "Hopi good heart." This ethos includes having trust and respect for others; being concerned for everyone's rights, feelings, and general welfare; seeking inner peacefulness; and practicing conflict avoidance. Even social factors such as whether a person lives in a small town or a big city have differential effects on altruism. In one study, a child was placed by experimenters on a busy sidewalk and instructed to tell pedestrians she was lost, then ask them to call her house. In a small town, three-quarters of passersby stopped to help; in a city only half. This may relate to Oliner's concept of "normocentric" behavior, the way that beliefs, models, and values absorbed from parents and communities become an internal compass of what "normal" people just *do*.*

In Monroe's study both the "rational actors" (entrepreneurs) and the Holocaust rescuers reported growing up with role models who had transmitted virtually identical moral messages: "honesty,

---

*The African term for humanness itself, *ubuntu*, means "a person is a person through other persons." The social ethic is so pervasive that in 1997 a South African government white paper officially recognized *ubuntu* as central to "the rights and the responsibilities of every citizen in promoting individual and societal well-being."

fairness, justice, equality, respect for other people." Were the rescuers somehow predisposed to take it to heart? But their attitudes, and ultimately their behaviors, were quite different: Why? Monroe notes in passing one peculiar observation: Altruists' deep humanitarian perspective was "evidenced at an early age." It again raises the question of whether there is some factor in the altruistic personality that can't be solely attributed to family upbringing, cultural influences, or moral training.

Psychologist Lawrence Kohlberg, who established a widely accepted schema of stages of moral development, noticed that children classified as highly gifted also used a higher level of moral reasoning than their peers, reaching a peak by their teens that only 10 to 15 percent of adults ever attain. Their helping behavior was exhibited so early in life that he reluctantly conceded it could not be entirely explained by his model of age-specific stages.

Tibetans refer to exceptionally bright and compassionate young children as *tulkus,* believing them to be reincarnated *bodhisattvas* who have practiced great kindness through a garland of lifetimes. They are given special instruction and placed in positions of spiritual leadership at an early age. Every society has taken note of children who are exceptionally giving, even in families and cultures that do not particularly encourage it. Sometimes, almost inexplicably, a lotus appears in a daffodil patch. The tenth-century Saint Luke the Younger (known as the Wonderworker for his legendary healing powers) was born the third of seven children to simple farm folk. He was said to be so naturally tenderhearted as a boy that he would give his supper to the hungry and strip off his own clothes to hand them to beggars. (His parents must have deeply loved him, entrusting him with sowing his father's fields even though he "was wont to scatter half the seed over the land of the poor.")

In our culture special children often fall under the heading of "gifted." Indeed descriptions of young saints, *tulkus*, altruists, and the highly gifted sound strikingly similar. For while the popular image of the gifted child has more to do with intellectual talent than tenderness, social psychologists have also remarked on an extraordinary quality some call "moral sensitivity." Linda Silverman, a specialist in gifted education, writes:

> We have dozens of cases on record of gifted children befriending and protecting handicapped children, becoming terribly upset if a classmate is humiliated, becoming vegetarian in meat-eating families, crying at the violence in cartoons, being perplexed why their classmates push in line, refusing to fight back when attacked because they considered all forms of violence (including self-defense) morally wrong, writing poems of anguish at the cruelty in the world, and fighting injustice.

She describes Sara Jane, who, at two and a half, brought her piggybank to her mother after seeing a TV report of a Russian earthquake that had left hundreds homeless, saying, "Mama, send them my money." The following Christmas she asked her parents to donate all her gifts to poor children: "I have everything I need. I wish you would give my presents to some little girl or boy who won't get any." At age six she organized donations for a soup kitchen. This sort of active moral response coupled with caring is not unusual, even in play. I was told of a gifted nine-year-old who was so upset to discover that, in a computer game called Neo-Pets, unwanted digital creatures were euthanized by "Dr. Death," she created original software to save them. Her "adoption agency" program allowed her and other children to rescue, "groom," and then give away the pets. She was uninterested in the stated objective of the game, which was to acquire as many creatures as possible for her own private menagerie.

One theorist claims that such children see the world in a way that constitutes a "qualitatively different new intelligence" he dubs "caring thinking." This includes not only "advanced cognitive abilities" but "heightened intensity of perception, of feeling and of experience, motivated by an intense social and moral conscience."

Pitirim Sorokin, the founding chair of Harvard's Sociology Department (who, like Kropotkin, escaped the czar's prison), devoted his career to studying human goodness. He took note of certain people he categorized as Fortunate Altruists: "Such individuals are loving and friendly from childhood. In the course of time they grow graciously in their love behavior...similar to the growth of beautiful plants." Sorokin, whose singular passion was the progressive "altruisation" of individuals over a lifetime (and of humankind over millennia), cites eighteenth-century Quaker John Woolman, who, recalling killing a robin as a child, later wrote how he had been "seized with horror, at having killed an innocent creature." Woolman grew up to be a forceful antislavery abolitionist, belying the notion that people who seem "hypersensitive" by nature are too fainthearted to be effective.

Such early bloomers appear in all times and places. They grow up to be people with an acute empathy for the downtrodden, a reflexive belief in one humanity, an intense thirst for justice, a tendency to cast off status and privilege, and a gardener's faith that the watered seed always flowers.

*F*ROM WHAT SOURCE, THEN, DOES ALTRUISM SPRING—NOT just in the "fortunate" and the "gifted" but in all of us? Is it possible that we owe as much of our moral activity to inborn instincts and emotional circuitry as to early pedagogy or the starry realm of conscience? The newest (and oldest) theories seem to

agree on this much: The heart leaps first, slipping past the cognitive gatekeeper. As one Holocaust rescuer put it, "The hand of
compassion was faster than the calculus of reason."*

Psychologist C. Daniel Batson, who was a skeptical grad
student during what he wryly calls "the dawning of the age of
Aquarius," was convinced that altruism was a rational, ego-driven
strategy, a chip off the old ice block of calculating self-interest.
After ten years' worth of rigorous lab studies, he did an about-
face, concluding that the "egoistic" hypothesis was not borne out
by scientific evidence and that what he calls "empathy-altruism"
is a prime force behind good deeds. He defines empathy in the
Greek sense of *empatheia*, "feeling into," and empathy-altruism
as a "motivational state" that bypasses conscious moral reasoning. That is, it is not a case of putting oneself in another's shoes
("perspective-taking") but a direct, swift intuition he compares to
a mother's unthinking response to her child's need.

Batson believes that the egoistic theory has held sway so long
because it provided an "Eden of simplicity," a single explanation
for a complex range of phenomena. Expelled from this narrowly
bounded paradise, science can at last embrace a "pluralistic model
[where] both egoism and altruism have legitimate claims." This
model is appealingly fluid, closer to our actual experience of a
sliding scale from me-me-me to you-you-you. "Contrary to the
beliefs of virtually all [research] psychologists," Batson sums up,
"concern for the welfare of others is within the human repertoire."
(*Alert the media!*)

---

*Darwin noted in *The Descent of Man* that people who had never risked their lives
for another will spontaneously jump into a torrent to save a stranger. He took
such deeds as evidence of "the greater strength of the social or maternal instincts
rather than any other instinct or motive, for they are performed too instantaneously for reflection, or for pleasure or pain to be felt at the time. Moreover, if
we are prevented by any cause from so acting, distress or even misery may be felt."

Batson's notion that the self can do a disappearing act—that between the perception, the feeling, and the helping hand no ego-shadow need fall—reminds me of the mystics' contention that compassion arises naturally when the ego gets out of the way. Contrary to the Freudian dispensation "Where id was, ego shall be" (ego's day job being to tamp down the id's base instincts), mystics believe that when ego exits the stage, it is not our baser instincts but the beneficence embedded in human nature that shines forth unobstructed.

Only a small number of Holocaust rescuers (16 percent, by the Oliners' count) credited religion or God per se as a factor in their actions, yet many described profound spiritual intuitions. One of Monroe's rescuers, a man named Tony, said: "I see the whole world as one living body, basically. But not our world only: the whole universe. And I'm like one of the cells." He added, "Gradually by opening your eyes, you see...everyone is you." I heard similarly mystical-sounding perceptions from other altruists. A woman I know who does countless deeds of charity told me: "I can remember being really young, lying on the sidewalk looking up at the sky and feeling that space was filled with this palpable energy. I could feel that same energy in people, understand what was going on inside them, especially their sadness. And I just let my heart go with them."

In Judaism the term *hesed* (steadfast love) refers to God's unbounded caring that never wavers—which we who are made in His image are capable of reflecting. One scholar calls it "the aspect of divinity which seeks to bestow love and blessings without limit." *Hesed* seems identical to *agape,* an ancient Greek word for the most unlimited, accepting form of love; the term was adopted by early Christians to describe humanity's proximate attainment of God's love for His creation. It is said in Genesis that He not only handcrafted each creature but saw that it was good. (One theologian has proposed that *agape* be translated as "seeing-good.") Key to *agape's* character, says a Christian ethicist, is "a feel for the preciousness of all human beings."

Here compassion is synonymous with a love not meted out according to merit but that falls like spring rain on the virtuous and the sinner alike. It appears to be a generative force, gathering strength rather than diminishing as it propagates. Those whom it touches, touch others. Said a student of the Hindu spiritual teacher Neem Karoli Baba, "What astounded me when I was around *Maharaji* wasn't that he loved everybody. After all, he was a saint, and saints are *supposed* to love everybody. What astounded me was that when I was around him *I* loved everybody. It's the kind of love that's contagious."

I have felt it in the presence of some givers, a peculiar radiance that makes the heart open wordlessly like a flower in a hothouse. Christian futurist Pierre Teilhard de Chardin claimed that love was a "radical energy," as real as magnetic lines of force, the pull of gravity, or the push of photons. If so, no one's yet measured it; indeed, it is by definition immeasurable.* But if most of us aren't radiating unconditional love, we're at least doing our fallible, level best to care. We shouldn't be too hard on ourselves if we don't measure up to some transcendental benchmark.

The real exemplars, far from being holier-than-thou, have always claimed to be flawed human beings like anyone else. I once heard the Dalai Lama tell a questioner: "I'm still practicing. Every

---

*Nonetheless sociologist Pitirim Sorokin proposed five factors, each with a sliding scale: *intensity* (from social gestures like giving up a bus seat to profound personal sacrifice); *extensivity* (from self-esteem, to romantic devotion, to the love of all); *duration* (from a single good deed to "great apostles of love discharging their love mission for decades"); *adequacy* (the degree to which compassion achieves its goal of helping); and *purity* (from "the thinnest trickle in a muddy current of selfish aspirations" to a "divine love").

practitioner is constantly fighting their inner enemies: attachment, hatred, pride, anger. So you see, I am not very holy!" One Holocaust rescuer, a German who was sent to a concentration camp for helping Jews (and who, amazingly, managed to continue his rescue activities from inside by bribing guards), joked that his morals were "only slightly better than those of an average American congressman." A woman named Margo, who as a consequence of her Resistance activities had been imprisoned six times, had lost contact with her young children, and had seen her fiancé killed, said: "I have my good sides and my disagreeable sides. I can be a bitch, and I can be nice. I'm nothing special." The LADs too scored high in the quality of "modesty" (defined in the study as "humble and self-effacing, though not necessarily lacking in self-esteem"). Zell Kravinsky told me he still rates himself as "missing the courage to be good...to push through to the moral life." Harold Mintz, expressing discomfort with what he called "that compassion label," said: "I have good days and bad ones—you should see me get pissed off in traffic." Rather than put altruism on a pedestal as an unattainable ideal, we might just take them at their word.

*P*ERHAPS BECAUSE ALTRUISM FALLS INTO A NO-MAN'S-LAND between our perfectly ordinary humanity and what sometimes appears to transcend it, it has been a battleground between spirituality and science, the former interested in the moral perfectibility of man—what we might be—and the latter in a factual assessment of what kind of creature-among-creatures we actually are. Is other-centeredness, not thinking of ourselves, a form of salvation or, as secularists have tended to regard it, an invitation to self-denial and self-delusion—to bloodless piety or even bloody messianism?

"Altruism's dark side needs to be held clearly in view," writes biologist Elliott Sober, "if we are to understand the moral dimensions of altruism and also its evolutionary and psychological character." He notes that self-sacrificing behavior on behalf of one's own group "can promote within-group niceness, but it also can promote between-group nastiness."

I was recently invited to a conference, billed as a dialogue between spirituality and science, where altruism proved to be the skirmish line. The event was flush with givers—clergy who ministered to the poor, healthcare workers, advocates for the marginalized, many of them members of the faith-based community. One speaker asked us to contemplate what would happen if all the faith-based volunteers were to disappear tomorrow. Society, he said, would grind to a halt: Who would be around to empty the bedpans of Alzheimer's patients, staff the soup kitchens, man the suicide hot lines, run the drug outreach programs, the orphanages, and the hospices?

The atmosphere at the gathering was genteel, but I could hear the subterranean rumble of plate tectonics along cultural fault lines. The audience sat politely as evolutionary biologists proposed that altruism might be accounted for by "misplaced nepotism" and religion itself by "a persistent cultural virus." They listened as speakers characterized their spiritual faith as "a byproduct of mental neural modules." Finally, an elderly, beanpole-thin man in a worn blue blazer, a philosopher-scientist able to quote both Darwinian chapter and biblical verse, took the stage. "I have a quarrel with the biologists," he said in a measured cadence. "They claim we are forced to describe ourselves in terms that are *alien* to our *intuition*." A native Coloradoan, he gave the impression of a slow-talking sheriff who'd finally had his fill of the town rowdies. His laptop was loaded with PowerPoint bullets, and he was ready for a showdown.

"All these theories designed to take the altruist out of altruism," he fumed, reciting them in a litany as they projected on a screen. "'Tacit, pseudo-altruistic reputation-seeking out-reproduces enlightened selfishness!' Conscience," he continued, "the still small voice that tells us how far we can go in *serving our own interest and get away with it*. Or how about this one: Thou shalt give the *impression* thou lovest thy neighbor as thyself! Well, those clever, *sneaky* Good Samaritans." He put a jocular lilt in his voice, but his mouth was pursed tight. "If Darwin is irrelevant to the understanding of solid geometry," he snapped, "why should he be relevant to the moral life?"

Though he was mostly shooting up a straw man, I caught his drift: These evolutionary biologists were trying to steal us blind of our nobility of spirit. Meanwhile, a biologist onstage had been listening with increasing impatience to one more Bible quote than he could stand. He burst out, his face flushed: "The flat Earth was taken off the table! Reasonable people took the God hypothesis off the table, too. If you want to put it back on, be my guest, but if you're here as a scientist, then play by the rules!"

I could sympathize with them both. At risk from the scientist's point of view was a reversion to superstition and wishful thinking (to say nothing of "creation science" mandated in biology class). At stake for the religionists was the holiness of compassion itself.

It was left to a tiny wizened rabbi to sort it all out. Rabbi Adin Steinsaltz, author of innumerable volumes of commentary on the Babylonian Talmud, master of countless languages, leader among survivors of unspeakable persecution, slowly mounted the stage, the very image of the unworldly religious scholar. "Look," he said in his old-country Russian accent, "electricity goes in both directions, positive and negative; that's why it works, yes? About seventy times a moment, back and forth. So you could say that in every deed of love, there is also some selfishness. They are not mutually exclusive.

"It's the *problematique* of being a human being," he mused. "We're practically divine on one side, and on the other side, this—this *kink* of hellish intention. The two parts come together to create a human being, a kind of angel put into the body of a gorilla! Look around you. It shouldn't be so astonishing that it works. Just do the best you can, and let the Creator who made this system in the first place take care of it." He twinkled. "After all, He's also somewhat responsible for it." He was offering an honorable compromise, a bit of rabbinical tradecraft: When faced with two irreconcilable views, choose both.

But is there no such thing, a questioner entreated him, as an unmixed motive? The man's careful articulation was at odds with the tremble in his voice, the question for him a burning brand. "Rabbi, sometimes a person can happen on pure grace even if he doesn't intend it. Isn't it possible that someone can be so lost in love of God, in *agape*," he said, asking for some reinstatement of the immaculate, "that he forgets himself entirely, acts out of pure love, isn't even *aware* that he's done good?"

The rabbi didn't miss a beat. "It may happen that the first time he isn't aware of it; but by the second time, he knows all about it. And by the *third* time, probably everybody else knows, too!" He waited until the cleansing laughter, the sense of relief at the popping of piety, had subsided. "Completely selfless deeds are completely impossible deeds," he said gently. "A person may spend so much time preparing to do the perfect deed he'll die before he does it! People shouldn't allow all sorts of noble intentions to interfere with the doing of good."

As he came off the stage, his wispy hair pasted down on his extravagantly furrowed forehead, he looked like some *shtetl* Merlin, five hundred years young. When I approached him, he greeted me with such expectant delight, such free-floating risibility, that I laughed before I knew what I was going to say.

"So," I blurted out, "if someone is trying to become more compassionate, is there some practice, some prayer in Judaism that helps?" The question seemed inane before it left my lips, but he savored it with an enigmatic half smile. He leaned in. "Just pray for grace. Pray for God to show you the way to do good. Pray sincerely, and he will reveal it to you."

He looked at me out of the corner of his eye. "You know, just join the crowd."

And I realized: The givers *are* a crowd, an embracing congregation. You could say we're all in the pews, even those of us beyond the pale. Whether we know it or not, the whole crowd of us: friends, family, strangers, enemies; mixed-up and wise, caring and craving; striving to transcend the mundane even as we cling to the status quo; opening our hearts, locking them tight, then opening them again when someone twirls the right combination.

Judaism talks about the Thirty-Six Lamed Vav, the unknown Just Persons who, according to the Talmud, are required for the survival of the world. Without them, it is said, the Holocaust would have marked the death of humanity itself. The rescuers, says one writer, "saved the concept of the human being as capable of goodness."

When those who stood by as the Holocaust unfolded were interviewed decades later, researchers noted a sense of "poignant isolation, viewing themselves as individuals who were alone and helpless: 'But what could I do to help, I, just one person alone against the Nazis?'"

But they were not alone; they only thought they were.

Rescuers touched others, not just their fellow conspirators, the paper-forgers and the people-smugglers but the bakers who sometimes silently portioned out more than the due ration, the farmers who wordlessly sold them cheaper vegetables, the occasional bureaucrat who turned a blind eye. They were too few and too far between, but thousands took tiny risks to affirm their humanity—risks that, without the rescuers, they might not have taken at all.

On the East Coast in summer, around dusk, you'll see a solitary firefly flick on like a miniature evening star; and then, as your eyes adjust, a myriad, an airborne processional: *blink-blink* in your yard, *on-off-on* at your neighbor's place, the green signal flares shimmering in code; and soon, all through town, this tango of light, as if choreographed by a cohesive intelligence.

So it is with us all. We signal each other, set each other off, turn on each other's inborn luminosity. Just look, really look, at somebody, anybody, laying down your defenses, not thinking for a beat about yourself, and there: the quick leap of tender flame, a little aureole of light. The knowledge is primal: wired in our brain, curled in our genes, thrumming in our nerves. Save each other, fail each other, hurt each other, help each other—it is always there, just waiting for us to notice.

THE ELIXIR
OF FORGIVENESS

I was angry with my friend:
I told my wrath, my wrath did end.
I was angry with my foe:
I told it not, my wrath did grow.

—William Blake

MY EX-PARTNER HAD BEEN MY ENEMY FOR EIGHTEEN YEARS, give or take a few yellowing calendar pages. He was, so far as I could tell, my worst (and maybe only) enemy, an arch villain in a business saga of trust betrayed, idealism tarnished, and labors lost (mine). I'll spare you the details, but they would rate a turgid Victorian subtitle, say, "Wherein I Am Utterly Ruined." The man's perfidy had swept me and my family into a whirlwind of trouble, sickened me body and soul, and plunged me into a dungeon of debt. Worse, it had broken my heart.

We'd set out to create a company whose mission statement was peace, love, and understanding. The business plan was progressive to the *n*th degree: flattened hierarchies and stakeholder employees, with yoga breaks and maternity leaves for all. I'd given it my all and everything, shouldering the day-to-day and the night-to-night of what grew into a dysfunctional, teetering multimillion-dollar business. Dazzled by the venture's endlessly spun potential, bamboozled by the partner's charming-boy fecklessness, I'd stayed on until he'd taken the best and left the rest.

Our venture was going to save the world; instead it had morphed into a snake pit.

It took me years to sift through the wreckage. I knew the drill: Pick yourself up, dust yourself off, and get over it. But somehow I couldn't. The Japanese have an expression for that feeling of grievance unredressed: *The belly is not satisfied.* It had been a clear case of Man versus Weasel. I got on with my life, but my hatred of the partner lingered, like a bare bulb dangling in the soul's basement, casting crazy shadows.

I tried all the spiritual home remedies. I told myself that my plunge to the bottom had taught me important life lessons, that my betrayer had done me a favor: I'd gone on to better things. I chewed over the notion that mean-spiritedness is its own punishment, that when you hurt another, you hurt yourself: instant karma. It was no good.

I'd sometimes catch myself idly planning a competitive venture to blow my nemesis out of the water. I dropped a disparaging word in the ear of a mutual business acquaintance in hopes of sinking his next deal. I imagined what I'd do if I ran into him on the street, flinging myself headlong on all six foot two of him, grinding his self-satisfied smile into the pavement. Thus doth resentment bring us low. Maybe I had a right to be angry, but I sensed I was paying a daily tithe to the Church of Mine Enemy, enmeshing myself in the big dumb cycle of retribution that already blights the planet. The question was: *How could I stop?*

I DO TRY TO BE LARGE-MINDED IN MY LIFE; THE TENACITY OF this thing was a little baffling. We all have some tendency to archive slights, indexing them for easy reference. We bank the smoldering fire of resentment so its embers need just a few twigs to kindle back into flame. More than likely, right now you can conjure up some big, painful humiliation. Such memories have a weird persistence; they leap all too readily to hand. The expression *nursing a grudge* is apt: We keep it on life support just to have the comfort of its brain-dead company. We imagine how sweet revenge would be (though we suspect it'd leave a bitter aftertaste).

Is there some evolutionary circuit that craves a settling of scores? Primates address social dilemmas through reciprocity: returning good for good, but also bad for bad, mandating a close accounting of favors and harms. Apes have been observed waiting for weeks or months before finding an opportunity to retaliate against a rival. Like us they seem to have an implacable recall for insults and a strong instinct to right the scales.

"It's your amygdala talking," a neurobiologist told me, referring to the ancient, almond-sized brain structure that primes our fight-or-flight responses. The amygdala is key (along with the nearby hippocampus) to the storage of long-term memory of emotional trauma. It is the likely home office of Grudge Enterprises and its wholly owned subsidiary Revenge Unlimited. It has recently been discovered that the amygdala is hardwired to the brain's center of higher reasoning, the neocortex, as well as to the visual cortex, suggesting that it is the culprit in our vivid recall of past slights and an unindicted coconspirator in the plotting of payback. Whatever the cause, surveys in several countries show that some 90 percent of men and more than 80 percent of women have had "fantasies about killing people they don't like, especially romantic rivals, stepparents, and people who have humiliated them in public."

A grudge, then, is no run-of-the-mill thought sprinting briefly through the mind. It digs in for the long haul, setting up house-keeping in a well-fortified bunker. We construct such a redoubt at our own peril; the maintenance costs are exorbitant. Says the *Dhammapada:* "In those who harbor such thoughts as 'he reviled me, he beat me, he overpowered me, he robbed me,'" "anger is never stilled."

Didn't I know it: Forgiving my enemy seemed like a primordial spiritual challenge. But I'd read about people who had faced it under far direr circumstances. Tibetan lama Garchen Rinpoche was jailed and tortured by the Chinese for twenty years yet had somehow, improbably, only strengthened his powers of forgiveness. "Ordinarily, if your enemy harms you, you will feel anger," he said. "This makes your mind like water frozen into ice by the cold. In order to melt it, we need sunlight, which is the cultivation of compassion."

I knew it was past time to let the sunshine in. I hadn't set eyes on my ex-partner since the previous *century.* The Berlin Wall had crumbled into chunks of graffiti-sprayed concrete; the late Pope Paul had apologized for anti-Semitism and kissed the chief rabbi's cheek; warring subcontinents had made peace. I had to forgive my enemy, but I knew I'd need his help.

I sat down and wrote him a letter: "Dear——, Scrolling through my mental PDA, your name still comes up in red letters. I'd like to strive for some forgiveness, after all this time. Would you be willing to join me in an experiment in reconciliation? Who knows, it might be for the greater good."

I was a little surprised when he promptly wrote back: "I am sorry to hear that you still harbor resentment toward me. I certainly feel nothing of the sort toward you. I would welcome the opportunity to see you. Time is a sparse commodity these days, but I would be happy to meet for a couple of hours. Kind regards."

His letter positively glowed with decency. What was he up to? Clearly, he wasn't going to acknowledge what had transpired. Translation of his "sorry to hear": "Whatever *you* think happened, didn't." Had he vetted this *billet-doux* with his lawyer? Still, I'd asked him, and he'd offered (making clear his time, as ever, was more precious than rubies). It would be small of me not to take him up on it.

As I planned my trip, I mulled it all over. If I forgave him without getting an apology, would I just be excusing his misdeeds? "Forgiving the unrepentant," says a Japanese proverb, "is like drawing pictures on water." It's so much easier when someone shows contrition, but what if he never did? I realized it wouldn't matter. I was persuaded by a remark I once heard Archbishop Desmond Tutu make: "To forgive is the highest form of self-interest. I need to forgive you so that my anger and resentment and lust for revenge don't corrode my being." I *was* corroding in my prison of ill-feeling. If I depended on my enemy to say he was sorry, he was my jailer. I resolved that no matter what happened between us, I would filch the key and set myself free.

I upped the odds of success by prepping a little for our meeting. I'd asked the advice of an international negotiator who was passing through town, a woman who'd gotten even Rwandan Hutus and Tutsis to sit down and forgive each other in the wake of genocidal horror. I'd been embarrassed to bother her with my petty grievance, but she'd waved off my objections. It's *always* the same story, she'd told me, whether broken friendships, marriages on the rocks, businesses gone sour, or war's grim remains of the day. The heart shuts down, encapsulating the injury. There's the denial of the other's human decency, the refusal to empathize, the memory button set on endless replay, the cosseting of grudges, the craving for revenge. The solution—to acknowledge your own pain, put yourself in the enemy's place, and try to let go—was wrenching, painstaking, but it was the only way out of the box.

She had assigned me a simple exercise. First, to lay out all my grievances, focusing more on my emotions than any litany of circumstance. I was surprised to find that much of my discontent stemmed from blaming myself. I'd felt deeply ashamed: I'd been a fool, a tool, a footstool of someone else's ambitions. I'd felt guilty that I'd dragged my family across the country for a fistful of funny money. I could also see that the intricate ways I'd been disappointed, all of which had seemed so unerringly personal, aimed straight at my heart, were just archetypal human pathos. Seduced, betrayed, abandoned? Reeling from your losses? Heart stuck in a rut? Welcome to Life 101.

A few months later, I showed up at my enemy's fortress, a small, sandblasted brick office building set in a stand of trees by an ambling city creek. "He said noon," his assistant told me, "but... [*sigh of affectionate exasperation for the Great Man who signs your checks*]...with *him* you never know."

Finally, the ex-partner strode in. I felt a surge of adrenaline. But at last I was face to face with the bad hombre who'd stolen my water, left me to the buzzards, and rode off with his saddlebags jingling with gold—*our* gold.

We sat across a table from each other, feeling that time-machine shock of twentieth reunions, each face a little older. I'd invited a mutual friend, a seasoned mediator, to give us some basic ground rules. I could talk as long as I liked; my adversary would listen. Then we'd switch. Finally, if we wished, we could talk together. Our friend would sit there, "holding the space." She asked us to take a few minutes in silence, then say a few words. I remembered I had resolved to ask him something that wasn't purely hostage to the past. And I was genuinely curious: Why had he agreed to meet with me?

"Because I knew it was important to you," he replied, "and I believe in healing. If I could make things better, I decided I would do it—to see what I could do for you, to strengthen my own understanding."

His answer—a *perfect* answer—threw me. He'd always been adept at dissimulating, talking the talk, a master at disarming in order to later stab you in the back. But if he were such an ogre, why was he even sitting here? After all this time, with all my painstakingly stockpiled bitterness, I was suddenly on the verge of tears.

"What I want to do," I said, my voice shaking a little, "is just tell you my side of the story."

As I spilled it all out, he listened, nodding occasionally: the shambles his hubris had made of everyone's lives, the fallout of his broken promises for me and the people I loved. When I became ill, he had dismissed me with a pittance. But it was his lack of caring that was most wounding. Without so much as a get-well card or a thanks for the memories, he'd acted as if I had fallen off the edge of the Earth.

As I talked and he took it in, I saw flickers of empathy in his eyes, glints of comprehension, not a spark of malice. But I detected something else: a blankness, as if it wasn't all quite registering. I was suddenly hit with an unwelcome thought: What if all of it, so utterly consequential to me, had been just a blip on his radar? What if he hadn't lost any sleep over it because it hadn't much mattered? What if—and this possibility was the most humiliating—he didn't even remember?

When his turn came to speak, he said as much. He did recall that some promises were made, but he couldn't quite place the details. He recalled I'd fallen ill, but not that he'd used the opportunity to dropkick me into the end zone. He was surprised to hear I'd been hospitalized not twenty minutes from his house. Whatever I'd been through had gone largely unnoticed; he'd had his own problems.

These he laid out, talking in ellipses about an "enterprise mis-
aligned with purpose" and "bad advisers" and "a certain naiveté
about the business," as if some malign imp had set about undermin-
ing the venture. Because of this occult force, "misunderstandings
took place" and "things didn't work out as intended." It was hard to
tell whether he admitted even to himself that he had used people
until he used them up. When it came to his broken commitments,
he talked about "the entrepreneur's reluctance to get pinned down
to entangling agreements," and his callousness became "not having the right emotional skill-set." He lamented his debts and the
relentless squeeze-plays by his investors.

But as he elaborated, he seemed to circle closer to the heart of
the matter, describing the desperation he'd felt to make the business
succeed. The international negotiator had also asked me to imagine my ex-partner's state of mind and heart, conjure his hopes and
fears as if they were my own. I was amazed how closely my guesses
were confirmed by what he was now telling me. "I felt I needed a
life raft," he was saying. "That I'd sink if I didn't take care of myself.
I had my family to think about." When he talked about feeling like
the Little Dutch Boy with his finger in the dike, I found myself
involuntarily nodding. I'd often used the same analogy; I had no
idea he'd felt the same way. "A person has an image of himself," he
went on, "as gentle, kind, and good. But others perceive him as
arrogant, narcissistic." He sighed almost inaudibly. "And then you
find there *are* things about you that are shitty and insensitive."

This rang a bell. If I were honest with myself, hadn't I also
pushed people too hard, though I would have claimed in the name
of the greater good? When he talked about his own life—growing
up feeling "invisible, always keeping the back door open so I'd be
able to get out when my family got too crazy"—even though he'd
been raised as the privileged scion of old money, I knew the feeling.

Now and again he'd come back to the issues between us. "It was hard to give you the consideration you may well have deserved. Besides," he hastened to add, "there was a certain lack of insistence on your part."

"You're saying that it was up to me to keep you from stealing my lunch money?"

He looked embarrassed. "Well, no, that wouldn't be right."

For the first time since we'd met, he seemed to really think about it. Abruptly, he began to talk about what it had felt like to come back from the Vietnam War, disillusioned and traumatized. "I still feel anger at all the lies. But the most hurtful thing was the feeling of betrayal." He paused. His eyes softened a little. "I can see how this would feel for you," he said, "that kind of betrayed innocence. It sears the soul."

Tears sprang to my eyes. I was speechless; this *was* how I felt. He'd reached deep down into his own feelings and pulled out a big handful of mine. That I was visibly moved seemed to draw him out further. "Look, I agree that you were not treated well. I didn't appreciate your efforts. I feel badly. I wish I'd done a better job." I looked at him, saying nothing. "Okay," he sighed. "If it helps for me to say it, I will: You probably *were* strung along."

He paused again. Then, out of nowhere, it came.

"And I'm sorry," he said.

The words could have been hollow, perfunctory, but they weren't. And suddenly it felt as if a stage set on which I'd been performing a long-running play began to recede on invisible casters, the houselights coming up, the audience stirring, starting to file out. I looked into the face of the man I'd made my personal demon. It seemed more open, warmer, more careworn; it was no longer lupine, just the face of an ordinary person, sometimes crappy, sometimes kind, contending with his own problems just like everyone. I felt something that would have been unthinkable a few hours before: a sense of empathy and more—a sort of soaring liberation I could only call forgiveness.

As we left the charmed zone of intimacy, chatting about politics, kids, people we used to know, the feeling persisted. We shook hands, briefly hugged. I thanked him for his time. "There's always time for this," he said softly. He left to get back to work; the business, he disclosed, wasn't doing so well. I hadn't missed any pot of gold, just decades of typhoon-class migraines.

As I took a cab to the train station, I began to think about my own role in the mess. Don't the soft-boiled idealists screw things up as badly as the hard-boiled pragmatists? Hadn't I also been hell-bent on success, inconsiderate, overwhelmed, out of my depth? How much, for that matter, had I ever thought about *him*? I was the talent; he was just the moneyman who signed the checks, the supernumerary who underwrote *my* globe-straddling contributions. I wondered how I'd missed the clues: my enemy, myself. We had been two young men out to conquer the known universe, using each other, and, God help us, brothers under the skin.

*I*N THE DAYS THAT FOLLOWED, I WAS A LITTLE BEWILDERED to find that the malignant miasma of my grudge had lifted. I could no longer understand how I'd allowed such a ludicrous state of mind to take hold in the first place. I'd planted a hard little acorn of resentment, fallen asleep, and awakened in the shadow of a towering, moss-draped oak. Where had my enmity gone? I didn't quite understand what had happened between us. He'd apologized, and I had accepted. But what *is* this epiphany called forgiveness? The field of psychology has tended to ignore it, treating it more like a religious mystery than a therapeutic modality. It is found in the indexes of few clinical texts. Sigmund Freud, in all his writings on healing the mind, hardly gave it a mention.

Lately, though, there's been something of a renaissance. The pace of scientific research on forgiveness has so quickened that more than forty laboratories around the world are now drilling down to mine for ore. Social scientists talk of "grudge theory" and "forgiveness transactions," of applying "game theoretic analyses" to the dynamics of apology. Evidence indicates that forgiveness increases self-esteem (that magic word) and decreases anxiety. In one trial men in a drug and alcohol treatment program who trained in forgiveness showed significantly less depression. And there are implications for physical health: While holding a grudge fuels anger and resentment, producing damaging stress hormones (cardiac patients who blame others for their initial heart attack are more likely to have reinfarctions), positive emotions like forgiveness lead to lowered heart rate and reduced blood pressure.

A new therapeutic subspecialty, forgiveness counseling, is making a bid for legitimacy, with volumes of theory and burgeoning self-help books in tow. A certain hyperbole has already crept in: One therapist calls forgiveness "as important to the treatment of emotional and mental disorders as the discovery of sulfa drugs and penicillin have been to the treatment of infectious diseases." And there is the inevitable controversy. Some clergy warn of a shallow secular dispensation, a forgiveness stripped of its most challenging moral dimensions, while some psychologists accuse *them* of guarding an exclusive religious franchise.

Some of the confusion may pertain to different degrees of forgiveness. At its most basic, forgiveness is an act of self-healing. I would rather have been hung by my thumbs than let bygones be bygones until I realized how much my burden of resentment was hurting *me*. Forgiveness begins with acknowledging one's own pain, shame, and sense of failure; healing the shattered sense of self-worth; and grieving the loss of faith in other people. To liberate ourselves from a hurt inflicted by another takes the psychological courage to open an old wound and pull out a tangled skein of issues we'd rather keep under wraps.

Many mental health counselors believe that this focus on personal healing should be where forgiveness begins and ends. In a recent poll of the profession, 66 percent said they "do not endorse activities that acknowledge and address the significance of the offender" and do not encourage empathy toward them. "The majority of respondents," concluded the survey, "appear to view forgiveness as a gift primarily to the self alone." One researcher quotes a woman who simply said, "Forgiving means to write the person off."

Though understandable—why *not* x-out the creepazoid who messed with your life?—I wonder if healing is really possible without striving to find empathy for the offender. President Jimmy Carter once defined forgiveness as putting yourself in the position of the other person and wiping away any sort of resentment or antagonism you feel toward them. Observes one clinician: "To forgive, one must have the capacity to identify with others and view them as more than simply extensions of oneself. One must be able to feel a modicum of social interest, a willingness to admit a personal role in relationship dysfunctions, and a genuine concern and empathy for others." Psychologist Heinz Kohut points out that a person who is too self-centered may be incapable of forgiving at all: The offending party is not seen as an individual in his own right, but as "a flaw in a narcissistically perceived reality." There can be no I-Thou when the Thou is subtracted from the equation.

One leading forgiveness researcher, Robert Enright, believes that without this Thou in the picture, forgiveness is radically incomplete. Enright founded the University of Wisconsin's Human Development Study Group in 1985, inaugurating the most extensive scientific investigation of forgiveness to date. He observed that a person may abandon a grudge only to be left with "detached indifference, writing off the offender as morally incompetent...and not worthy of our time." In that case, rather than forgiveness, we "end up replacing resentment with alienation." After a study of the existing psychological literature (along with the beliefs and the practices of the world's religions), Enright concluded that there is a deeper level of forgiveness, a kind of spiritual transformation he calls "a willed change of heart." He encourages his clients to strive for an attitude of "compassion, generosity, and even love" toward the offender.

It raises hackles among some social workers, who tell of domestic abuse victims counseled to forgive a perpetrator only to suffer new injury at his hands. Forgiveness horror stories make the rounds. Writes one clinician: "Some counselors have worked, as I have, with parents and grandparents who 'forgave' the behavior of drug-addicted youth, resulting in not only failure to treat the addiction, but, in some cases, the murder of the 'forgiver.'" At the very least, they caution, letting go of vindictive feelings can mean relinquishing necessary self-respect and needed self-protection.

Some kind of warning label seems well advised against what could become a forgiveness fundamentalism or just a mishandled new tool on the therapeutic utility belt. But a preponderance of time-tested wisdom points to the power of forgiveness to restore relationships, to heal communities, even to kick-start something akin to unconditional love—love that is not dependent on the other person's conforming to our expectations or being instrumental to our needs.

This sort of forgiveness is a form of mutual healing. Desmond Tutu speaks of reconciliation as a human necessity: "It is important that I do all I can to restore relationship. Because without relationship, I am nothing, I will shrivel."

S OME YEARS BACK, IN A YOUNGER, CRAZIER TIME, I DISCOVERED that a good friend had had a brief affair with my girlfriend while I was away on a months-long business trip. The news felt like a serrated steak knife between the shoulder blades. It seemed an unforgivable breach of trust. With an icy-cold voice, I declared our relationships null and void. I refused to talk to either of them.

But to my amazement, they refused to accept my edict of banishment. My girlfriend called every other day, sending roses and handwritten letters and notes of apology. My friend, stricken, told me, "I'm just not willing to lose your friendship. Tell me what I have to do." He didn't wait for an answer but contrived various tokens of apology and expressions of remorse. Though I'd turned to stone, they kept up their campaign of almost daily erosion. I could see that both of them were genuinely suffering. After a while I couldn't hold fast to my sense of outrage: It was making me feel small, even cruel. They had so empathized with me that their pain about the pain they'd caused me had made *me* feel for *them*.

Eventually, I relented. I forgave them. Our relationships were restored and grew mysteriously stronger in the broken places. My friend became, in the fullness of time, my best friend. My girlfriend and I affirmed a deeper, less contingent love; though we separated years later, we remain close. I know that if I had clung to my first wounded impulse, my life would have been incomparably poorer.

I had to wonder: *What was it about being the injured party that was so paradoxically seductive?* In the early days of Internet spam, marketeers discovered that people would readily open any e-mail whose subject line read "I'm So Sorry," proving that most of us feel somebody somewhere owes us an apology. I had to acknowledge the truism that we judge most harshly those who embody our unadmitted failings. Had I ever cheated on a romantic partner? *Yes.* Had I ever acted on a selfish desire and hurt another in the process? *Yes.* Had my friends, then, been my tormentors or my scapegoats? Christ's words on the cross, "Forgive them, for they know not what they do," is compassion's holy formula. We all miss the mark in our blindness, ensnared by ego and self-deception; we miss it more than we care to acknowledge.

Thinking of my business nemesis, it seems that none of it was personal. Wrapped in his own private fogbank, he'd hardly even *seen* me. An old Buddhist fable: A ferryman is taking a rich nobleman across a river. It is a misty night; he can see barely 10 feet ahead. Suddenly, another boat glides out of the murk and rams into his prow, spilling his finely dressed fare into the water. The ferryman is furious. Cursing, enraged, he lifts his pole, readying himself to strike the other boatman as his craft sweeps past, only to see—an unmoored, empty boat.

Maybe it's possible to forgive others' trespasses by realizing how blindly they harm us. Like empty boats, adrift on their own currents, colliding with us by happenstance, they're not quite all there, and neither, if we can admit it, are we.

Unless we are solitary anchorites, cartoon hermits with beards down to our toes, we live in relationship, which guarantees we will be hurt by others and inevitably will hurt them. Forgiveness, the binding of wounds, is indispensable to our lives together. To accept our own hurt, taking it in rather than projecting it out, distills the healing elixir.

Unresolved emotional pain is the great contagion of our time—perhaps of all time. This does not deny the struggle for justice: There *is* a world out there, and it cries out for rectification. But those who cannot sense the pain of the one who wounds them will dispense, under the banner of righteousness, a misshapen justice and create yet more enduring wrongs. I could be deep in goody-two-shoes territory, but I suspect that the final extension of forgiveness is just as Lao Tzu said: "It is the way of the Tao to recompense injury with kindness." The spiritual consensus is too wide to ignore. As Rabbi Pinhas Ben Yair once boasted of a favored disciple, "My Raphael knows how to love the most wicked evildoers!" The other day at lunch, I even got the message from my fortune cookie: "The way to get rid of an enemy," counseled the Peking Noodle Company, "is to make a friend."

I've concluded, at least in theory, edging toward practice, the same. I'm persuaded that the theologian Paul Tillich put forth an ideal worth striving for: "Forgiveness," he wrote, "means reconciliation in spite of estrangement; it means reunion in spite of hostility; it means acceptance of those who are unacceptable; and it means reception of those who are rejected. Forgiveness is unconditional, or it is not forgiveness at all."

I'm inspired, but it's still lofty enough to give me vertigo. We have all experienced that hardness of heart that makes reconciliation seem unattainable. God, I still get miffed when an acquaintance passes me in the market without a warm enough hello. I know people for whom a simple social snub has fueled a lifetime of rancor. To forge my own minor act of forgiveness had taken decades.

And aren't there some individuals we *should* place beyond the pale?—the ones who've tromped on our insteps without a murmur of apology, who've screwed us in the past and, given half a chance, would stick it to us again, this time with a little more torque? And what of the rotten people, the cold-blooded calculators and hot-blooded haters, the ones we justifiably loathe? In the Greek New Testament, the term used for compassion toward one who has wronged us is *splanchnizomai,* from the word for "intestines" (to pour out one's insides: forgiveness is gut-wrenching work). Sometimes it just feels impossible.

But now and again we hear of people who have forgiven the unforgivable. How do they keep their hearts open amid the buffetings of true malice? I was about to find out.

LOVING THE MONSTER

What shall we make of our darkness?

—Blaise Pascal

*I*T'S A FOUR-HOUR DRIVE FROM ATLANTA TO THE TELFAIR STATE
Prison down a lonesome stretch of I-75, which slices through
central Georgia like a straight-razor cut. I put the tuner on scan
and, just as I pass the Pinetucky Church of God, catch a burst of
pure southern gothic, some ballad about a dying preacher who
"a-laid his bloodstained Bible right in that hooker's hand." In the
staticky desert of rural bandwidth, where the choice is either Black
Sabbath oldies or the Good Book's greatest hits, I'll take a good
sermon, where the story of Mary and Joseph at the inn becomes
"the Bethlehem Motel Six *refused* to take their credit card!" I play
a mental game, slugging in my own translations for the more over-
wrought scripture thumping. When the preacher shouts, "Friends,
I wouldn't live a day without Jesus," I think, *without compassion,*
for what else was he, and amen to that. "Repent!" becomes *take a
frank and fearless inventory,* and I try: The truth is, I'm more than a
little nervous: I'm on my way to meet a stone cold killer.

The murder had shocked the down-at-heel Atlanta neighborhood of Vine City. Residents there were no strangers to crime, but
the victim had been an angel. Forty-three-year-old Patricia Nuckles

had come up from those very streets, gone away to college, and then returned to her roots, working as a librarian, tutoring kids, doing charity work in her spare time. Trish, as everyone knew her, had had an unusual upbringing: an African-American woman raised by a white couple, Hector and Susie Black, who'd moved down in the 1960s to do grassroots civil rights organizing. There in the Deep South, the Blacks, their three other daughters, and Trish had formed an unlikely, fiercely devoted family.

Trish's cousin Michelle was the first to hear. Watching a news bulletin about a homeless crack addict who had burglarized a home and murdered the owner—a drearily familiar tableau of flashing police cruisers and yellow crime-scene tape—she realized with a ripple of horror that she was looking at Trish's house. Not long after, police caught thirty-two-year-old Ivan Simpson hiding at his mother's place. "What type of animal could have done that, killed her the way he did?" Michelle asks me. "Trish would literally give you the clothes off her back. She helped the homeless too; she would have helped *him* if he'd asked."

The case was a prosecutorial slam-dunk. When Simpson pleaded guilty, the district attorney shifted his focus to getting the death penalty. As the crime's terrible chronicle was read into the court record, Hector Black, who had driven down from his Tennessee farm, felt thankful that his partial deafness made some of the account inaudible. He could hardly bear to glance at the powerfully built black man, head down and shoulders drooping, sitting in the courtroom.

The defense attorney recounted how Ivan Simpson had been born in a mental hospital to a severely disturbed mother. His life had been a nightmare of violence and deprivation. When it came Hector's turn to read his prepared victim impact statement, his feelings were in turmoil. Standing with his sport jacket thrown over his bib overalls, he told the court of his joy when Trish had come into his family.

"Although she was not our child by any claims of birth," Hector told the judge, "she was our child by every claim of love." He had watched her bloom from the thin, neglected child of a neighborhood alcoholic into a woman intent on making the world a better place. He opened his briefcase and took out his favorite picture of Trish as a beaming eight-year-old, telling the court of the mortal dark that had swallowed their lives, of his feelings of abandonment by a God, whose eye, he'd once believed, was always on the sparrow.

Such statements are usually a platform for crime victims to hammer home the enormity of their loss and demand the maximum penalty, but Hector had a starkly different purpose. "I know that love does not seek revenge," he told the court. "We do not want a life for a life." Facing the startled judge, he read the words he had written to the murderer: "I don't hate you, though I hate with all my soul what you did." Then summoning a reserve of will, Hector turned around to speak the last lines directly to the prisoner: "My wish from my heart is that God would grant all of us peace who have been so terribly wounded by this murder—including you, Ivan Simpson."

Hector remembers the moment: "It was almost like I was grabbed to turn around and look at him. He lifted his head, and our eyes met. Tears were just streaming down his face, such a look of...oh, God, like a soul in hell. It was one of those rare moments when the raw wounds strip away all pretense or falseness."

As he was being led away, Simpson asked to speak. Turning to face the family, he said, "I am so sorry for the pain I have caused. I am so sorry." Even the court's victim representative, accustomed to stony silence, false contrition, or even cruel mockery from the accused, told Hector she felt a sense of awe. "This is something we rarely see, genuine remorse." Simpson was sentenced to life without parole.

*T*HE TELFAIR PRISON GUARD TOWERS RISE MIRAGELIKE IN the swampy sunlight like giant mushroom caps on gray concrete stalks. Behind them low, boxy buildings warehouse some thirteen hundred violent prisoners, a third of whom are doing life without parole. The assistant warden, a whippet-thin bleached blond woman in her fifties, agrees to take me on a quick tour of purgatory.

We walk the path outside the yard, passing knots of marble-eyed men with time and blood on their hands who pause in their furtive talk as we approach. A young man with a shaved head saunters by, an enormous blue swastika tattooed on his skull. There are hundreds upon hundreds of terrible crimes contained within these walls, she tells me, and she pretty much knows them all. My curiosity morbidly piqued, I ask her to describe a few. She glances at me sharply, quizzically. "Isn't Ivan's crime monstrous enough?"

She leads me to a fluorescent-lit room, its walls decorated with fake flower wreaths and a pastoral painting of hunters and hounds chasing down a fox. Four brass ceiling fans whisk the soupy air. I'm seated at a conference table with twelve chairs, like a jury room. "He's probably going to cry," the warden says dourly. She puts a roll of toilet paper on the table.

Ivan Simpson is led into the room, wearing a prison-issue white jumpsuit. I expected a glowering, manipulative sociopath or some feral con man behind whose mask I'd spot the hard gleam of cunning. I am unprepared for this man with an abject air of guilelessness, speaking in soft, country cadences.

When I ask him about his childhood, he tells me of the morning his mother, a schizophrenic who had been in and out of mental hospitals since he was born, had awakened him, his four-year-old sister LaToya, his brother Chuck, and two other siblings for an early outing to the local park. He felt excited and happy. They were at the edge of the swimming pool when his mother, raving that they were all "a threat to God," scooped them up and plunged into the water. His sister LaToya drowned before his eyes. Ivan managed to thrash free and pull his brother Chuck to safety while the others struggled from her grasp.

Ivan was adopted by his great-aunt. He recites his ghetto coming-of-age story in an emotionless monotone. Hotwiring cars at fifteen. Moved up to "B an' E"—breaking and entering—earning a two-year prison stint. Then the revelation of crack cocaine— "just a few minutes of everything's-at-ease." He supported his habit through "property crimes, lying, and manipulating," sometimes stealing his aunt's rent money, watching as she lost her house, her car, and her job. The crack, he says, "seemed to take away all my caring for other people."

Had he ever really cared? I ask him. "Oh, I grew up in a loving atmosphere," he says in his slow, heartful drawl. "My adoptive mom, Marie, she raised me good. She loved us, just loved us." A tear meanders down his cheek. "I never had thoughts about hurting nobody."

Despairing over his addiction, he tried to kill himself several times before being admitted to a treatment center. Clean for a few years, he'd been given a car and a furnished three-bedroom house by a woman at a local church, where he, his common-law wife, and son lived in exchange for simple upkeep. It was a stroke of inconceivable luck, but soon he was addicted again. After picking his gift-house clean of anything he could fence, he wound up back on the street. Finally, he moved back to Marie's and got off his habit again. But one night, walking to the convenience store to buy cigarettes, he ran into his old dealer, who offered him a rock of crack. Soon high and craving more, he impulsively decided to do a burglary. Chance led him to Trish Nuckles's darkened house.

When Trish unexpectedly walked in on him, he knocked her down and tied her up. After that he remembers having a strangely cordial conversation. Trish, trying to calm him down, had asked him about himself. He said he was hungry. She urged him to take some cooked chicken and ham and sodas from the fridge. She even told him, as he was leaving with her computer and stereo under his arm, that he should try to get some help. He promised he would, adding he would just use her car to drop off the stolen goods and leave it parked where she could find it, next to the Chinese restaurant up the street.

He remembers thinking she was a nice person, even remembers telling her to be sure to install some outside floodlights and put her lamps on timers to deter future burglaries. "And then I just left." I can hear the relief in his voice. "Just *left.*" For a moment he is back at that crossroads, as if he could turn around and walk the other way, as if the story could end right there. His cellmate hears him in his sleep sometimes, saying, "I'm leaving, Trish, I'm leaving."

Instead, Ivan scored some more crack. As he sat in Trish's car, smoking it, he was startled to hear a voice, ghastly cold and glacially clear: *Go back and kill her.* He looked over at the passenger seat; the voice had issued from thin air. He re-creates his hallucinatory dialogue.

"I said, 'I ain't gonna kill that lady. She didn't see my face. Her glasses fell off. She can't ID me.'"

You go back now and kill that lady, said the voice. *You go back and* kill *her.*

Ivan knew then he was remonstrating with a demon, a demon, he says, "name of Legion." He smoked more crack, then returned to the house. "Legion want me to kill you," he told the still-bound and now terrified Trish. He remembers her asking why after he'd been "so nice up to now," her begging him to just take her car. He told her he wanted to have sex. She said he'd have to kill her first.

"The only thing I remember," Ivan claims, "is watching myself...strangle her. That's...that's all I remember. Standing above. Watching." A slow cortege of teardrops rolls down his cheeks. He swears he'd never been violent before in all his years of crime. "I don't know why she had to die," he mutters, "or I should say—why I took her life."

> For Jesus had commanded the evil spirit to come out of the man. Many times it had seized him, and though he was chained hand and foot and kept under guard, he had broken his chains and had been driven by the demon into solitary places.
>
> Jesus asked him, "What is your name?"
>
> "Legion," he replied, because many demons had gone into him.

The ranks of the possessed—by personal demons of defeat and dysfunction—*are* legion in the world. Ivan Simpson had had what psychiatrists call a "command hallucination"; crack, which addicts call Kryptonite, is notorious for them. I am revulsed by Ivan's crime, by his vile massacre of an innocent. Yet I think of a prayer by the Dalai Lama: "Those who, maddened by the demons of delusion, commit violent negative actions that destroy both themselves and others, should be the object of our compassion."

Navajo tribal healers who treat modern mental illnesses, like the violent flashbacks of soldiers returned from war, call it all *nayee* (monster). "What is the essence of the cycle of violence," writes a Navajo lawyer, "in which children who are abused or neglected become offenders themselves? *Nayee.* Antisocial personality disorder? *Nayee.*" Just as his mother had been "told" to kill his little sister, Ivan, in some awful restaging (a psychologist would call it repetition-compulsion), had been ordered by a phantom to snuff out a blameless young woman's life.

*H*OW COULD I HATE THIS MAN WHO HAD SUFFERED SO MUCH as a child?" Hector wrote in his diary after the day in court. "Someone so tormented by what he had done?" Hector had been unable to sleep that night. For the first time since the ordeal began, the coils that had wrapped themselves around his heart had loosened a little. He knew he'd done the right thing to oppose the death penalty. But there was something else, something he hadn't expected. "I knew then that I'd forgiven him," he says, the echo of surprise still in his voice. "And though I found it an awful stretch to think I could be concerned about the man who'd destroyed Trish, I also knew I had to write to him, encourage him that his life wasn't over."

Hector stayed up until dawn trying to find a way to put his new feelings on paper. He wrote to Ivan Simpson:

> The thought of being in prison for the rest of your life must be very hard. But it doesn't have to be the end. You can still find ways to help people who need help. You can be a force for peace and for light in dark surroundings. Patricia tried to make the world a better place. We should also try. If you will let me, I would like to keep writing to you. It would mean a lot to me to hear from you, especially knowing how hard it is for you to do this. Please try.

He signed it, "A Brokenhearted Father."

Ivan tells me that after his arrest he had only one purpose at his trial: to die. "I felt like for what I did, I deserved to go. I done took someone's life. Even though my dying wouldn't make up for it, why should I still be here?" He had told his lawyers, over their objections, to plead guilty. He'd wanted justice to take its course, straight to the electric chair. When they told him about Hector's opposition to the death penalty, he was baffled.

"Come on! How can someone not want me to die, and I just took his daughter's life? And Hector, how can he get up in court and say he hated what I did but he doesn't hate *me*?" He looks at me wonderingly. "Eyes can tell you a lot about a person. I saw his eyes, and he was for real. And, at first, I really didn't want that forgiveness. Fact, right now, up until this point, I ain't really forgave myself for what I did."

His voice catches only slightly. His head sinks in shame. He is stern as he weeps. He will not permit himself the indulgence of a sob. I strive to withhold my empathy, as if allowing myself to feel anything would be collusion, would betray the life he took. It's not easy to do, sitting with a man forever condemned to dry his own tears.

Hector continued writing to Ivan sometimes as often as weekly, the correspondence growing into a thick sheaf. He sent Ivan a letter with a leaf of scented geranium, but the censors confiscated it as contraband. He regaled him with the quotidian doings on his farm—the struggle to keep the grass in the orchard under control after heavy rains, chasing a neighbor's escaped cows.

Hector told Ivan about his skateboarding grandson and the teenage kids from the halfway house he invites out to climb around his property's waterfalls and savor a few unfettered hours. And Ivan wrote back in a scrawled pastiche of block letters and cursive about "the thorn in my side," about how the hardened inmates "think I'm crazy because I cry some nights about what I did." He described persuading a despondent man who had killed his own children not to hang himself, and breaking up fights and arguments between people "who literally want to see blood." He was trying every day, he said, to do good.

"The hardness I have against myself," he wrote Hector, "is a sort of strength to help others that I draw from. I used to pray for myself, but I realize it's not about me. From the moment I came to realize the hurt, pain, and grief I caused, I can pray for others now. It's hard going, giving up anger, jealousy, lies, and pride. But I am trying."

"Sometimes," Hector tells me, "I doubt myself. Are you crazy, writing to the man who killed your daughter? What kind of strange bird am I? I do have to wrestle with my feelings." But somehow, improbably, he'd grown to care for a man struggling in the grip of damnation.

What had happened to create such an overturning? Hector's plea for clemency had been on moral and intellectual grounds. But even with his Quaker philosophy and his big heart, he had hated Ivan's guts. "When I found out Trish was raped, especially," he says quietly, "I tried to demonize him. I felt like he had power over me, like someone was shoving my face in the mud. I had these horrible pictures in my head of the murder; I just couldn't shake it."

But when Hector saw Ivan sitting at the defense table, facing a sentence of death, in a courtroom "filled with our family, folks from our church, and he all alone, nobody there for him," he had felt something shift. Saint Paul said that higher morality is "written on the heart," not in the canon. Studies have shown that belligerents in war will feel sympathy when shown a picture of an enemy soldier in pain. When photos of a frightened, bedraggled Saddam Hussein being dragged from his spider-hole were beamed around the world, many people expressed oddly ambivalent sentiments for the Beast of Baghdad. "I felt pity to see this man destroyed," a Vatican cardinal was quoted. "Seeing him like this, a man in his tragedy, despite all the heavy blame he bears, I had a sense of compassion for him."

Perhaps it is easier to be magnanimous when we have the upper hand, gazing down on a human being prostrate in defeat. (One biologist told me: "I suspect brain structures for nurturant behavior fall in a rough range of candidacy: helpless, defenseless, weak, the underdog.") But religious doctrines often enjoin their followers to imagine even a superior enemy as weak and fallen, trumping the mind's logic with that of the heart. Martin Luther King used to portray his racist adversaries as broken people, living in spiritual exile, in need of forgiveness only the oppressed could grant them. He inspired among his followers a paradoxical sense of empowerment: It was only they, the victims, who could heal the damaged souls of their enemies by moving them to mercy and leading them out of hatred's wilderness.

There is an intellectual component to understanding the fruitless cycle of revenge and a moral component to understanding the willed extension of humanity to a hateful other. But compassion goes beyond moral decision-making. It is an irresistible force, breaking down the thickest fortress walls that separate us from each other. Psychologist Pumla Gobodo-Madikizela, a member of South Africa's Truth and Reconciliation Commission, had taken it upon herself to interview the jailed former security chief of the apartheid regime, Eugene de Kock. Chief planner and sometime triggerman in the government's brutal shadow war, de Kock was the mastermind of the infamous Vlakplaas "death farm," where the worst killings and tortures had taken place. He had by his own hand murdered and maimed. For the horrors he had visited on so many, he became known to the public by the sobriquet "Prime Evil." Gobodo-Madikizela's prison interviews began as a detached study of a specimen of inhuman detritus through a psychological microscope.

Convicted as a common criminal on murder charges, de Kock surprised everyone by asking to meet the widows of three black policemen who had been killed by a bomb he himself had planted. Gobodo-Madikizela was further astonished when one of the women told her after the meeting, "I couldn't control my tears. I could hear him, but I was overwhelmed by emotion, and

I was just nodding, as a way of saying, *yes, I forgive you.* I hope that when he sees our tears, he knows that they are not only tears for our husbands, but tears for him as well." The widow's response went beyond empathy; she had offered de Kock a priceless gift, a reentry into the human community: "I would like to hold him by the hand," she said, "and show him that there is a future, and that he can still change."

Gobodo-Madikizela's own friends criticized her for the equivalent of sitting down on a first-name basis with Adolf Hitler. She herself was shocked as a rapport grew uninvited. She had been "dumbfounded," she says, to discover that she and de Kock shared the same birthday: "I had to steady myself just to consider what it meant to share something so personal with a man whom many would consider a mass murderer." But meeting with de Kock, so close she could sometimes feel her skin crawl, she saw in spite of herself a man whose remorse was so deep he was wearing "an intolerable shirt of flame." She found over time her revulsion was challenged by the suffering of the human being sitting before her, leaving her deeply conflicted—consumed, she writes, by a "fear of stepping into the shoes of a murderer through empathy." She was taken by surprise by her own conclusions.

In her book *A Human Being Died That Night,* Gobodo-Madikizela's writes, "Empathy reaches out to the other and says: 'I can feel the pain you feel for having caused me pain.'... There is something in the other that is felt to be part of the self, and something in the self that is felt to belong to the other."

You in me, me in you. "I know it's a cliché," Hector had told me, "but deep down I'm not that different from Ivan Simpson. I really believe we each have a capacity for evil as well as good. What kind of person would I have been if I'd been born into his circumstances?"

Somehow Hector's open heart is having an inexorable effect. More than penitence, Ivan is absorbing into his charred soul Hector's unpretentious lovingkindness. When Hector sent him a small money order, Ivan was amazed: "How *can* he, I'm wondering? Where was his hate at? 'Cause I have to tell the truth, if the shoe was on the other foot, if someone took a loved one from me, I couldn't send them nothing. But *he* goes, 'Here's ten dollars.' He asks me to use it to buy something I need, some stamps or a candy bar. It just felt funny, it really did, for this man—I'm gonna have to say it—for him to love me. And I really believe he loves me. Even when I couldn't love myself. When I look around and wonder, *Is there really some love left, or care, or kindness?* here he is."

Theologian Paul Tillich wrote, "God's forgiveness is independent of anything we do, even of self-accusation and self-humiliation." But Ivan Simpson is the lowest of the low. I was sitting across a table from a man who had killed a sweet young woman out of sheer depravity and then—there is no delicate way to put this—returned to ghoulishly rape her body. Yet I could not help but see in him what Hector saw: a person possessed not by demons but by an unmistakable spirit of human worth he struggles daily to reclaim. That Hector's love is a force working on the very substance of Ivan's heart, I cannot doubt.

*D*OWN A FEW TWISTY BACKROADS AND DEEP IN A TENNESSEE holler, there's a sign that reads, "Entering Spring Creek Sanctuary: Animals and Plants Protected." Hector's house is a little farther on, a modest affair concealed in a green jumble of vegetative exuberance. When I walk up the path, his big dog doesn't let out a hint of a bark at the stranger but trots up to amiably nuzzle my hand.

Hector's farm grows everything from chestnuts to cherries, but it's the blueberries that are running riot this season, the fields spread with an azure impasto as far as the eye can see. A big carton of fresh blueberries sits in the living room. There's blueberry wine, blueberry preserves, blueberry muffins, and thick blueberry juice dark as indigo, at once sweet and tart, steamed right from the fruit. Homemade, all of it, as are the exotic plant jellies set on the dinner table by Hector's wife, Susie, who trundles around the kitchen with cheery efficiency despite being wheelchair-bound from rheumatoid arthritis. They have a stand at the farmers' market every week with the Quakerish motto, "Plain But Delightful."

Hector on first impression is just a tall, snowy-haired farmer in Liberty-brand overalls with tarnished brass buttons, a folksy sort who calls his combination fax-printer a "watchamajiggit," uses "okey-dokey" as his preferred assent, and reserves "humdinger" as an accolade for a stellar occasion. He's an atypical local—his degree, from Harvard no less, is in social anthropology—but he'd gone to agricultural school just before World War II and is clearly at home with anything that issues from the dirt.

"If it bears fruits or nuts," he says cheerfully, "I'm interested in it." He raises exotic plants as a member of the intrepidly named North American Fruit Explorers. As we walk through his nursery, he offers me a calamondin, a tiny fruit with a sweet skin and a sour inside. His current passion is autumn olive from the Himalayas. "Just loaded with antioxidants—and it's nitrogen-fixing." A gaggle of Russian plant biologists came through recently, conveying in thick Slavic accents their admiration along with a certain covetousness.

All they needed to do was ask. Hector's an open hand. He'll likely just give away most of his blueberry crop this year. He sold 80 acres to a community land trust at a no-interest steal.

Hector is a grade-A giver. He grew up in a family of them. His aunt Mollie inherited a pot of money, gave it all away to charity, and went back to her day job. His mother was so generous with her table during the Depression that the hoboes used to mark the house with chalk. He is another with that quality sociologist Pitirim Sorokin called "generativity"—something in him that likes fostering and the provision of sustenance. "You just like taking care of things," I tell him mock-accusingly. "People, plants, the dirt under your toes..."

He considers this, then nods. "I never looked at it that way, but maybe that's about right."

He talks about Trish, remembering "this little kid with impetigo sores on her legs from lack of sanitation and nutrition who was like a starved plant. She absorbed all the love you could give her, then just bloomed." Trish had passed that same love along, he says, taking in a young girl from the neighborhood and seeing her through college and marriage.

"When she died, I was in darkness," Hector says. His voice is ruminative, far off. "Susie reminds me that the first night, I was wild, crying, saying, 'I'd like to kill that bastard!' I don't have any answer why forgiveness happened. It was like a hand pulled me out."

His eyes mist. "I wanted to find something good in all the horror. I'm one of these people who don't believe in accidents. Though I do have a hard time figuring out what the hell happened and why this guy Ivan's in my life now." Then he laughs, and the laugh shocks me with its uproariousness, a burst of cosmic humor to shoo off any lurking grief-buzzards.

*I*T IS SURPASSING STRANGE. THE PURPOSE OF THE JUSTICE SYStem in capital cases, after all, is vengeance. Either the killer is himself killed, terminating his tenure on the same Earth his victims' loved ones must walk, or else he is buried alive where they will never have to know he still exists. Either way, victims are offered the grail-cup of final closure.

I once attended a meeting of a group called Parents of Murdered Children. Around the circle where a dozen mothers and fathers of varying ages, races, and backgrounds come together to cope with the ultimate tragedy, the current of outrage ran deep—at the "slimebucket killers," at the "donut-eating detectives" who couldn't catch them, at the "injustice system" that couldn't convict them or hold them or execute them.

The stories they told were heartrending. So were their lives. The past haunted them, the wound still as fresh as yesterday. One woman proffered the thin consolation that "you do get numb after a while, but you're never the same again because a part of you has been torn away." Legal retribution held out the only hope of peace from torment.

But for many that peace seemed more elusive the longer they sought it. I was struck by a woman who had brought along a white plastic bag filled with memorabilia about her daughter and her case. She carried it everywhere. "They call me 'the Bag Lady,'" she said acridly, her mouth a tight slash. Her daughter had been killed—"at the age of twenty-seven years, five months, eight days, twelve hours, and four minutes old"—in a hit-and-run on Christmas Eve while making a charity delivery of food. The Bag Lady thinks she knows who did it. She has collected Ziploc baggies of paint chips from the cars of potential suspects and collated boxes full of evidence, from the coroner's report to mortician's notes. She may yet have the triumph of justice long denied, but meanwhile it's eating her alive.

"I'm more full of rage than a 7-foot, 350-pound man," she said as she tugged from her bag of sorrows a framed picture of a beautiful long-haired young woman and passed it around the circle. "I was one of the best Christians you'd ever meet, but now I'm like a pit bull on steroids. This has made me a bitter, angry

person. I know some people who are my targets *shouldn't* be, but..."
She trailed off.

An elegant British woman of about seventy with swept-back gray hair, a blue shawl over her floral dress, smiled at her. "Well, I may not be a pit bull," she said, her diction gentle and precise, "but I *am* a British bulldog." Her son had been kicked to death by three men outside a bar, and the wheels of justice were grinding exceeding slowly. She'd been complacent about the legal system, she said. "Now I tell them, 'I'm sorry I'm not easy to deal with, but that is of *no consequence.*'" She looked over at the Bag Lady. "I might want some of those rage drugs you talk about next time I go in there." I got the impression of a crew of diligent carpenters constructing something that, with each turn of the screw, became too deeply joined to ever dismantle.

No one can judge how another deals with the most tragic of losses and certainly not whether they ever choose to forgive. Notes one clergyman, "We sometimes speak of forgiveness as though it were some sort of coin you can reach into your pocket and hand someone. There is no 'cheap and easy grace.'"

And Hector's decision has not led to any cut-rate closure. Ivan Simpson has become, from within his entombment, a vital presence in Hector's life. Rather than consigning him to state-sponsored nonexistence, Hector has chosen to receive his letters, think about him, care about him. To forgive someone who has eclipsed the very sun of joy—to gaze into his soul and find some indwelling virtue, no matter how besmirched—seems a form of spiritual heroism few could muster. Hector claims that he is the one being healed. "I just can't imagine that I would be the person I am if I had not forgiven," he says, "if I hadn't continued to write to him. In recognizing his humanity, I found my own again."

And granted it to another. It has been said it is not the wrongdoer's repentance that creates forgiveness but the victim's forgiveness that creates repentance. This is where forgiveness enters a realm of paradox and panacea, becomes a mysterious gift offered to one who does not merit it, becomes the essence of compassion itself.

*I*N A FAMOUS SCENE FROM VICTOR HUGO'S *LES MISÉRABLES,* Jean Valjean, a desperate man just released from nineteen years in prison for stealing a loaf of bread, is taken in by a kindly bishop. The cynical ex-con repays his hospitality by stealing the church silverware in the dead of night. But when Valjean is caught by the gendarmes, with the cutlery in his sack, the bishop lies that he had given it to him as a gift, pressing upon him two more silver candlesticks. Valjean's humanity is reawakened by this single gesture, and he begins a new life of virtuous service to others.

But what could Ivan Simpson possibly give back?

"Oh, I have a chance to give a lot," he tells me. "I'm in a place where a lot of people are going through pressure, having flare-ups. I try to point out stuff to them, keep 'em out of trouble, maybe just that day. I believe if each man just sat down and not dwell on his past but look over his life to see what he started, the envy and strife and how his attitude is making him now, it would humble him. I learned this: A soft answer to anybody'll turn away wrath. Sometimes you can hear two people yelling at each other; tensions are building. If one of them answers in not a harsh way, the other's going to stop. 'Cause you gotta have wood to make a fire burn."

Suddenly, I burst out laughing. I can't help myself: Ivan Simpson has become a *peacemaker.* Silent Simpson, the men in the yard call him; Quiet Ivan. Ivan, the crackhead killer, is making this harsh world of murderers and madmen, within its razor-wire circumference, a better place to live. The assistant warden and a guard sit on the couch, leaning forward, listening in, expressionless. I don't want them to think I'm being conned, chatting and laughing with the man as if I've forgotten who he is, what he's done, the lives he's blighted. But I can no longer hold, any more than can Hector, to a strict taxonomy of inhumanity.

Every day, Ivan says, he reads Psalm 88, a song of abandonment and of impossible faith.

> O Lord, God of my salvation, when, at night, I cry out in your presence,
>   let my prayer come before you; incline your ear to my cry.
> I am counted among those who go down to the Pit; I am like those
>   who have no help...
> You have caused my companions to shun me; you have made me a
>   thing of horror to them. I am shut in so that I cannot escape...
> Are your wonders known in the darkness, or your saving help in the
>   land of forgetfulness?

"It's when David thought the Lord had forsook him," Ivan explains, "but he was just trying to show him that he's always there." It strikes me as unutterably sad, but Ivan insists, "That's a *good* song, a song of hope."

I ask him what hopes he could have. "There's another passage says be of good courage and wait on the Lord," he says in his deliberate way. "I didn't know whether it meant to wait on him, like, he'll show up so don't rush, or wait on him like a waiter or waitress. So I try to do both. I wait for him, and I try to serve him by helping." But how could he help, in lifelong lockdown, with his faith at once puerile and profound? "I pray," he says simply, "for inmates, for officers, for everybody. I try not to pray for myself. That goes back to the life I've taken. I know Miss Patricia did touch a lot of lives. I believe if I ask for someone else, he'll help them. And if I can get to see that, see it manifest a little, that's good."

I ask Ivan if he thinks about the future. He's quiet for a minute. "I'm going to live out my natural life in prison, so I have to treat this as my home and do what I can to make my home a peaceful place. My future is to speak right or just walk right, try to be an example if I can. If I can. Encourage someone no matter where they at. That's just how I look at it."

He stands up and juts out his hand. It's cool and dry, the grip light, tentative, not making contact. He expects no warmth from the clasp, no friendship. I rein in any urge to offer solace, even to hug him, but I know he senses it. I almost regret my glimpse of this man's private suffering because I have been unexpectedly pierced. Weeks and months after I return home, I see his indelibly stricken eyes. Though Ivan Simpson is by any conventional measure a monster, a ghoul, he is also a figure of deep pathos and improbable hope.

*A*S HECTOR AND I HIKE UP A HILL—I'M PANTING, HE'S BARELY winded—he recites a running inventory of the critters he's spotted on his property: river otter, deer, muskrats, mink, scarlet tanager, indigo bunting, mourning doves, whippoorwills, great blue heron, vultures—even the bald eagle's coming back, he says. We come to a stand of dawn redwood trees that marks Trish's gravesite. The grave is a homespun affair, bordered with hand-laid rocks and blanketed with pink and red impatiens, aka Busy Lizzy, which bloom all summer long. The simple headstone reads: "All the darkness in the world cannot extinguish the light of a single candle."

It would be glib to say that light is growing. But though Hector may be "a strange bird," as he puts it, he's part of a flock of others who have managed to fill the mortal void of loss with living compassion. I'd expected them to be a gaggle of church ladies in deep denial, bringing hot soup and hand-knit socks to hardened cons who laughed up their sleeves at them the minute they left. Instead I've found people who have become, without setting out to be, agents of social healing.

There's Jennifer Bishop-Jenkins, whose pregnant sister was murdered in 1990 by a teenage thrill-killer from a wealthy family. Now serving three life sentences, the murderer has never explained or apologized let alone asked for forgiveness. "I'm not doing it for him; I'm doing it for me," says Jennifer. "I've heard it said, 'Hating is like drinking poison and expecting the other person to die.' It's not going to kill them; it's going to kill you." Her sister's last act, she tells me, was to write "I love you" on the floor with a finger dipped in her own blood. "I'm not going to second-guess the power and sacredness of that message," says Jennifer. "We need to be about the business of loving, of trying to solve our problems and making society a less violent place."

Jennifer has been a leader of Murder Victims Families for Human Rights, a group that has grown from a small number of victims' families bearing witness against the death penalty to an activist organization of more than five thousand members. Hector is one of them. So was Mamie Till, the mother of Emmet Till, the teenager whose lynching in 1955 in Mississippi awakened the nation to the horrors of racism. Another member is the son of James Byrd, whose gruesome 1998 death by dragging in East Texas was a reminder of hate's virulence unquenched. Members have been accused of being, as one puts it, "either not good enough or too good to be true." They've been told to their faces by support-ers of capital punishment that they are betraying their dead loved ones. (One member recalls being invited to talk to an audience of bereaved who, alerted to her viewpoint, held aloft miniature nooses all through her talk.)

But the group is part of a larger movement, a society-wide, even worldwide, search for a justice that heals. The quest to bal-ance justice and compassion is one of historic provenance: On one side stand those who counsel restoration, restitution, and absolution; on the other, those who favor some variation of the eye-for-an-eye tradition of what is known as the Talionic Code (from the same root as *retaliation*). In the Jewish *Sefirot*, the Tree of Life, the branch of justice (*din*) is balanced on the opposite side by compassion (*rahamim*). Hassidic tradition says that God himself struggles to tip the balance to overcome his trait of judgment (*midat ha'din*). Indeed, in many traditional cultures the justice system is weighted heavily toward compassion. Leading Navajo jurist Robert Yazzie points out that his people's word for justice, usually translated as "reparation," is actually a verb meaning "to enter into a respectful discussion of the hurt" or "to be made whole." Navajo law focuses less on punishment and more on healing and reintegration with the group, working to restore relationships between offender, victim, families, neighbors, and community.

Programs of reconciliation that bring together victims and offenders—usually matching those in different states not linked to the same crime—are becoming common. For some offenders it is the first time they have understood the impact of their deed on the lives of real people. "I knew I had hurt my family and friends who trusted me, yet I never considered the wider effects," writes one prisoner who took part in the program. "I was so caught up in the actual event that brought me to prison that I hadn't even thought of reconciliation. These classes opened my eyes to the world, the way we're all connected. I will never be the same. Maybe one day, I'll get to tell my victim's family, 'I'm sorry,' face-to face."

We live in a world where's there's a lot to say "I'm sorry" for. Archbishop Desmond Tutu helped found South Africa's Truth and Reconciliation Commission so that everyone could finally apologize to each other. Some have criticized the commission as an extreme application of the principle of Christian mercy, allowing wrongdoers to escape punishment through public confession, placing the reweaving of the social fabric above rightful justice. Others see it as a continuation of a radical experiment begun two thousand years ago. When Peter asks Jesus how many times he should forgive, the Rabbi answers: "I tell you, not seven times but seventy-seven times." Far from being cheap grace, seventy-seven times takes everything and more.

Once Tutu had to sit and listen to a police torturer who had killed a man and used the grisly photos to intimidate his next victims. "He said of the man's death, 'It leaves me cold.' Then he told the person's name, and I nearly fainted. This was a friend of mine. And I put my head down on the table and wept. What could have eaten at the vitals of this man's humanity?" Only one perspective had gotten him through it all, Tutu explained: "When you are dehumanized, inexorably, I am dehumanized. If I want to enhance my humanity, then whether I like it or not, I must enhance yours."

I suspect it will be written into some future history that, after eras of assuming only real saints could ever get the hang of it, it was in our time that the doctrine of forgiveness finally took hold—took hold because it had to—from individuals forgiving individuals to entire peoples reconciling with those who warred against them. (For aren't all wars waged by parents of murdered children, children of murdered parents, brothers and sisters of murdered sisters and brothers?)

I wonder if we aren't seeing prefigurations of an age when the binding of wounds takes precedence over the binding of captives, the beginning of a new covenant to heal the damage done by not caring passionately enough what happens to one another. I get the feeling history has written only the first provisional lines of that story. If we can stick around awhile, it's going to be a page-turner.

A LITTLE PEACE
OF THE HEART

He maketh wars to cease unto the end of the earth;
he breaketh the bow, and cutteth the spear in
sunder; he burneth the chariot in the fire.

—Psalm 46: 8–10

WHEN I WAS IN THE THIRD GRADE, MY YOUNGER SISTER broke my favorite toy. I yelled at her, she screamed back, and then, to my surprise, she launched herself at me in a fury, scratching me hard on the arm. My reaction was blind, unthinking; I raked my own nails down her forearm, making furrows that, to my shock, began to ooze blood. I was punished, but nothing cut so deeply as the guilt I'd felt at her pain.

I've wondered from time to time what happened in this primitive, instinctual tit for tat, a variant of any playground fight. Some kid pinches you, and you pinch them back: *There, now you know how it feels!* The word *revenge* doesn't quite cover it; in an odd way, it's more like enforced empathy, a need to make others feel, firsthand and in rough proportion, the suffering they caused us.

It's not such a leap from the dynamics of schoolyard rivalry to the logic of clan warfare: *Here's* what it felt like when you dishonored my family, terrified my child, killed my brother. Carried to its extreme, it is the twisted reasoning of warfare itself: *This* is what it is like to have your church destroyed, your crops burned, your city ruined. See how *you* like it.

On a typical day, some fifty conflicts rage on the planet, from armed clashes of massed troops to guerilla skirmishes, civil uprisings, and border incursions, most of them classified as "low intensity" (though scarcely so for the forty thousand whose lives they claim daily). The differences between sides—religious dogmas, nominal ethnicities—are often so tragically trivial they only affirm the combatants' commonality. Even the most "just" wars seem heartbreakingly preventable had the victors in a previous conflict been kinder to the defeated, who rose up to become aggressors in the next. Despite their specifics, the basic narratives of territory, ideology, and historical grievance are so standard that all that's required is to fill in the blanks with the countries' names.

If we really want to heal our world, we'd better find an antidote beyond the topical remedies of truces and treaties. If war is an infection in the human system, its cure must lie in strengthening what it most directly attacks: compassion itself. If enmity draws a bayonet-sharp distinction between self and other, only empathy can cross that line (*you in me, me in you*). If strife builds up impenetrable armor (emotional, literal), compassion calls for mutual vulnerability. If fighting is justified by some historic grudge, forgiveness destroys its rationale. If war is the repayment of blood debts, peacemaking assumes the infinite debt of love.

But how do we get there from here? We may all be in this together, but when I pick up the newspaper I want to throw in the towel. Every official road to peace has a dotted white line running down the middle of it, like a perforation that says "Just Tear Here."

*P*ALESTINIANS AND ISRAELIS ARE AMONG THE PLANET'S unhappiest cousins, keeping the small house they cohabit in such constant uproar that it threatens to drag down the neighborhood. From an aerial view, the ancient sibling rivalry between the children of Sarah and the children of Hagar—*Just get over it! No, you get over it!*—looks like a pointless dustup in a sandbox. But it's also a tinderbox that could set the world afire.

Here every square inch of soil is claimed by great narratives both congruent and contentious. Here God is said to have been last seen face-to-face—the One whose angels broke bread in desert tents, whose only Son was crucified and rose, whose last Prophet ascended heavenward on a white stallion. Underfoot are ancient bones cubits deep, every step a genuflection to the past. The living feel upon them the watchful eyes of ancestors whose begats go back to the Beginning of It All. Would that the Holy Land were not just hallowed ground but a seedbed for the peace that passeth all understanding.

That isn't the latest bulletin from Bethlehem, but there is news behind the news, and it comes down to this: three teenage girls sitting, knees nearly touching, their ancient enmity for now foresworn, trying to make a little peace of the heart. Amal, an eighteen-year-old West Bank fundamentalist with streaked blonde hair, is telling an Israeli girl that Muhammad was the last Prophet and the Koran the final Book.

"God gave us all the land. He orders us into *jihad*—not just war, but holy war."

Rachel, a fair-skinned Israeli girl in blue jeans, flushes deeply. "By Jewish law, all Israel is for the Jews. By Muslim law, it's all for the Arabs. The only way possible to fulfill these laws is by killing millions of people!"

Fatima, a dark, curly-haired Palestinian born in Israel, is caught in between. "I feel lost. I'm half-half. I can imagine the little

child who saw her daddy shot by soldiers in Jenin *and* the Israeli
kid whose mommy was blown up on a bus. My father was killed.
Everyone I know has lost their cousins. I'm sick of these mean
leaders who only want their place in history. Stop hurting each
other—that's all I can think of."

The three are part of a group of some thirty girls* flown from
an eternal war zone to a borrowed lakeside estate deep in the heart
of rural New Jersey. Under the auspices of a program called Building Bridges for Peace (part of a larger organization called Seeking
Common Ground), they will live together for two weeks, sleeping
in one big room on air mattresses, their relationships a microcosm
of internecine strife and a litmus test for any hope of resolving it.

"I feel like I live in the middle of a stupid world," Rachel tells
Amal and Fatima. "All that's important to me is you, and you. We're
destined to live together in the same place at the end of the day. If I
don't know you, it's easy to hate you. If I look in your eyes, I can't."

Amal shrugs elaborately. "When we're here, who knows,
maybe we're friends. When we return, you are my enemy again.
My heart is filled with hatred for Jews." She says it bluntly, coolly,
planting her flag. But I detect wistfulness, the barest hope that her
burden—of poisonous rancor, of history's dolorous weight—might
somehow be lifted from her shoulders.

"History," wrote James Joyce, "is a nightmare from which I am
trying to awake." This is no high school civics debate, and Rachel's
"stupid world" is no typical teenage plaint. There are Israelis here
who one day soon will be girl soldiers carrying rifles that could be
pointed at Amal—at sad Amal, whose uncle was arrested, released,
and soon after shot dead in his home by soldiers; haunted Amal,
who will never forget; vengeful Amal, who admires the *shaheed*,
the suicide bombers; hard-hearted Amal, who has come here a
hater but may secretly hope she can learn how to love.

---

*Some names have been changed.

A child of the second *intifada,* Amal has never met Jews who don't wear fatigues and combat boots. "She's one of the generation that 'did not know Joseph,'" says Melodye Feldman, the preternaturally calm American social worker who founded the programs. Melodye grew up as one of only three Jews in her Florida grade school. She remembers one of her friends groping the top of her head to feel for horns; she remembers being jumped, kicked, thrown into puddles, coming home to her parents and sobbing, "If only they knew me, they would like me."

It could be the motto of her program. She has been bringing together Israeli and Palestinian teenagers for the past ten years with no other agenda than to place them in fertile soil for compassion, give them water and sunlight, and hope they grow. Melodye, who was an Orthodox Jew and a staunch anti-Palestinian until visiting East Jerusalem in 1989, was inspired to act after seeing firsthand the mounting despair among the youth of both sides. Meeting sometimes in secret with Palestinian counterparts, she proposed a program whose only goal was to shatter the stereotypes of the enemy. "I didn't know what I was doing," she admits freely. "I just wanted to do something to give young people some hope." She designed a camp-style retreat for young women that would use every tool of empathy she could borrow or improvise. What resulted is a sort of living lab for peacemaking, its protocols honed through trial and error.

At the first Building Bridges program, some girls, in close quarters with their adversaries for the first time in their lives, were desperate to leave, but Melodye had shrewdly confiscated their tickets and passports. "You're not your nationality here," she told them. "You're not your ideology, your religion, your history. All that counts is who you are as a person." The Palestinians staged a demonstration, refusing to share tents with the Israelis. But then a freak storm blew in, full of Old Testament thunder and Koranic lightning. "They all got in tents together fast," says Melodye, "and snuggled up during the night."

The next morning one Palestinian girl confided how soldiers had come to her home, beat her family, and, upon discovering they were mistaken, left without apology or offer of medical care. Using a technique known as "compassionate listening," Melodye asked a Jewish girl to repeat the story in the first person, then describe the emotions it had made her feel—terror, anger, vengefulness, sadness. The Palestinian girl burst into tears. "My enemy heard me!" The Israeli girl wept with her, and they became fast friends.

Melodye, a cheerful, unflappable forty-five-year-old whose sharp eyes, set in a soft, open face, convey the impression little escapes her, knew she was onto something. "As the saying goes, God gave us two ears and one mouth," she says, and so she created a program devoted to listening.

There hasn't been much listening in the Middle East. Even if the two sides were so inclined, the shouted slogans, crackle of small-arms fire, explosion of bombs, and grinding of tank treads muffles the dialogue. These are children of war, Melodye says. They've known little but stress and trauma, life in a garrison state, an occupied town, a refugee camp. Many have never met anyone from the opposing side. They are dispatched to her program by their respective communities, thinking they will champion their cause to the enemy's face.

Instead they wind up literally taking their enemy's pulse: The first thing Melodye has them do is gently grasp each other's wrists. "They've never touched their 'enemy'; they have no idea what they feel like. Then suddenly it's like, 'Oh, warm! I feel blood beating!'"

A few of the kids have been to other programs—"youth diplomatic corps," one put it a little sarcastically—the kind where issues are debated and coexistence extolled. But Melodye doesn't want them to merely coexist; she wants them to care about each other. She's insistent on keeping it personal. "Keep your hate, if you must," she tells them, "but now just touch her hand, her face, look in her eyes, speak your heart." These kids have yet to pick up weapons, but their minds are locked and loaded, ready to go off half-cocked. "Here, you just give those stares that could kill," Melodye tells them. "When you get back, you could do much worse. This could be your last chance to know the other side, their hopes, their dreams, what they're really feeling."

Melodye will try anything to get them to drop their canned historical laments and encounter each other as people. They make life masks out of plaster, molding the wet goop over each other's faces, tracing the unknown contours. She gets them to form a soft machine by connecting to each other with motions and sounds, or sit in a circle singing nonsense songs, patting their own legs and those of their neighbors in a blur of rhythm. They're from a part of the world where symbols count, and the games are rich with metaphors: At their first meeting, staff members, mostly Palestinian and Israeli kids who've been through the program, loop rope "handcuffs" around the girls' wrists, entangling them in binational pairs, challenging them to get free of each other when tugging on one end only pulls the other end tighter.

I chat with a Palestinian girl wearing a T-shirt with a cartoon gun shooting a little flag that says *bang*. Kids on both sides talk of violence with stunning casualness. "I had all these boys who wanted to marry me," she tells me. "One said if I didn't, he would bomb himself." I'm shocked, but she just giggles: Threatening to strap on a suicide jacket is a common boast of lovesick West Bank suitors. Her fiancé is with the Palestinian intelligence service; his job is to ferret out the *ameel,* the collaborators—find them, report them, maybe hurt them. For her, the *intifada* is always and every-where; for the Israelis, it's wondering about the next bus bomb, worrying if, as citizen-soldiers, they'll be sent across the green line into the occupied territories.

*B*UT AT THIS CAMP THE ONLY DIVIDING LINES ARE THE ONES the girls bring with them and carry inside. I eavesdrop as they talk their teenage flotsam and jetsam of shoe styles and skin care, boys and CDs—girls who on both sides are every hue from freckled white to dark olive, who by their ancient genome are vir-tual half-sisters. I find it hard to comprehend how deeply Other they are to one another.

Psychologist Karen Horney once wrote that an enemy is an economical way to form an identity. Economical but surely not cheap, with its costs amortized in collective tragedy. The Israelis are raised hearing about the horrors of the Holocaust and their state's David-and-Goliath victories over Arab foes bent on their annihilation. "We're shown the old family photos, and it's 'Hitler got her; Hitler got him,'" Rachel tells me. "Every year on Holocaust Day, survivors lecture in the classrooms. One history final exam is mostly about the Holocaust. And then we all join the army."

The Palestinians grow up hearing about the *Nakba,* the Catas-trophe of 1948, when, according to dueling versions of history, they fled or were driven from their hereditary lands as Arab armies marched into battle against the Zionist Jews creating a nation in their midst. In the wake of utter defeat, living as refugees for gen-erations, a stateless people in their own diaspora, they have taken guerilla commandos and suicide bombers for heroic role models.

"After fifty years of occupation, chaos, and resistance," sighs one of the Palestinian staffers, "we're all fucked up. To live as a refugee, it's the same as being subhuman. We're going to need years of national therapy. The whole Middle East needs therapy!"

Therapists have taken a keen interest in the conflict as a case study in how war and hatred take root in the human psyche and how they might be extirpated. Each side in the conflict, says Israeli psychiatrist Yitzhak Mendelsohn, sees itself as a victim of history struggling to survive in a hostile world, with the other side the ultimate threat to its existence. Individual biography is woven into a collective narrative of woundedness—what he calls a "dependence on negative memory. People get hooked into a potent resentment that primes them for revenge and escalation. Hate becomes a way to create the illusion of power."

Mendelsohn, a quick, intense man with a neat black goatee, comes to his specialty in "ethnic national conflicts" from an intimate perspective: Grievously wounded in a Palestinian terrorist attack on a restaurant ("I got two bullets and needed twenty-five units of blood"), he is a self-described "victim without hatred." He is, he says quietly, "personally familiar with the psychological obstacles to peace." The task of reconciliation, he believes, is to break down the "symbolic scars that bind people to the group" and offer "some larger sense of 'we' to replace the victim identity."

Melodye has her own diagnosis. "Nations are stuck in a developmental phase approximating an adolescent identity crisis," she says, "refusing to compromise, seeing everything in black and white." It's hard to argue the point: geopolitics as teenage wasteland. An adult personality can selflessly give, but the world's nationalities are grabby, cliquish, defensive, obsessed with ego-boundaries. They announce, "It's my room and I can do what I want in it," leaving a mess for others to pick up after them. They gang up on weaker kids; they're hypersensitive; they lash out explosively. There is a line in the *Chatu-Shataha Shastra:* "Buddhas see delusion as the enemy / And not the childish who possess it." How many posturing politicians and gung-ho generals have the

courage of these coltish girls who struggle to see through delusion
to reality's shades of gray—and beyond, to life's true colors?

These kids who could soon be gazing down gun barrels at
each other are just teenage girls with half-articulated thoughts and
inchoate longings, still safety-pinning their identities to fit: One
minute they're mouthing the slogans of the *intifada* or proclaiming
the tenets of Zionism; the next they're tooling around on the pink
Schwinn they found in the garage or teaching each other American country-swing steps.

"First they need to define the box they've placed themselves in,"
Melodye says, "then they can step outside it." In an early session,
they're asked to list, in order, their most defining characteristics. A
Jewish girl says, "Family, friends, music, Jewish religion"; another
says, "Being from the city, being a high school student, clothes,
travel." Other Jewish kids put "human being" first, or the environment, or love of animals. But for most of the Palestinians, the
list is more circumscribed: *Arab, Palestinian, Muslim, colonized,
refugee.* It is the template of oppression, of a people defying erasure by carving a collective face in granite. If each side is living in
an identity-jail, the Israelis' is medium security, the Palestinians'
more like twenty-three-hour lockdown.

"Self-esteem is in large measure a function of the esteem
accorded to groups of which one is a member," writes one social
psychologist. As a result, he notes, "The sources of ethnic conflict
reside, above all, in the struggle for relative group worth." It reminds
me of a T-shirt I saw on a marcher in one of New York's ethnic
parades: "It ain't where you at, it's where you from." (*No,* I wanted
to say. *It* is *where you at. And here is a recipe for peace: [1] Cut pride
into bite-sized pieces. [2] Chew. [3] Swallow.*)

This is not to argue against ethnicity, which is in any case a
fact on the ground. In a homogenizing global society, with the

unique wisdom of entire cultures being lost as surely as languages themselves are going extinct almost weekly, we need a counter-weight against punch-card citizenship in a corporate McWorld. But without the translucent overlay of a common human identity, real peace is a mirage on the horizon.

"We're all of us brainwashed," Fatima, the Israeli-Palestinian, says to the circle. "We accuse each other with these phrases, but don't know what they mean. We want freedom? What is it? Words someone told you to say, not really coming from your heart. Seri-ously, where did you get all that stuff?"

"What do you think causes war?" Melodye asks them.

"History," says one.

"Injustice," says an Arab girl in a headscarf.

"Religion...leaders...misunderstanding," offer others.

"We do," says Fatima. There's a silence as it sinks in. "All of us. Without people buying into it, it wouldn't happen."

As the days go on, identities become more fluid. One minute they are pouring salt into each other's wounds, the next probing them as tenderly as private-duty nurses. They talk it through, feel it through, first in anguish, then in relief: "I don't want to kill *you.*" "Well, *I* don't want to kill you, either!" I hear ululation drifting in from the sunporch used by the Palestinian delegation, the yearn-ing, keening vocals of Arab pop music mingling with sinuous Israeli rock from the dining room.

They're having a great time, but this isn't just Camp Kumbaya, telling stories by the campfire, singing and eating s'mores. Their ability to resolve their blood feud is a field test for peace on Earth. If these girls can't find a way to love one another, what then? I find myself walking around with a lump in my throat, thinking how it has fallen to them to do what their foolish leaders will not.

O NE DAY, PAPER BAGS LABELED WITH THE TOUGHEST HOT-button issues are put in the center of the room, and each girl is asked to write down a phrase that best expresses her feelings about it. The responses are scrawled in magic marker on big white pieces of paper and posted on the walls.

Under "Zionism," an Israeli has written, "idealists who fought to come back to their country," and a Palestinian, "an evil organization that wants to kill all the Arabs in the world."

Under "Palestine," a Palestinian has written, "a dream that will come true, my homeland forever, my soul," and an Israeli has scrawled, "hostile territory, a danger for my existence."

Under "suicide bomber," the Israelis write "a killer" and "a dead murderer"; and the Palestinians write, "a blessed person," "a winner in the next world," and, chillingly, "what I hope to be."

The kids shuffle from poster to poster, subdued, disbelieving. Now it's all been shoved out into the open, every threat and calumny; their faces are ashen at this secret ballot of fear. I can hear everyone's heart thud in the silence; it's suddenly a roomful of hunted rabbits.

"I see these words and I feel scared and angry and want to leave," says one Israeli girl.

Tears tremble on eyelashes, overspilling rims of reddening eyes as they attempt to smile through the pain, as if to spare others, or cling to their sinking hopes. A passed tissue box quickly empties.

"It hurts so much that each of us has deep hatred for the other. It's like you've been sleeping in the same room with a person who wants to get rid of you." My notes don't say whether this was spoken by a Palestinian or an Israeli; it's irrelevant.

The dire mood is fleetingly broken by the town's Funny Bunny Ice Cream truck careening around the corner outside, blaring its tinny recording of the Disney anthem, "It's a Small World After All." A few kids who recognize it laugh at the irony.

As the tears dry, the girls are more curt, defensive; they put on their game faces. "I feel proud to be Arab, proud to write these words about *jihad* and *shaheed*," says Amal defiantly. They trot out their litanies of grievance, their sullen prejudices. But they also seem to recognize that something momentous is occurring. For once in their young lives, the truth has been laid bare, a force to be reckoned with—unpredictable, frightening, liberating.

"These words on paper are our biggest fears," says Fatima. "They're what we're hiding behind our laughing faces, being dishonest one to the other. I want to learn about them from you."

Later they are asked to build a bridge out of craft supplies. As they sort through Popsicle sticks and pipe cleaners, Rachel and Fatima tell Amal, "We're here to listen to anything you want to say." But Amal shakes her head. She doesn't want to talk. "I just want to draw a bridge," she says tersely. "A bridge that's been broken."

It sometimes seems the bridge has been broken since time began. What are the root causes of war, of millennia of hatred and strife? Those who study conflict look at everything from politics and economics, to history and religion, to child-rearing methods and marriage customs. But some point to a key human (and, for that matter, primate) emotion that, in individuals and nations alike, seems to drive the cycles of violence: humiliation. "People would often rather die than live with such a sense of shame," writes one psychologist. "Even considerations of self-interest become irrelevant."

The need for recognition, to be heard and seen, is universal. The Nazis cunningly appealed to restoring German pride after the crushing settlement imposed by the victors of World War I. In 2001 a nameless man—was it in the streets of Cairo, Karachi, Jakarta, Damascus?—cried out from among a crowd that cheered

9/11: "You Americans think we are nobody, like you are the only human beings," he said. "Now you have heard us. Now you know we too are men!"

Shame is a wound to the very sense of self. Palestinians speak of the daily humiliations of border crossings ("We're herded into a chute like cattle," one girl tells me bitterly), of grinding poverty and strutting Occupation soldiers. One girl tells me how her father died in an ambulance held up for four hours at an Israeli checkpoint outside Jenin even as his heart gave out. He was forty-seven. "I had thoughts about becoming a bomber," she says. "But I realized when I came to this camp last year that there was nothing worse than to lose my life to make others die. The responsibility for this suffering, it's not Jew or Arab; it's this circle of history, of violence with no beginning or end."

Humiliation is surely not just the province of the Arabs. "For Jews in general and Israelis in particular," says a writer in the Jewish magazine *Tikkun*, "there is a lasting form of shame associated with having been vulnerable and victimized during the Holocaust...a determination 'never again' to be subject to such humiliation as to be helpless prey to a ruthless predator."

*T*HE HOLOCAUST MUSEUM IS A MARBLE BUILDING LIKE OTHERS in the nation's capital, a massive stone cube devoid of postmodernist histrionics, built to last for as long as history shall endure. As I walk through the entrance, passing a sculpture of a deconstructed black swastika, its arms twisting to the sky, I see a quote by President Jimmy Carter carved into the wall: "We must harness the outrage of our memories to stamp out oppression..." In the company of the Palestinian and Israeli girls, bussed down for an all-day fieldtrip, it strikes me as a very Middle Eastern sentiment: Isn't this what the Palestinian *shaheeds* think they are doing? And the far-right-wing Israeli settlers? All over the world, there is no problem harnessing outrage; the problem is jerking back the reins.

A museum guide highlights the exhibits she feels are "pretty neat—check them out"; the atrium, she suggests, is "a fabulous place to take pictures." But the museum is not designed as a tourist attraction. It is a funnel into moral blackness. To walk its corridors is to follow the saga of a civilization's premeditated murder of compassion itself. First were the Nazi book-burnings, harbingers that failed to kindle the world's alarm. Then the artificial creation of stark ethnic divisions: here the lurid charts of racial mugshots; there a poster promulgating laws against "racial defilement" and a glass case full of "scientific" meters of curious design—calipers to measure skulls, and eye- and hair-selection guides in hand-held compacts for white-gowned nurses to classify children for extinction.

The visitor's claustrophobia grows as exhibits show all cultural institutions—art, music, theater, medicine—suborned in service of the deranged hygiene of ethnocentrism. In his 1906 book *Folkways*, William G. Sumner catalogued the ubiquity of the self-versus-other distinctions made by tribal cultures the world over. "Each group nourishes its own pride and vanity, boasts itself superior, exalts its own divinities, and looks with contempt on outsiders."* There are only a few insidious steps to regarding the

---

*In a poll taken in Kosovo in 1997, two years before the genocidal "ethnic cleansing," Serbs and Albanians living in that province were asked to choose which words they thought most accurately described themselves and each other as a group. When it came to themselves, the Albanians selected adjectives like "hospitable, peaceful, courageous, clean, honest, intelligent, united, and hard-working." The Serbs characterized themselves nearly identically. But Serbs described Albanians as "united, those who hate other nations, treacherous, backward, rough, hard-working, exclusive of other nations, and selfish." And, predictably, the Albanians chose virtually the same words to describe the Serbs. With ghastly consequences, both groups lay claim to laudable traits for their own identities, while threatening traits are projected outward.

other as subhuman; it's astonishing, unthinkable, but, to anthropologists, sickeningly familiar. Sumner notes in a later work that nearly all the tribes he had studied called themselves by names that meant simply "'men,' 'the only men,' or 'men of men'; that is, 'We are men, the rest are something else'..."

Modern anthropologists point to the Amazonian Yanomamo, whose fierceness seems to derive in part "from their belief that they were the first, finest and most refined form of man to inhabit the Earth, and that all other peoples are a degeneration from their pure stock." Among the headhunting Amazonian Mundurucu, rival tribes were linguistically lumped with game animals, providing a conceptual frame to overcome the natural aversion humans have, along with all other creatures, to methodically killing their own kind.

The Holocaust Museum corridors narrow as Hitler's power grows and the tapes of crowds *Sieg Heil*'ing themselves hoarse grow louder, engulfing the visitor in a gathering dark. The museum's architects have designed passages that dead-end in cul-de-sacs, emplaced red-and-white-striped barricades. You don't know where you're going until you get there, and even then you're not sure you haven't been treading a no-exit circle. One exhibit tells the saga of the Lodz ghetto, sealed in April 1940, trapping 164,000 Jews behind bricks and barbed wire, forcing them to live with overcrowding, starvation, disease, and the stench of raw sewage, the first of four hundred ghettos created to wall off the millions.

From there you traverse a wood catwalk and embark on a journey into Hades: a railcar with a thin shaft of light falling onto a blood-red wood floor; pathetic piles of abandoned luggage, hand mirrors, hairbrushes, and toothbrushes. The malignant efficiencies of industrialized murder: canisters of Zyklon-B; a narrow bunk from one of the Auschwitz barracks where skeletal prisoners lay awaiting the fire. Relics of Dr. Joseph Mengele's infamous Block

10, where the most gruesome medical experiments were performed; photos of sterilized children, of bodies disassembled like department-store manikins. A line from Elie Wiesel: "Never shall I forget the little faces of the children whose bodies I saw turned into wreaths of smoke beneath a silent blue sky..."

I see one girl who'd proclaimed herself a would-be *jihadi* in tears. An Israeli, overcome, sags against the shoulder of a Palestinian friend, who clasps her tightly. I see others walking slowly, arms around each other's waists.

When the dark corridors open out at last into the muted, sifting sunlight of the white marble Hall of Remembrance, I finally break down and weep. When I emerge, I see Amal and two of the more militant Palestinian girls in checkered *hijab* photographing each other as they sign the visitors' book in Arabic. I feel touched.

Yet there is something odd as they mug for the camera, flashing their V-signs. A whisper goes through the bus on the ride home, building to an agitated buzz. An Israeli who reads Arabic says the girls wrote something terrible, something unthinkable. What they had inscribed, in large, curlicuing letters, was: "Death to All Jews."

By the time they get back to camp, all the girls are in an uproar. They gather in knots to scream and to cry, beside themselves.

"It's none of your business what I write!" shouts Amal. She claims it's freedom of speech. "The guard told me to write what I felt, and this is what I feel. If Jews went through all this suffering, why do they make us suffer, too? *I've* suffered. I get to say it."

"So now it's public!" a Jewish girl yells back. "It proves you want to hurt us, to exterminate us! I can't believe I spend a week with you, and now I know you want me dead."

"Don't you feel sad at the piles of bodies, the millions who died?" another Israeli demands, in tears. "For a few hours, you couldn't just leave off your suffering and feel ours?"

But this is just the point. A quiet, lissome Palestinian who has barely spoken all week shouts: "We've seen bodies, too! What do you expect? We go through hell because of you. A ninety-year-old Holocaust survivor at least has had some happiness now, for himself, for his children. I don't know how much longer I can go on. One day when I'm sick and tired of all this, I might blow myself up!"

A shocked gasp goes through the room. It takes me by surprise, too, though it shouldn't have: Many Palestinians saw in the museum not the sorrowful history of the Jews but a mirror of their own plight. They did not, *could* not empathize; the pain of the other only reminded them of their own.

"Ghettos, checkpoints, identity cards—this is my reality back home," one told me. "A camp with barbed wire, surrounded by soldiers, the streets filled with sewage. My dad grew up in a refugee camp, and then me. I saw *me* in that museum—me every day, not fifty years ago. I can't compare it to medical experiments and extermination. But I felt defensive: This is happening to us too."

Amal will bend only this far: "I should have written death to all Israelis, not death to all Jews."

One of the Israelis spits out, "You expect to be treated as a human being, but you don't act like one. You don't *deserve* human rights!"

Amal's eyes go hard and glossy, her face immobile as a basilisk. The lowest blow, for them, for anyone, has been struck. "It's the Israeli soldiers," she says, her voice finally breaking a little, "who shout at you, 'You don't deserve to be treated as human.'"

SHOAH. NAKBA. MY PEOPLE'S HISTORICAL DISASTER IS MORE horrible than yours; its wounds fresher, its losses more enduring, its anguish more palpable, its injustice a sharper blade. But is there no end to it, each tragedy planting the seeds of the next? The Serbs who oppressed the Muslims in the ethnic cleansing of the late 1990s felt *they* had been oppressed by the Muslim Ottoman Turks, the injury of their defeat still throbbing after six hundred years. The unhealed wound is the psychoanalytic nubbin of the problem; everything else, the fighting and the oppression, can seem like mostly acting out. The whole planet is wired with big red sticks of dynamite like an old Warner Brothers cartoon, the close-packed explosive of unassuaged anguish, a fuse waiting for the right matchstick of a hatred only kindness can snuff out.

"If we could read the secret history of our enemies," wrote Henry Wadsworth Longfellow, "we should see sorrow and suffering enough to disarm all hostility." But in many places around the world, this equation is forbidden to have an equals sign. "The Jewish community would be up in arms," says Melodye, if someone dared to compare one people's ultimate tragedy of genocide with another's of exile and oppression. "They would be called a self-hating Jew, anti-Israel."

In May 2004 Israel's justice minister, himself a Hungarian-born Holocaust survivor, criticized a plan to demolish Palestinian homes in Gaza. As quoted in a *New York Times* story headlined "Offering Empathy," he told Israeli radio: "I did think, when I saw a picture on the TV of an old woman on all fours in the ruins of her home looking under some floor tiles for her medicines—I did think, 'What would I say if it were my grandmother?'" His remarks created a wave of national outrage. Scolded a fellow cabinet minister: "Any analogy, even hinted at...has no place in any form."

Primo Levi writes with grim eloquence in *The Drowned and the Saved* of the pain seared into collective memory: "The injury cannot be healed; it extends through time, and the Furies, in whose existence we are forced to believe...deny peace to the tormented." But it must be healed, lest the injury be transmitted down through generations, forever blighting new lives. There is hardly time to wait for national policies and official proclamations.

What's needed are private edicts of empathy, little peaces of the heart. The work couldn't be harder or more humbling: the hearing and the telling of the world's most painful stories; the emotional truths that are too hot to handle alone.

I watch as Rachel and Amal attempt to mirror each other's feelings in front of the group, trying to neutralize even a scintilla of the elemental toxin. Their body language says it all. Arms folded, legs crossed, heads turned to the side, barely glancing at each other, they are stoic, removed, their looks searing. They repeat each other's words with smirks and rolling eyes. They interject their own opinions, Rachel taking a moral position, citing history and ethics; Amal an emotional one, claiming the Jews are blind to the suffering under their noses.

It seems as if there can be no meeting ground, for nobody's pain is dispensable, not even for a second. The conversation advances a few notches—"We need to point to the tragedy for humanity," a Palestinian suggests—but I notice something happening that is beyond words. Even in the midst of their outrage, the kids, Israeli and Palestinian alike, are treating Amal not with ostracism but with an outpouring of affection. She had done her worst, walked up and detonated her nail-bomb of hate-speech in a supreme shrine to memory, and yet they refuse to not love her. She pretends not to notice at first, or to care, but when Rachel, leading a game, asks Amal to come play, I see a quick flash of relief. She hesitates only a moment before joining in.

The next day has been scheduled on the calendar as a day of silence. Before it officially begins, Rachel approaches Amal, who today wears a black T-shirt spelling *Mustard* in jagged yellow letters. "Look, I know I will never fully understand your pain," she says awkwardly, her tone struggling against formality, "but I'm sorry for what happened to you in your life. I might seem only angry at you, but I was hurt too. I know you wrote those words because you thought no one knew your suffering." Amal, gazing into the middle distance, finally nods with the faintest of smiles. Rachel tells me later: "All that day we communicated with looks and hands. And when I could turn to her with words, we were talking again about this and that."

Rachel later wrote a short story that is, for an Israeli, a traitor-ous heresy, comparing the Hebrew concept of *milhemet hakodes,* the holy struggle to preserve one's humanity against all that seeks to erase it, with the "holy war" of *jihad.* Could these vile acts, she wondered, stem from the same desperate drive of a people to assert a sense of self-worth?

"People call me a moral relativist for seeing both sides," says Melodye. "They pat me on the head and say I'm naive for thinking I can make peace this way. But I know that even the smallest steps are good. I tell them it's messy work here on the ground, but one by one people really do change; and those who do, change others. It may take generations, but real peace will come."

In small ways it already has. One of the Palestinian staff, Muna, confides to me, "I used to completely deny the Jews' suffer-ing. Then I became close to an Israeli and realized, all this horror happened just fifty years ago. Their parents are orphans. They're all in recovery." Her sense of empathy had come to her unexpectedly. Muna's brother is still, after years, in Israeli administrative deten-tion. A former athlete, he has nerve damage in his wrists, which she claims came from a prison beating and from "being stretched" in interrogation.

"Years ago, when I came here, I was ready to blame," she says. "I was prepared to respond to being attacked, but when you see they're actually listening, saying, 'I'm really sorry you go through this,' it shocks you. It was my first contact with Israelis other than the guards at the checkpoints, the soldiers who hurt my family. It left a stamp on me, inside of me." She became friendly with one

Israeli girl. "I realized we were both sixteen-year-olds who can't live without fear, both of us. Why can't I invite her to my home—*why?*

"My hopes and dreams for a country haven't changed," she adds. "We need a homeland. I won't forget my suffering, but I'm willing to forgive the minute that suffering is recognized. We're looking toward the fruit; not us, but later, thirty years ahead, for our children."

More than four hundred girls have crossed Melodye's bridges for peace. All have been changed in some way, some more visibly than others. There have been Israeli girls who resolved to endure the social stigma of not serving in the army. Some have become peace activists. One Palestinian is now a leading environmentalist, enlisting people on both sides to save the fragile desert ecosystem they all share; another, to the ire of the fundamentalists in her community, has become a feminist.

R'wan, a Palestinian staff member with blue hair, a pierced tongue, and a tattoo of a Chinese ideogram she says means "Love, Woman, Friendship," first came as a stone-thrower in the Bethlehem *intifada*—a "hardcore militant," she says. But she was touched when, months later, an Israeli who had been her arch nemesis at camp was the first to call her when her school was bombed, even before any of her Palestinian friends.

"I have to take it from my society for this," R'wan says, "for saying that I love Israelis." She would cry when an Israeli bus was bombed, while her cousins cheered. "I had to worry if I went back with new ideas I'd never be accepted in our society, even in my own family. Peacemakers are so rejected in our community." She's studying to be a schoolteacher, hoping to reconcile the alternate-reality curricula, the warring maps imposed on the same geography. In some Middle Eastern schools, the scurrilous forgery of the *Protocols of the Elders of Zion* is still read as nonfiction. Palestinians are taught that Jews secretly run the world. Jews believe the Palestinians aim to complete Hitler's unfinished project. Each people defines itself as a victim of hatred and oppression, a refugee and an outcast.

After their day of silence, the schedule calls for a "spa night." Their only instructions are to pamper one another, make each other feel special. Once again there's laughter as they massage each other's hands and feet. I flash back to my time with the bonobos: social grooming behavior, female alliance. They are subverting war and hatred and death with red toenail polish. Tentatively, but with growing courage, these children are doing what their childish leaders are afraid to do: open their unguarded hearts.

TIME IS GROWING SHORT. SOON THEY WILL BE GOING HOME. Now it's in earnest, their heads bent toward each other, the talk urgent, intimate. Suddenly they're on fire to say everything and anything.

"We haven't finished the job we started," Amal tells me. I detect an unexpectedly wistful note in her voice. The signs still leer menacingly from the wall: Settler: "someone in my family I love"; "someone who deserves to be killed." Israel: "place I love"; "place I hate." But the enmity has flickered on and off like a worn-out light-bulb filament. Curtains have parted, letting in shafts of natural light.

What they say they want in their circle today is so ingenuous: "I hope to have a best friend here, to visit each other when we get back, to meet each other's family." When a Palestinian says, "I only hate soldiers who kill my neighbors," one militant Israeli, a middle-class kid in a horse-camp T-shirt, allows, "If someone was doing this to me, I might hate them, too." One girl, the nationality doesn't matter, tells me incredulously, "I wanted them to know I have pain, too, but that's exactly what they're telling me!" Can the chain of violence be weakened, link by human link, until it finally snaps?

The final night is a gala feast, a kosher shindig thrown by a local Jewish organization: homemade *gefülte* fish and matzoh ball soup, pot roast and roast chicken, potato kugel and carrot *tsimmes* with little marshmallows. An elderly man in a toupee, one of the organization's board members, approaches a cluster of Israeli and Palestinian girls that includes Amal. He introduces himself as a Holocaust survivor and, pointing to the Palestinian girls, counts jocularly: "One, two, three, four—after this week, I'll bet we have four less suicide bombers."

Amal's face drains of blood. The room grows still. "You think we're all *terrorists*?" She looks as though she will faint. Then her eyes flash back to life, and something shocking occurs. Amal the warrior, Amal the stoic, Amal who has carried her hard ball of pain like some priceless heirloom—Amal cries. The invisible chalice of tears she has balanced without spilling a drop falls, breaks into a thousand shards, splashes out all its contents. Amal cries, and she can't seem to stop.

And the girls gather around Amal, their own angry one who had secretly gotten used to being treated like just herself, who had opened just a little in the sun of their affection, who had begun to sense what it might feel like to be sprung from identity-jail. All of them, Jews and Muslims and Christians, Israelis and Palestinians and Americans, surround her, telling her: You are *not* a terrorist; you are *not* the enemy; we *know* you—you are *Amal*. The man, too, stricken, apologizes for having missed what was essential but invisible to the eye. And Amal's smile, that fugitive always running, always hiding, darts back in for a moment.

"Soon she's returning to the *intifada*," says Melodye. "They all are." But one of the militant Palestinian kids, the one who had talked about blowing herself up, has approached her quietly, surreptitiously, about training as staff. "She's recognized that what she's been taught in books, what the media has portrayed, what both sides want them to believe about the other—it's all false. She told me, 'You can't make borders to keep people's hearts from meeting.' She says she wants to be a force for change."

They all will be, in their own way. These children belong to families, and families to clans, and clans to villages, and villages to nations. Have these two weeks implanted an antivirus of compassion that will spread slowly through their own societies? There's no telling how far the tentative words of peace they have spoken to each other here will reverberate. In the desert air, voices carry.

*J*OSEPH SEBARENZI KNOWS WHAT IT IS LIKE TO STRUGGLE TO affirm his humanity. Or so I'd been told. A friend had suggested I look him up if I was ever in Washington, D.C., saying only that he was a Rwandan refugee with some stories to tell. But when I call to confirm our two o'clock meeting, Joseph tells me in a soft voice he's had a few friends over that afternoon and they're running late. Might I come by closer to suppertime?

I have only a few hours before my train, I tell him, insistent. I really need him to fit me in. True, I'd scheduled our meeting on short notice—as an afterthought, really—but I'm hard-pressed to understand how he would prefer hanging out with his buddies to a chance to speak on the record.

When I ring the buzzer in the lobby, he doesn't buzz back but comes down to greet me. Impossibly tall and gracile in the Tutsi way, he refuses my hand and with a broad smile bends from his lofty height to give me a hug. When we enter his apartment, he introduces me as "my friend" and gestures to an imposing man with gold teeth and a dull yellow sport jacket. "Please meet His Majesty." I think he's joshing until the big man offers his card, embossed with a simple "His Majesty King Kigeli V of Rwanda."

Another man in the pink clerical shirt of an Anglican priest gets up from the couch to shake my hand. He turns out to be Rwanda's archbishop. I'm mortified to realize that Joseph has interrupted a long-planned, high-level meeting to see me, too polite to refuse.

Joseph's face has a sweetness to it that belies his bitter life story. He was born in the 1960s during the first civil war and remembers having to flee into the bush with his parents. In 1990 the nightmare began all over again. The dominant Hutu tribe had acceded to power and set out to destroy their hereditary enemies, the Tutsi, once and for all.

The Hutu leaders took a page from the bloodstained playbook of Hitler and Stalin, Pol Pot and Milosevic. First came the society-wide propaganda campaign through the radio, newspapers, and leaflets. "They would make ugly proverbs about us," Joseph recalls. "Like, 'If you invite a Tutsi to be a guest in your home and give him the living room to sleep in, by morning he'll be in your bed.'" The Tutsi were soon forced to carry Identicards. "A card with 'Tutsi' stamped on it meant 'enemy.' You'd interview for a job, all the requirements were met, but there was a policy of quotas. I had a sociology degree, but I couldn't be hired." (Social theorists call this process "badging": An in-group finds ways to distinguish itself from an out-group, whether through genetic traits like skin pigment, stature, hair texture, and facial features, or through artificial signifiers of clothing, adornment, headgear, and tattoos, or through manners, rituals, etiquette, and speech patterns. "Irrational beliefs serve the purpose far better than rational ones," one anthropologist has noted. "They are easier to produce.")

Soon enough, cards and quotas were supplemented by an official campaign of bizarre racial slurs. "They called us *inyenzi*. It means 'cockroach.' You see," Joseph says with a sad smile, "a cockroach is an insect found everywhere; you try to kill them and kill them, but you're never finished." The word grated ceaselessly from every radio in the country: *Inyenzi, inyenzi,* or sometimes just "snake," free-associating the Tutsis' tall, thin stature with a symbol of evil.

It amazed him, Joseph recalls, how the incessant barrage of racial propaganda wormed its way into his own brain, making him ashamed of how he looked, of the way he walked, the Tutsi's long, graceful stride. "It can shape your mind until you no longer admire even the beauty of the woman you want to marry," he tells me, shaking his head.

Seeing the writing on the wall, he sent his wife and infant son away and, after he was jailed and then released, fled the country. A month later the genocide began. The virus spread fast, replicating its malignant memes through the pamphlets and the broadcasts that inflamed the Hutu populace to turn upon Tutsi neighbors who had once been their friends, even murdering their own Tutsi wives and half-Tutsi children. (The radio exhortations so fanned the deadly grassfires that a pop singer whose malicious melodies had dominated the airwaves would be among the first war criminals brought to trial in Rwanda.)

Between April and July 1994, as many as a million people were massacred, most hacked to death with machetes. Joseph's father and mother, who had insisted they could weather the new crisis until suddenly the roadblocks and killers were everywhere, perished along with his seven sisters and brothers and many of his nephews, nieces, and cousins. "It is a pain that is difficult to describe," Joseph says, his eyes welling up. After a long minute of silence, he says almost apologetically, "I cannot find a word to express that."

In the aftermath of the war, Joseph returned to help in reconstruction, creating an assistance association for the survivors. He was eventually elected to parliament. Many Tutsi, he says, wanted him to avenge their abuse from his new position of power: "Friends would tell me, this guy or that guy should be arrested. Sometimes I would refuse; other times I would say, 'Yes, I'll arrest them,' and then do nothing. I had friendships with Hutus, but I had to keep this secret or I would be seen as a traitor.

"From talking to them, I knew that the Hutus who'd participated felt guilty. They had killed and killed, they told me, out of fear the Tutsi would come back and kill *them*. I didn't want revenge. I knew their sense of guilt could make them more dangerous in the future.

"Besides, I had no courage to arrest the Hutu people in my village."

I'm puzzled—Joseph certainly seems like a brave man. Then I realize he's using the word in the French sense: He didn't have the *coeur*, the heart for it.

"Yes," he agrees, "I had no feeling, no power inside me, to hurt these people back."

Helping translate between imprisoned Hutus and their Tutsi captors, he could see they were in "the same situation of dehumanization as we Tutsi had been. And one day," he says with some amazement, "I ran across the man who had been the mayor of my village, who had been very active in the genocide. He was probably the one who oversaw the killing of my family! I remembered how I used to see him in the village, official, powerful, beautifully dressed. Now I saw him in a prison camp, suffering, in rags, reduced to nothing. And I instantly felt sorry. I had some money in my pocket and I gave it to him."

An ambiguous smile plays around Joseph's lips. "I really don't know why I did that."

In 1997, to everyone's surprise, Joseph was elected as a compromise candidate for Speaker of the Parliament, the country's third most powerful post. He argued staunchly for a policy of reconciliation. "I made a speech that said if there was revenge, the virus would never stop. We are all already victims. I can't bring back my family. I didn't want it to be that the one who's powerful today overcomes the weak one, because then tomorrow it will be reversed all over again. Our children and grandchildren would be killed. So I do this for my grandchildren. I told the Hutus that I hadn't come to hurt them, that they shouldn't cry; but they all cried anyway, even though it's considered bad for a man to do so!

"I live for the idea to not pay back evil. When I returned to my home village, I hugged the people who I knew had helped to kill my family."

I must look a little dumbfounded. "You see, after the genocide," he explains, "it was a time of anger. I was thinking all the time, *How do I care for my life but also take care of others who are suffering?* I saw that both were the same thing. The anger and resentment I felt toward those others was killing *my* body. *I* could have a heart attack and die."

More than that, it had dawned on him that the survivors had a great and difficult duty. "I realized reconciliation maybe doesn't come first from the perpetrators but [from] the victims," he says thoughtfully. "Maybe victims must take the first step. They should help the oppressors to move from guilt to apology to reconciliation." He seems surprised when I mention that this was one of Martin Luther King Jr.'s great doctrines: the paradoxical power of the oppressed to restore the oppressor's blighted humanity. "This is good," he says with his big smile. "I like this. I am glad I am not alone in my crazy ideas."

Joseph and Melodye and a smattering of Middle Eastern teenagers do not a mass movement make. They are ordinary people who decided to take the ideals of the great social prophets and apply them right here, right now. They are trying to grasp hold of a peace beyond religion, ethnicity, and politics, one that can be manually fashioned with their own hands.

"I don't want my opinion attached to some stupid political leader or to any country," seventeen-year-old Fatima told me at the peace camp. "I'm an Arab, yes, but I feel like I'm a world citizen. I've seen people change if I just listen to them, even when what they're saying are the hardest things to hear. Everyone around me says I should get real," she says, rolling her eyes, "that I haven't seen the way this world is. But I'm going to keep my water clear of anything that could poison it. I think that innocence is realism too."

Once King Solomon dreamed that God appeared to him and offered to grant his fondest wish. Solomon asked only, "Give, then, Your servant a listening heart." Can something as simple as listening and being heard liberate the world? Would it be too much to agree, once and for all, that the heart is the country to which we all belong and love the only state to which we owe our allegiance?

Rachel, Fatima, and Amal finally did finish their bridge, a span of green Popsicle sticks over which walk three resolute, fluorescent pipe-cleaner figures. Amal had pressed her blue paint–saturated hand onto the construction paper, joining their palm prints of pink and purple. Like the hands outlined in ochre on the cave walls of Lascaux, bearing witness to people thirty-five thousand years distant, theirs was a primeval act of self-declaration: *My blood is your blood. I too am human.*

THE BELOVED COMMUNITY

Grandfather
Look at our brokenness.
We know that we are the ones
Who are the divided
And we are the ones
Who must come back together.

—Ojibway prayer

The end is the creation of the Beloved Community...
It is this love that will bring about miracles in the hearts of men.

—Martin Luther King Jr.

I CAME TO NEW YORK A FEW DAYS AFTER 9/11, INTO A STRICKEN city of the walking wounded. A charnel breeze, burnt and bitter, blew through the ghost town of Tribeca, making the lungs and the heart ache. Like everyone, I couldn't sleep; I'd snap on CNN at three in the morning, nod off with it still murmuring. Below my window, ad hoc choirs of passersby serenaded firemen at the stationhouse next door, its bricks festooned with Missing posters, homemade floral wreaths, and kids' crayon drawings of skyscrapers blooming with flame and cherry ladder trucks zooming to the rescue. I watched friends straggle back toward faith or lose it.

U2's bittersweet ode to love, loss, and bravery, "Beautiful Day," was on the airwaves. Beneath tragedy's skin, there were invisible sinews of tenderness. Even my most tough-minded friends seemed surprised at how catastrophe had catalyzed a sense of mutual belonging, had reawakened—on the street, in offices, cabs, and elevators—some instinct to be better, to love more. Despite the news testifying to an ineradicable streak of human brutishness, you could feel what anthropologist Stephen Gould called "the victorious weight of innumerable little kindnesses." It became impossible to relegate compassion to mere sentiment, to a poignant lump in the throat or a one-off act of charity. It was as basic as air.

But things gradually drifted, in fits and starts, back to normal. "Everyone was wide open," observed a friend, "but then they crusted over again." As the months passed, there were fewer uncalled-for hugs, tears, and smiles. Down went the "Our Grief Is Not a Cry for War" placards on Union Square; up went the velvet ropes that let some in and kept most out. Subway riders no longer wedged their bodies into a closing door so stragglers wouldn't be left behind. New York's patented *get-outta-my-way-I'm-going-places* street pushiness made a comeback. "People loved that tender we're-in-this-together feeling, however awful the cause," said my friend, a lifelong Manhattanite. "But they couldn't quite hang onto it."

How to understand this mysterious force at once fundamental and fugitive, emerging in crisis as our natural endowment, only to be crowded out by our pressing little agendas? To say nothing of our national ones: the notion of building a more compassionate world quickly took a backseat to the dictates of security. The then secretary of defense sardonically quoted Al Capone: "You will get more with a kind word and a gun than with a kind word alone." The peacemakers were banished to the kids' table with the rest of the utopians. It's said we've crossed a historic threshold, from an interregnum of innocence to a new age of terror.

I don't believe it. Yes, there is awful public tragedy, wrenching private sorrow, the dire clangor of arms. Plague-dogs of rage and cynicism roam the planet's nameless back alleys (and some name-brand front offices too). And we are *not* safe. I read it in the *Times;* I can read it in Thucydides. It is a long battle, this struggle between love and hate. But if love is ever to triumph, it's not enough for us to just knock the haters off their thrones. We need a regime change of the heart.

That somber week in September, the barricade-keepers by the "pile"—terse Irish cops and narrow-eyed young soldiers with M-1 carbines—looked shell-shocked. Behind them grim truths were being excavated by the hour. The sky above was a mottled bruise from the lingering miasma of vaporized glass and steel and bone; fused elements new to Earth sifted down from the plume over Ground Zero. There seemed to be nothing to do but mourn and leave the cleanup to the uniformed municipal employees who now straddled the truncated skyline. I felt useless, but I couldn't imagine what I could do—what help I could be to the guys scooping up the horrific wreckage with cranes and dump trucks. I was unaware that behind the barricades something—something heartening, even wondrous—had escaped the jaws of darkness entirely.

Its epicenter was Saint Paul's Chapel of Trinity Church, an eighteenth-century architectural gem at the foot of the towers, that had survived miraculously unscathed ("standing defiant," in the mayor's phrase). A team of young parishioners and clergy had immediately reopened the chapel, and the entire world had flooded in. The site had attracted givers from every compass point (disaster experts call this the "convergence phenomenon"), some with official sanction, others fast-talking their way through police lines, all intent on supporting the rescue workers. Those city crews faced a disheartening task, searching around-the-clock for survivors in what was turning out to be a mass grave. But out of the cauldron of despair arose something beyond the ubiquity of death: a community based on, in the words of one volunteer, "trying to outdo one another in the showing of love."

Theologian Courtney Cowart, then forty, was in a church office a few blocks from the towers when the planes hit. She'd heard the percussive roar of a hundred floors pancaking, endured a sudden dark night as her building's ventilation system sucked in the black soot. She had made her way out through the chaos, managing to shepherd some visiting monks and clergy to safety before the second tower fell and she had to run for her life. "I was one of those gray ghosts coming up Fifth Avenue covered in ash," she tells me over breakfast in a Greek greasy spoon. It had been a near-death experience, she says, one that had kindled an overwhelming desire "to walk back into the enormity of the void" and somehow be of help.

The church's corporate types seemed bureaucratically paralyzed and virtually incommunicado. Instead, a makeshift community of helpers sprang up of its own accord, like proverbial grass blades poking through pavement, and the ensuing stories are legend: giant vats of Cajun food cooked up by a crew that materialized from New Orleans, truckloads of brand-new boots donated to workers whose own had virtually melted off in the smoldering pit. Under the auspices of the chapel's Reverend Lyndon Harris, and with Courtney as newly minted chief of staff, what had begun as a ragtag collection of food and aid stands planted amid knee-deep debris became a twenty-four-hour, all-volunteer support operation for the men and the women digging through the rubble.

But there was a story behind the story, she says—a mystery, a revelation of something so marvelous that many who witnessed it are still grappling with its impact. Ten thousand volunteers of every political stripe, income level, race, and sexual persuasion, of every religion and no religion, had transubstantiated tragedy into an ad hoc affirmation of humanity's indestructible goodness of heart.

It was a defining event for those who experienced it, a harrowing of their old ground of belief and the planting of new, still-unknown seeds. Joseph Bradley, a hardhat crane operator who had helped build the World Trade Center when he was twenty-two, had volunteered to help pull up the wreckage. Like so many workers at the site, he was overwhelmed by the carnage at the pile, sinking to the curb after his first night under the savagely bright arc lamps, his head cradled in his hands. "That's when the Salvation Army kids appeared," he remembers, "in their sneakers with their pink hair and their belly buttons showing and bandannas tied around their faces. They came with water and cold towels and took my boots off and put dry socks on my feet.

"And then, when I got to Houston Street, a bunch more of these kids, all pierced and tattooed with multicolored hair, had made a little makeshift stage. They started to cheer as we came out, and that was it for me. I never identified with those people before, but I started crying, and I cried for four blocks. I can't tell you—I was taken so off guard.

"I got home and saw my wife, who asked, 'Joe, are you okay?'

"'Sure!' I said. You know, the bravado came back.

"But she said, 'Are you sure? Go look in the mirror.'

"There I was with my filthy dirty face and just two clean lines down from my eyes."

A community of love was the last thing anyone had expected to find in the mouth of Hell. Douglas Brown, a monastic prior, had stood upon the still-smoking pile and imagined he was standing on a new Golgotha. The awesome devastation, he said, was "like a place of crucifixion." To him fell the soul-crushing task of blessing human remains as the heat of the wreckage coursed up through his shoes and the naked, crazily canted gothic arches from the tower's first floor seemed to mock all sacraments.

One day he saw a small, aged fireman digging through a slope of debris, searching with his comrades for his missing son, who had last been seen trying to rescue people in the collapsing South Tower. A week later Brown saw a news photo of the same fireman tenderly carrying a body from the pile. He prayed that the man had found what he had been seeking.

"It struck me then, on the spot, that what I was seeing, acted out in front of me, was all that Jesus said about the shepherd who leaves the ninety-nine of his flock and goes looking for the one who is lost—this obsessive commitment not to leave anybody behind, even though it was clear no one would ever be found alive, that they still needed to be found, they needed to be cherished and honored."

S AINT PAUL'S, WITH ITS GOLD-ENCRUSTED ALTAR AND SPAR-kling chandeliers, was the church of the eminent and the powerful. George Washington had once bowed his head in his own reserved pew. The altarpiece—Mount Sinai wreathed in clouds and lightning—was the work of Pierre L'Enfant, designer of the nation's capital. It was Wall Street's chapel, where titans of American finance had searched their souls, seeking benediction (and maybe absolution) for the keenness of their enterprise. Now it became a church dedicated only to the fruits of compassion.

In place of Stations of the Cross, the enactment of Christ's tortured journey, there were instead what one called "stations of compassion" that grew to include gourmet meals and clothing, massage therapists and grief counselors. Everything was donated in a spirit the people who were there still remark upon. "Everybody who walked in that door experienced the same amount of love," recalls one volunteer. "It didn't matter who they were. It was so unconditional and so overpowering. And when you were there, you knew that every creature in that room was loved as much as you were—and you were loved more than anybody. I mean, there was no quantity to it."

Few of us, it seems, feel deserving of uncontingent goodness, yet here it was in flagrant abundance. Maybe it was embarrassing to know, really know, that it had been there all along, free for the taking and the giving. Martin Cowart, a fifty-three-year-old Tribeca restaurateur, was recruited by his cousin Courtney to run the food service. He's no sentimentalist. Only blocks away was the charred hulk of the bank where he'd once worked as a numbers-juggling financial wizard. He'd traded his pinstripes for downtown hipster black in his second career in the viciously competitive New York food trade. His last venture, a shabby-chic neighborhood coffeehouse, had just lost its lease before the planes tore into the towers. He remembers his awe at the small miracle that became known by the shorthand "Nine-Twelve" by those who were part of it. "People helped each other because there was nothing else *to* do," he says. "The emotional need was so great that it was almost like madness, a human madness of giving and receiving to each other no matter what that was. It was such a strong current, you could not resist it."

Many who were there commented how shared suffering had engendered a sense of wholeness, even joy, a profound paradox one summed up cryptically as, "Most pain, best time."

"For me, it was hearing the story of a person who lost a loved one, every single day," says Martin Cowart. "I felt this deep, deep sense of human pain that I don't remember I had ever felt. I think the common denominator is the breakdown of your ego to a place of vulnerability. We are brought up to think we all want to be happy and comfortable and *up*—and that's what we're programmed to go for. And I don't think anybody in their right mind would want to go for the other. But when you have been put there, you become aware that you can relate to others who have been there as well— hearing firemen talking about finding bodies the night before and feeling the pain they were going through. And it wasn't morbid. It was just...connected."

With that connection, all barriers seemed to tumble. Jews from a nearby synagogue helped celebrate the Eucharist. A clergyman laughs at the memory: "'You did the *what*?' I asked them. 'Yep,' they said. 'We did. This is our church, too.' It was a full-service chapel for everybody. Even the atheists were happy."

Another parishioner remembers being deeply affected as a rabbi stood at the pulpit to deliver a memorial sermon. "He said, 'The crucifix is one of the most beautiful symbols of mankind because it points straight to heaven and across to each other. Now is the time to strengthen that "across."'" In the Church of Nine-Twelve, "across" became the only hierarchy. New York's notorious codes of class and signifiers of status disintegrated.

"When somebody asks, 'What do you do?' and I say, 'sanitation worker,'" says Tony Palimeri, "I always have in the back of my mind that they might be saying, 'But you're a *garbage man*.' But everybody was so great. They didn't care what I did. They didn't care I was heavy. What they cared about was me as a person. Nobody had any agenda. No one was trying to outshine anyone. Just people coming together saying, 'You help me. I'll help you. We'll help each other.' And I started to learn a little bit about people—that we all need each other."

Mary Morris, assistant to the dean of the seminary and wife of an Episcopal priest, recalls her astonishment as the staid institution's pecking order turned upside down: "I saw a bishop cleaning toilets at Saint Paul's while a sanitation worker was preaching!

Every time I went down there, and I encountered somebody I would never ever have spoken to in my real life, it's like my soul went up in love. Our facades were stripped. It was like it pushed Mary Morris, egocentric human being, aside. What Nine-Twelve taught me, absolutely concretely, is we're all in it together and we're all the same. And when you are equal, there are endless possibilities of communion and community."

Each person in his own way felt he was bearing witness to something unprecedented, some proof positive that a less troubled world was possible, one where simple compassion made the carnage splayed at their feet seem a vestige of some bygone dark age. Was the experience at Saint Paul's a freak exception in troubled times, a temporary resurrection of what theologians call "the primitive church"—or a homing beacon of the future?

"Up until that point, universal love was theoretical for me," says Courtney Cowart. "I'd only read about the idea, and then it appeared in our midst, this microcosm of the Kingdom on Earth made visible. Then it was gone, vanished, with only the people who were there knowing how real it was—and still is." To her the story of the little church that stood was not a symbol of defiance or evidence of the indomitability of a faithful nation. It was a harbinger, a living prophecy of the caring society to come.

It was what Martin Luther King Jr. had glimpsed one day in the spring of 1966, after the March to Montgomery, as he gazed out over several thousand homeward-bound marchers who had been delayed at the airport. Amazed and touched as he looked out over the crowd, King wrote in *Where Do We Go from Here:* "As I stood with them and saw white and Negro, nuns and priests, ministers and rabbis, labor organizers, lawyers, doctors, housemaids and shop workers brimming with vitality and enjoying a rare comradeship, I knew I was seeing a microcosm of the mankind of the future."

For Courtney Cowart, Nine-Twelve changed everything. Whatever she'd thought was important, her rising career as a theologian, was reshaped in the crucible. What she had seen was more than what the Church could be. She had seen what the world could be. "I realized I would not be able to go back to arguing over altar linens," she says wryly.

That September she had been thrilled to have lunchtime colloquies with the archbishop of Canterbury. Now, she spends two hours each day feeding lunch to Mr. Pierre, the paralyzed, speechless father of a Trinidadian friend. "I didn't know where the treasure was," she says. "In God's economy you put the other first. That's what makes us thrive and feel most joyous." Wasn't this, after all, the original impetus behind every church and synagogue and mosque and temple: an affirmation that compassion *is* a contagion, its flame leaping heart to heart, blazing without being consumed, like the miraculous desert bush?

I've heard other anecdotes of this mysterious conflagration that fires souls, melding them together. My friend Svetlana grew up in the old Soviet Union, where joining the Young Pioneers was obligatory and college students were expected to volunteer to serve the state. One summer she and a few other young women were put in charge of a rustic retreat for forty hard-luck kids, mostly preteen victims of child abuse.

"We were scared at first," Svetlana remembers. "We'd been dumped at this place in the woods with all these screwed-up kids, no training, no teaching materials, no structure: good old Communism! What did we know?" Then, unexpectedly, something shifted. "The strangest thing," she says. "We fell in love with them, the most helpless kind of love. These kids were such a mess, so needy, that it just drew it out of us. Maybe it was our maternal instincts waking up with a bang, but we were *drunk* on unconditional love, and they felt it; they began to change, too, under the influence of this power."

Svetlana's not one for feel-good kitsch—she has, if anything, a certain Russian dolor—but she fills for a moment with a kind of wonder, smiling at the memory: "We found out we could easily teach them all their school subjects, all the ones they'd been miserably failing at, and they just soaked it up like sponges. I'm convinced we could have given them advanced calculus, and they would have learned it from us, under the force of this love. Honestly, it's something I've never felt before or since. As the summer ended, I found myself wishing I could adopt them all. It was devastating to leave this community we'd all made."

*M*ANY SCIENTISTS REMAIN SKEPTICAL THAT THERE COULD be such a thing as a truly caring community. Some seem almost gleeful in wiping the moue of self-satisfied virtue from the do-gooder's face, in stifling the trill of the pie-eyed optimist. "No hint of genuine charity ameliorates our vision of society once sentimentalism has been laid aside," wrote biologist Michael Ghiselin in a famously acerbic passage. "The economy of nature is competitive from beginning to end...What passes for cooperation turns out to be a mixture of opportunism and exploitation..."

Science is a tough job, and someone's got to do it, but—those sharp little teeth, rending at our most cherished beliefs. It's a view that doesn't conduce to sunlit idealism, but maybe that's the point. There have been enough utopian pipe dreams about what society *could* be, based on dangerous wishful thinking about human nature ("scientific socialism," anyone?).

But we sense that the picture Ghiselin and his ilk are showing us is only the torn-off corner of a much larger one. While those who sourly assess our possibilities have looked in one direction, some scientists are starting to look in another. A recent Emory

University study showed that when players of a game called Prisoner's Dilemma decided to trust each other and cooperate rather than betray each other for gain (as the game allows and even encourages), a part of the brain associated with feelings of joy lit up. Forget "Greed is good": Social cooperation has its own neurological reward-circuit, portioning out the endogenous dollops of pleasure that are evolution's good housekeeping seal of approval.

The study of such "prosocial" (as opposed to antisocial) feelings is so new that it's still possible for scientists to put emotions on the map that hitherto hadn't been named. Jon Haidt, a professor of cognitive psychology at the University of Virginia, wasn't setting out to be the heart's Magellan; it's just that he'd gotten his own broken, and it hurt like hell. Miserable, Haidt had a sudden insight: "Hey, there's an actual pain here; an aching heart isn't just a metaphor." His dashed romance temporarily eclipsed by scientific curiosity, he began asking colleagues in the Biology Department how they would explain his feeling. The general consensus was the vagus nerve that ferries signals back and forth between heart and brain.

It made Haidt wonder about another heart sensation that had always intrigued him: that warmth in the chest (often accompanied by a "choked-up" feeling) that we sometimes get when we witness a good deed. Haidt found that this response, which he dubbed "elevation," usually occurred when witnessing someone helping the downtrodden, the sick, or the weak. He quotes an interview with a woman who was driving home with three friends after a morning of volunteer work for the Salvation Army. It had been snowing hard, the flakes piled up in a thick blanket, when they'd passed an old woman trying to shovel her driveway. One of the men in the group asked to be let off. "I didn't think much of it," the woman said. "I had assumed that this guy just wanted to save the driver some effort and walk the short distance home. But when I saw him jump out of the backseat and approach the lady...I realized that he was offering to shovel her walk for her.

"I felt like jumping out of the car and hugging this guy," the woman reported, still surprised at her strong reaction. "I felt like singing and running, or skipping and laughing...I felt like saying nice things about people, playing in the snow like a child, telling everybody about his deed."

That this small act of kindness had a specific and disproportionate effect tipped Haidt off that a built-in biological response might be at work. The woman had experienced such a profound lifting of her spirits that she gushed about it to her roommates, who in turn clutched their hearts and smiled. Why *are* we so moved by good deeds? he wondered. A neo-Darwinian to the core, Haidt was sure that evolution must have had something in mind to install such an automatic response. Elevation also seems to be unusually contagious, often accompanied by what he academically labels "changes in the thought-action repertoire." When he asked his respondents if the feeling had made them want to do something, they described an almost overwhelming desire to "be with, love, and help other people."

Feelings of elevation also seem to foster admiration and a desire for closer affiliation with the good deed–doer. Said the woman in the snow-shoveling incident, "Although I have never seen this guy as more than just a friend, I felt a hint of romantic feeling for him at this moment." (I wonder if this attraction isn't a sign that evolution is tickled by the prospect of a few more altruistic genes in the pool.)

Film directors, noted critic Roger Ebert, have learned they can reliably tear-jerk any audience anywhere by having the hero perform an act of noble self-sacrifice. Haidt has collected enough descriptions across cultures and through history to conclude that elevation is a universal human trait. A forty-six-year-old Japanese housewife described how she felt when she saw people volunteer to help after a natural disaster: "The heart brightens up [*akarui*] and I feel glad [*yokatta*], relieved [*anshin*], admiration [*sugoi*], and respect [*sonkei*]." A primary school principal in a small village in Orissa, India, reported a feeling of joy (*ananda*) and a tingling sensation in his body when he saw people in his school step forward to defend a teacher wrongly accused of having stolen some books. Thomas Jefferson wrote to a friend about his "elevated sentiments" upon seeing "an act of charity or gratitude," describing the feeling in his chest as "dilation." (Think of the expression "My heart swelled.")

A Unitarian parishioner told Haidt of his "tears of celebration" when his church voted unanimously to become a Welcoming Congregation (a church that officially invites homosexuals) after a gay member stood up and publicly came out for the first time. The man described it as "a tear of receptiveness to what is good in the world, a tear that says, 'It's okay, relax, let down your guard, there are good people in the world, there is good in people, love is real, it's in our nature.'" It reminded me of a comment made by one of the Nine-Twelve communicants: "I discovered the emotional magnificence of life. The joy of being human. Living that love for real. The beauty of it. The glory of it. The confirmation of it. The glee of it."

Elevation opens a picture window onto the expanse of our nature. It implies that we are drawn to each other's goodness, hardwired to exult over it. The elation seems to stem, as much as anything, from sensing oneself part of some common stream of virtue—an apotheosis of *you in me, me in you;* a sort of *we in us.*

Haidt uses a secret weapon in his lab studies: an *Oprah* episode that he claims is a surefire tearjerker the flintiest heart cannot resist. "Bring it on," I told him. I popped his "induction sequence" into my DVD as soon as it arrived, settling back to watch with a certain can't-make-me-cry stoicism. It was the story of a ghetto kid whose life had been turned around by a kindly public-school music teacher. The young candidate for the thug life had instead gone on to fame as a jazz trumpeter, but he had never forgotten his crucial father figure. Years later it influenced his unexpected decision, at the pinnacle of his career, to become a public-school teacher. As he told his story, the camera panned to his old mentor planted in the audience, head bowed, overcome with emotion.

Then Oprah surprised the young man by showing a video of *his* students thanking him for changing their lives, and, well...the teardrop-shaped stain on this page is not the manufacturer's watermark. Afterward I trundled over to the HeartMath equipment still set up in a corner of my living room and confirmed, as Haidt's own studies have shown, that his devilishly sappy video increases heart-rate variability. My balloon was floating in the stratosphere: I was certifiably *elevated*.

"The effect is real, all right," Haidt tells me. "One of my pet peeves is this notion that you can explain away virtue as just secret selfishness. Scientists haven't looked at it in the right spirit. We really *do* have some beautiful things in our nature."

He is particularly intrigued by elevation's "power to spread. A witness to good deeds," he writes, may "soon become a doer of good deeds... If frequent bad deeds trigger social disgust, cynicism, and hostility toward one's peers, then frequent good deeds may raise the level of compassion, love, and harmony in an entire society." I might once have taken this for a Chamber of Commerce brochure from the Wonderful Land of Oz. Now I'm not so sure.

S TILL, LET'S FACE IT: FREQUENT GOOD DEEDS ASIDE, THE WORLD of frequent bad deeds is still very much with us. Hatred too is a contagion—and sometimes a pandemic. I found myself in the

Balkans a few years back, not long after Serbia's ethnic-cleansing campaign had been halted by NATO's bombardment. The war was over, but war and peace are more than the victories and the defeats of armies. Even in Dubrovnik's fanciest hotel, the grim-faced maître d' seemed a vestige of the old police state, still uncertain whether to greet the guests, guard the buffet table, or round up the diners for questioning.

I was in Croatia for a conference of peace activists. That week the country had advanced to the World Cup soccer quarterfinals, and bedlam ruled. Young men ran through the cobbled streets of the Old City waving flags and pounding the roofs of passing cars. A thoughtful Serbian student protest leader remarked that it had been like this when the malignant nationalism had taken hold in Belgrade. In every bar, he said, you could hear the hoarse bellowing of fight songs, see drunks tumbling into the street in hard knots, accosting passersby. There was a woozy, tingling excitement in the air. "You were expected to join in this euphoria, in everyone losing themselves in the group mind, or you were looked on with suspicion."

I've never been in a war. The idea of a whole society deciding to hoist a warm gun instead of a cold beer and turn it on their neighbors is mystifying. Supposedly, there was still sporadic shooting a few hours away in Mostar, even years after the conflict's end. I convinced a young Croat named Igor who knew the town to drive me there. We pulled into a charming city center dominated by the snaggle-toothed stone walls of old Roman ruins—or so I thought, until Igor informed me they were bombed-out buildings, this one an office complex, that one a department store, here a mosque, there a church, now gutted and tumbledown. At one point, he said, opposing forces had arrayed themselves on opposite sides of the main street and simply blasted away at each other.

The bridges of Mostar over the meandering River Neretva, once famed for their beauty, had become infamous symbols of the gulf between the Muslim and Croat quarters of a newly divided city. At the height of the conflict, if you were a Muslim attempting to cross into a Croat area or vice versa, you stood a good chance of having your forehead drilled with a small, neat hole by a waiting sniper.

"How could they tell who was who?" I asked. Muslims here are mostly light skinned and often blue eyed; everyone looks alike. Well, Igor said, sometimes it was the ethnic giveaways: a scarf on a woman, the size and the composition of family groups. But mostly, since it was a small town, people knew each other on sight. The idea confounded me: If you recognized a former neighbor who was now your newly designated enemy, said Igor, "Maybe you just plugged him, *pam!*"

I was reminded of how, a few years ago, authorities in my town had taken a sixth-grader into custody, confiscating a select list of classmates on which he'd penciled the word *Kill* next to each name. (I live in the Columbine shooting state; there's no such thing here as a schoolboy prank.) The student told police he'd created his roster based on which kids "looked weird" to him: a boy with freckles, a girl who was too skinny. The Balkan madness seemed just as arbitrary: the sociopathy of small differences; the mind's gearbox seized up in low, stuck in some primitive sortition of good and bad, friend and enemy; its talent for abstract distinction turned, during a time of derangement, into a murder motive.

We wandered into the Muslim part of town, finding ourselves beneath a seven-story mosque, its minaret crowned with a curlicue of metal flame, the speaker system blaring a recorded *muezzin's* call to one o'clock prayer. But the people themselves were taciturn. The streets were reservoirs of silence, brimming with terrible secrets.

We finally stumbled by accident across a little office with a sign that read "Human Rights." A stocky, dark-skinned man in his late forties excused himself from a meeting of Muslim and Croat young people—reconcilers in whom all hope for the future resides—and came over to talk. He wanted to explain what had happened here. Igor translated as he began his story where everyone did, with recitals of territories seized and retaken over centuries, capped by the rise of the crazy men, Franjo Tudjman and Slobodan Milosevic ("an idiot lost in space and time"), who used boundaries and ethnicities to fuel their megalomaniacal ambitions.

But what had really *happened*? I asked. In this city every third marriage was a mixed one, with residents living side by side in an ethnic patchwork locals compared to stripes on a tiger skin. He shrugged: Mostar had been a symbol of harmony, a rendez-vous of East and West, and so, of course, it had to be destroyed. The propaganda machine had cranked into overdrive. "Who you prayed to, where your family was originally from, suddenly became all-important—to get people to hate each other. People are not poultry," he sighed, "but they behaved that way."

He described the night they'd come for him. "They burst into my apartment in their black ski masks, and I thought I was dead for sure. But then I suddenly recognized the one holding the AK-47—he was the son of a neighbor! I recognized him from his voice, his eyes. 'I know you,' I said. 'I know your father. I knew you as a child.'" At first the man tried to disguise his voice by lowering it to an ominous growl, but then he hesitated, softened for a moment, and spared his neighbor's life.

I kept pushing for more of an answer, though I was beginning to realize there wasn't one. We'd lapsed into French by this time, his fluent, mine such as I could retrieve from the undergraduate mists.

"*C'était les têtes vides,*" he finally sputtered. "The empty-heads! Without a brain! People in town, one after another, people you knew, people you'd *always* known, all were *tout-à-fait* empty-heads!" For

some years, it seems, the Empty Heads had been the region's dominant political party.

Or perhaps it was not so much a case of empty-headedness as
heads stuffed with loony ideas, minds hijacked by roving gangs of
delusions, brains infected with some mutant cultural spirochete
against which they had all too little resistance. "Men will die like
flies for theories and exterminate each other with every instrument of destruction—for abstractions," notes an all-too-prescient
1938 paper on aggression and war. What was it Gandhi said about
your thoughts becoming your destiny? Here was a textbook example of the power of mental fixation to paint reality in any color—in
this case, dead black.

The mass mind-meld was, per usual, incalculably amplified by
media, fueling the descent into society-wide paranoia. Says Milos
Vasic, editor of *Vreme,* the only independent magazine in Belgrade
during the war: "All it took was a few years of reckless, intolerant,
warmongering propaganda to create enough hate to start the fighting." To understand what happened, Vasic says, "Imagine a United
States with every little TV station everywhere broadcasting Klans-
man David Duke. You too would have war in five years."

I remember a conversation with a student leader, half-Bosnian,
half-Serbian, who belonged to an interethnic youth organization that called itself the Post-Pessimists. She told me how, at the
height of the war, she had been horror-struck to see Serbian television news footage of an atrocity committed by Bosnian troops.
A few weeks later, sneaking across the border to visit her Bosnian
relatives, she had seen the same footage again, only now it was
attributed to *Serbian* troops. "For all I know," she said, "it was some
old footage from World War II!" She looked at me and said, half
in plea, half in declaration: "So, do we just keep our parents from
killing each other, or do we change the whole human equation?"

*T*HAT'S EASY: CHANGE THE EQUATION. BUT IS THERE ANY
inoculation that *could* prevent the next outbreak of this dread
social pestilence, this anti-elevation that turns friends to enemies
and town squares to ancient ruins? Violence is not just the doing
of crazy men, who'd remain street-corner ranters if no one saluted.
Real peace seems to depend on a culture's baseline immuno-
competence, some self-healing system that kills hate germs dead
on contact.

Colombian priest Leonel Narváez so believes in social healing
that he is leading a government-sponsored, historically unprecedented experiment in mass psychotherapy. With the goal of helping
tens of thousands of ex-combatants from his country's brutal civil
war reintegrate as civilians, he has organized cadres of therapists to
address combat traumas that, left untreated, would inevitably trigger renewed conflict. Leonel had spent long years working in what
he calls "The Kingdom of the FARC," the rural villages controlled
by the insurgent Fuerzas Armadas Revolucionarias de Colombia,
mediating between the guerillas and the government.

Leonel grew up in the same small town as the former FARC
leader, nicknamed Tirofijo, or "Sure Shot," after his flair for killing
enemies with a single bullet. They even shared the same birthday,
although they couldn't have been more different. The town's old
people said of Tirofijo, "The desire for vengeance ate him up."
Leonel, now in his late forties, has long been consumed with the
desire to make the only permanent peace—the peace of the heart.
"I was once trying to explain to Tirofijo that hatred and anger
mostly hurt the person who experiences those feelings. Tirofijo
just snapped, 'Get down from the clouds, priest!'"

Leonel, head in the clouds, maybe, but feet planted on terra
firma, has moved ahead with a series of bold social initiatives,
founding Schools of Forgiveness and Reconciliation known by the

acronym ESPERE (Spanish for "hope"), which are slowly spreading throughout the country. He doesn't plan to quit until he's turned his whole war-accursed nation into a beloved community. Though he is a strong believer in justice and human rights, he is convinced that what he simply calls "tenderness" is the ultimate antidote. "The heart is where violence is born," he says, "and so it is there where peace is reborn."

Leonel knows that the world has had its fill of grand social engineers, the ones with the Big Ideas who pretty well screwed up the twentieth century for everyone else. He just wants to ensure that brotherly love and forgiveness aren't "a monopoly held by churches and priests but indispensable elements of everyday life." His ideas may look simple in the extreme, but that simplicity is deceptive. "Against the irrationality of violence, it is necessary to propose the irrationality of forgiveness," he says slyly.

For him it's not just about the FARC or the government or the right-wing paramilitaries. It's about the sodden meanness of the streets, the domestic violence against women and children, the police who "model aggression to the citizens," even the human rights workers who, he says, "have so much anger and hate they're also in the trap." His "reconciliation schools" represent a crucial step from peace treaties to peaceful entreaties, from truce enforcement to truth-force. He recites his classrooms' core curriculum: "I decide to move from darkness to light; I choose to forgive; I see with new eyes; I share the pain; I accept the other within me." It's a new pledge of human allegiance.

"We need new ideas of conciliation," says Leonel. "Not just techniques because they don't get to the root." This is more than just a wistful lament from a new-age Catholic priest who wishes everyone would just be really, really nice to each other. The mayor of Bogotá has asked Leonel to help him transform the city of 8 million into a new urban paradigm based on mutual understanding.

"We're going to try to transplant it into civics," says Leonel. "We're proposing a citywide network of reconciliation. We're going to try to reverse the historical and cultural attitudes that say you react to violence with more violence, that you should punish a crime with a crime. It's hard even for me to believe, but now there's a bill in the Congress for a new law based on restorative justice. We're training the police not to speak the way their gun speaks, but to speak with their hearts. We need a whole *culture* of reconciliation, where even people who get aggressive behind the wheel learn to drive with compassion."

Tirofijo died before Leonel could realize a fond wish: "To be the one to say to *him,* with great respect: 'Get down from the clouds, Don Manuel. Without forgiveness and reconciliation there is no future. Not for you and not for anyone!'" Leonel's goal, he says, is to help build a new city from the inside out.

I CAN'T ALWAYS SEE IT, THIS GLIMMERING HOPE BECOMING A reality. Nor hear it, for that matter, what with Alpha Chimp Björn rolling his orange war drum down too many of the world's Main Streets, slam-banging for all he's worth. But I like to think he already senses he's a creature of the past, making a big noise while he still can. With the day fast approaching that a handful of angry, calculating people can blow up not just a restaurant but the city that lists it in the Yellow Pages, the good of each is tied to the good of all. What happens in our own hearts is suddenly as big as the whole world. It's true our human task is made harder by the institutionalization of hurt and harm, by an accumulated investment in the ruin of our own prospects. But we are, collectively, wiser than our leaders, kinder than our institutions, and more open-hearted than our dogmas.

On my better days, I feel I'm witnessing, across the planet, the subversive innervation of some neural net of kindness whose filaments are so fine as to be invisible (but like threads from a spider's spinnerets, more tensile than steel). It no longer seems far-fetched to imagine a kind of compassion insurgency—a revolt against all the wasteful diversions of our creativity; a Good Society Movement, if you will; a self-emergent, adaptive cultural mutation. Could the sum of all the little changes be a popular uprising of the heart that will burst forth, as did the soft revolutions of ironclad Eastern Europe, seemingly out of nowhere? Is our global organism developing prosocial antibodies against the plague that has too long infected the body politic?

I know citizen-negotiators who have reconciled Azerbaijanis and Armenians—nationalities with centuries of murderous grudgery—using just skills of compassionate listening and bearing witness to each other's hurt. I know a freelance mediator who believes that parties in conflict want nothing more from each other than empathy. Marshall Rosenberg has brought the technique he calls Nonviolent Communication to nearly sixty countries, from Afghanistan to Turkey. He travels around the world with a guitar case and a suitcase full of silly props—a jackal puppet (to symbolize paranoid, judgmental thought and speech) and giraffe ears (to signify an ability to listen openly—giraffes having the animal kingdom's largest heart-to-body ratio). He's seen how kindness spreads person to person, he says. He's seen the techniques he calls Nonviolent Communication taught in a hundred schools from Ashkelon in Israel to the Navajo nation. He's an utter eccentric, plainspoken and deliberate, with a mournful look that disguises the sly, slow-dawning sense of humor that has helped to reconcile Tutsis and Hutus, rival street gangs, and battling spouses.

"I feel like there are two different worlds," he tells me. "There's the world I'm living in, where every day I meet people who are doing all these wonderful things. And then there's the world of these folks," he says, gesturing to the complimentary copy of USA

Today lying on the bedspread in his hotel room. He shakes his head. "They don't seem to connect at all."

It does seem that we suffer from a collective cognitive dissonance. We know the children are starving; the ice caps really *are* melting. We know our designer sweats are connected to designer sweatshops, our automobiles to the turbid atmosphere, the food on our table to the dwindling water table and the chemicalized soil. We sense that life in the developed world has become a desire machine cranked up to maximum RPM, spinning out a dizzying succession of induced wants for which satisfaction is supplied, scratches for itches, at fair market price—no matter the cost. We also know there's already enough to feed, clothe, house, heal, and educate everyone, without exception. It's less a shortage of resources than a shortchanging of imagination: compassion being an ability to imagine—to *see*—the connection between everyone and everything, everywhere.

From that standpoint, isn't that connection love itself? Isn't it love itself that underlies all wanting? Don't we only consume the Earth in our hunger for a love already abundant in our own hearts— and waiting in each other's? And if, enriched by that love, we took less and gave more, would we not see the Midas world we've built recede, and the outlines of the Beloved Community emerge?

*T*HAT COMMUNITY'S FOUNDING MEMBERS ARE THE ONES WHO root for the other team, the people Martin Luther King Jr. prophesied we would become when "our loyalties...transcend our race, our tribe, our class, and our nation." I know a young Bosnian woman named Nadja, who was terribly wounded by Serbian shrapnel during the siege of Sarajevo. After the war, watching one of the Serbian soldiers who had rained death on the city weep during his televised trial, she wept, too. When her brother angrily scolded her, telling her this could have been the very man who'd lobbed the mortar round at her, she said: "I can't keep a separate heart, one for my friends and one for my enemies." Nadja's no pushover: She has gone on to become an effective global campaigner against child slavery and the abuse of women.

She echoed a Burmese activist named Ka Hsaw Wa, who told me he learned to feel empathy—what is called in his language *ko gin ser* ("my heart is trying to be your heart")—for the government soldiers who have attacked and tortured him and his people, even as he opposes their brutality with the nonviolent weapon of international law. He is an effective activist—his group won a case against a California oil giant complicit in brutalizing villagers to build a pipeline—yet he confides he prayed for the corporate exec who lost his job after their victory.

He and growing numbers of others are the loyal subjects of the Country of You in Me, the Empire of Everybody. Behind the daily headlines that give little hint of it, I can't help but see the obvious: a world yet poised on the brink of self-discovery, awakening to the fact that if we are to go anywhere, we must all go there together.

ALL MY RELATIONS

We are caught in an inescapable network of mutuality.

—Martin Luther King Jr.

Truly, universally, relations stop nowhere.

—Henry James

I RECENTLY SAW A LOCAL NEWS STORY ABOUT A BOY WHO became lost in the Colorado woods in the dead of winter. As hypothermia set in, he saw emerging ghostlike out of the swirling snow two large elk. Feebly, he threw stones at them, shouting until his voice gave way, then lost consciousness. Early the next morning, he awoke to find himself sandwiched between the two great beasts, which had laid their warm bodies next to his through what would have been a fatal, freezing night.

Or so he told the search team when he staggered into a clearing and was rescued. They were skeptical—hallucinations are a side effect of extreme duress—until he led them back to his sleeping spot. There, in the snow, they saw the concavities made by two enormous animals, the imprint of a small boy in between.

Why would the animals bother? Why not just curl up with each other for some languorous elk-frolic through the wintry night? (Three's a crowd, and besides, in these parts people *shoot* them.) There are a million stories of our fellow creatures being kind to us for no good reason—from dogs who, with no rescue training and at risk to their own lives, rush into the flames of burning buildings to drag strangers to safety; or dolphins who nose drowning swimmers to the surface, wait for human help to arrive, then take off with an errant tip of a flipper. There are inexplicable ways compassion radiates through the world, some spirit of sympathy drawn toward any distress like white cells to a pathogen. When William Wordsworth spoke of "a motion and a spirit that...rolls through all things," he was talking about the systole and diastole of some universal heartbeat.

Mitakuye oyasin, say the Lakota: "All beings are my relatives." We are just starting to get the implications. Recently, the Tumbling Creek cavesnail, a creature so tiny it's invisible to the untrained eye, was put on the federal list of endangered species. Scientists had noticed the snails dying off in large numbers. They finally realized that not only was the Missouri cave stream where they lived polluted but also the aquifer that supplied the stream on which animals *and* people depended. All of nature is now the canary in the coalmine.

But is it enough to calculate the cost/benefit analysis of "preserving the environment"? Given our shaky collective plight, knowing nature's "value" may not be enough; we may need to *love* it (that, or start looking for an evolutionary niche).

Julia Butterfly Hill, notorious for the two sentinel years she spent camping atop the redwood tree she named Luna, is intimate with nature. When she lectures—pacing the stage barefoot, weeping, laughing, doing uncanny imitations of a chainsaw's splutter and the crashing of great trees onto the forest floor—she appeals for not just the preservation of the wild but a blind passion for it. Her over-the-top antics get on some people's nerves. Environmental activists are one thing; actual nature lovers are quite another. We don't entirely trust them: Like all lovers, they seem prone to exaggerate.

Besides, love is for people, not for plants. We know the stories of people who can open their hearts to their prize rosebushes and lavish their love on dogs and cats but have a heart hewn of granite toward the people next door. But why for one second should love of nature and humanity be mutually exclusive? Sociologist Kristen Renwick Monroe observed that many of those who rescued Jews from the Nazis seemed to have altruistic feelings that extended "beyond the world of human beings to include all living things. Margot talked about the humanity of dogs. Lucille spoke of not harming any living thing, even spiders. Others spoke of 'the good earth' itself (Knud) or the animal and vegetable kingdoms (Tony). Life itself was something to be valued for these altruists."

Perhaps our ultimate human assignment is to extend our sense of kinship beyond family and clan and strangers to *all* creatures. (We turn out to share a surprising percentage of our genome with everything from trees to fleas to manatees.) I believe Julia Butterfly Hill when she says, "I'd come to value Luna as myself, my own body. When she was cut, I felt that a loved one had been attacked." The emotion we feel toward those we love—wonderment at their uniqueness, desire to foster their complete unfolding, appreciation not for their uses and benefits but their inviolate worth—might be the only force potent enough, *tender* enough, to save the world.

I spent part of last winter staring at a potted amaryllis bulb someone had given me for Christmas. I was firmly in the grip of seasonal affective disorder, and this thing seemed in similar straits. It was a typical watched pot; nothing stirred. Then one day a pert green spatula extruded, then another. The longer it sat there, growing, the more baffled I felt: *So, an inert lump of vegetal matter, plus dirt, plus water, plus light, plus...what? A lattice of info-molecules? Self-emergent properties of sufficiently complex matter? Élan vital?* And then this slow-motion *kerplow* of impossible creativity.

I thought of Dylan Thomas's line: "The force that through the green fuse drives the flower." *What* force, and what was nature thinking, making it so unnecessarily gorgeous? I wanted to call friends to rhapsodize about it, to tag it as forensic evidence of some divine immanence. Sometimes I almost caught it looking back at me, one living thing to another.

Mystics and shamans have long claimed that all of nature has an emotional life. Peruvian shaman Pablo Caesar Amaringo once commented: People may say that a plant has no mind—a plant may not talk, but there is a spirit in it that is conscious, that sees everything, which is the soul of the plant, its essence, what makes it alive.

Some years back I met a gruff, disheveled former detective and polygraph expert named Cleve Backster, an investigator of plants' secret lives. He'd had the bright idea to affix skin galvanometers, which detect changes in the electrical response associated with emotion, to the leaves of philodendrons. He noticed that when he cut the leaf of one plant, the tracings of other nearby plants spiked in what looked for all the world like a sign of distress. (The plants reacted in the same way when he rigged a nearby device to kill tiny brine shrimp at random intervals.)

During my visit to HeartMath, Rollin McCraty decided to administer a coup de grâce and reveal his ultimate Stupid Heart-trick. He took some yogurt from the fridge and dumped it, along with its resident colony of acidophilus and bifidis bacteria, into a petri dish. He took out a tan metal box with a dial and a needle called a "portable bioresponse meter" and placed its electrodes in the dish. As expected, the needle just sat there. "We're measuring the baseline electrical activity of bacteria, which holds pretty steady," he explained. "Biophysics would say that the needle shouldn't move at all."

Then he asked me to think of a deeply disturbing emotional experience. Rummaging through memory, I had a sudden flash of my sister's death, and I was flooded with a surge of grief. At that very moment, all by itself, the needle on the meter buried itself in the red zone, then oscillated wildly back and forth. We hadn't touched anything. The box was hooked up to nothing but the yogurt (strawberry, my favorite). Nothing in the room had changed but my feelings. When I switched my mental focus back to my surroundings, the needle went still.

"Okay," McCraty said, "now think of an incident of physical pain." I called to mind a recent medical checkup that had involved giving several blood samples. The needle kicked fitfully, like a man disturbed in his sleep. Then he had me remember a moment of profound embarrassment (I'm not telling), and, again, the needle twitched abruptly as if in response. What was being revealed here, he claimed, was that all living creatures, from microorganisms to pets to people, resonate to the field effect of the human heart.

Yikes! Just as an empathic person feels the pain of another, do other living things respond invisibly to the suffering and joy, hatred and love, that surround them? Is it possible we live in a universe that is not only sentient but deeply feeling?*

---

*Though McCraty attributes the effects he is measuring to the proximate electromagnetic field of the heart itself, William G. Braud, PhD, senior research associate at San Antonio's Mind Science Foundation, believes them to be related to "nonlocal mind," postulated as a sort of omnipresent field of consciousness. In one of Braud's studies, red cells drawn from volunteers were placed in a solution with low salt content, which normally would cause them to rupture. The volunteers were told to try to mentally "protect" their own distant blood cells. Measurements made with a computer-linked spectrophotometer revealed that nearly one-third of the participants had succeeded, seemingly, in mentally slowing their cells' destruction. The odds, gleaned from sixty-four separate sessions, were nearly 200,000 to 1 against chance. Overall, Braud has performed more than five hundred such experiments, all aimed at detecting the nonlocal influence of human consciousness on biological processes as diverse as the spatial orientation of fish, the locomotor activity of small rodents, and the brain rhythms of people. Consciousness, he has concluded, produces verifiable biological effects in bacteria, neurons, cancer cells, enzymes, fungi, mobile algae, plants, protozoa, larvae, insects, chicks, gerbils, cats, and dogs.

Starting with René Descartes in the eighteenth century, ascribing an affective life to our fellow creatures has been considered scientifically disreputable. Mr. I-Think-Therefore-I-Am, though he had an expansive brain, seems to have had a constricted heart. He once remarked that animals had no feelings whatever: If a cat being vivisected yowled in pain, it was only the mechanical noises of an "earthen machine." If this sounds archaic, bear in mind it wasn't until 2003 that scientists announced they had "discovered" that a hooked fish feels pain (so *that's* what all that agonized thrashing was about).

Acknowledging a sentient world might make us kinder, gentler citizens of a planet that has already had to endure more than its share of our cruelties. Besides, a world filled to the brim with awareness is a livelier place because it implies an infinite variety of relationships. As I was sitting here writing these words on a hot summer day, a fly began buzzing around the room. It was a metallic iridescent bluebottle, the kind that always sparks a jolt of irrational hatred. My official policy is swat on sight, but it had set right down upon, as it were, the topic at hand: a manuscript page with "All My Relations" in the bottom margin. I just couldn't.

Just then it landed on my forearm.

I looked down at it in the light of my desk lamp, trying hard to overcome my distaste. I admired its glittering carapace, which was, I had to admit, a marvel of nature's design shop. I did tonglen, contemplating the poignancy of its—his?—too-short, flit-about life. I breathed out love and appreciation for his job as nature's sanitation engineer. I pondered that he and I shared some 85 percent of our DNA.

Then a ridiculous idea occurred. I *talked* to him. "Why don't you just keep sitting there," I said reasonably, "and instead of trying to kill you, I'll put you back outside." I got up, keeping my arm level. I looked down. He hadn't budged. Moreover, he seemed to be hanging on, even when my office fan's full-tilt breeze hit his wings with enough gust to make them ruffle. He clung there as I ambled down the hall, stayed put as I reached for the doorknob, and was still there when I opened the front door and stuck my arm outside. "Okay, *shoo-fly!*" I said. And he did.

Okay, he'd probably just dozed off on his union-mandated break. But I felt good about this exercise in what Hindus call *ahimsa* (nonharming). It could now be truly said of me, "He wouldn't hurt a fly."

This is not to say I've become the Fly Whisperer. I tried my trick a few nights later when his big fat brother wriggled through the hole in the screen and began dive-bombing me. The closest I got to a kindly attitude was to recognize that he was buzzing frantically through his life, trying to get his needs met like the rest of us. I can't say I didn't long for a sturdy yet flexible swatter.

S TILL, I CONFESS: I'M GOING SOFT AND GOOEY ON ALL CREATURES great and small. It's been getting a little out of hand. The other day, shopping for a houseplant, I felt a wave of affection for every living thing in the store, from clerks to customers to the store's pet parrot, who, when I approached him, gave me a cheerful hello.

"Hello," I said.

"*Hel*-lo!" he said.

"Hel-*lo!*" I said.

"Hell*ooo!*" he said.

This seemed to be, with varying inflections, his only conversational gambit (though maybe he concluded the same about me). Every time I tried to walk away, he'd shout his greeting, and I found it hard to leave him there famishing for small talk.

So imagine how Aimee Morgana must feel. She's raised her captive-bred Congo African Gray parrot, N'kisi, in her Harlem apartment across from the old National Geographic Explorers

Club since he was a fuzzy little chick. Now, at age seven, he's as unalterably attached to her as a toddler. He loves her, and as the world's most verbose parrot—twelve hundred words thus far—he *can* count the ways.

I ask her how she trained him. She didn't, Aimee insists. "He learned to speak like any child," she explains. "I talked to him—a lot—just using language creatively, and he picked up on it." Like her friend Jane Goodall, who first approached chimps with her hand outstretched in a gesture of submission, Aimee, in her experiments to "explore avian language," decided to give N'kisi dominance in their social relationship, figuring it might facilitate learning. Whatever she did, it worked beyond her wildest dreams. "He was actually ahead of human children for the first few years," she says with parental pride. "He'd be using ten-word sentences versus their two-worders. Now we have actual conversations."

The fact that African Grays can sensibly "talk" rather than randomly mimic was first demonstrated by MIT professor Irene Pepperberg, who trained a bird named Alex to identify ordinary objects and classify them by color and shape. "Alex proved parrots know what they're saying," says Aimee, "but it's pretty dry stuff—linguistics tests by behaviorists, using rewards. I don't give N'kisi any rewards, so he won't perform on cue." Her role was more playing Annie Sullivan to his Helen Keller. "I'd show him water and say 'water.' Then if he said the word 'water,' I'd just give him a drink.

"Basically, we just live here together. I'm home-schooling a parrot," she says with self-amused irony. But then she gets closer to the truth: "I live in a magical world with a talking animal." Her apartment decor suggests a faculty lounge at Hogwarts Academy. Aimee, who makes her living as a TV production designer, has turned her place into a cabinet of curiosities, filling it with a bricolage of animal skulls, giant crystals, and cases of luminous blue Morpho butterflies.

N'kisi doesn't just talk, Aimee says. He has revealed a mind of his own, an interiority, a feeling-life. "I've discovered compassion, humor, altruism—the philosophy of an animal mind."

Hmm-mmm, oh-kay...

"I wanna fly over there now," N'kisi suddenly announces. Congo African Grays are big birds. When he flaps over, the downdraft fans my face. He perches on the arm of the couch, his foot-long, bright crimson tail feather hanging off the edge, peering sidelong into my eyes. His normal speaking voice is a digital recording of hers, but he says "Hel-*lo!*" to me in a hearty male voice, like a conventioneer doing a grip-and-grin at a regional sales conference. "That's his 'guy voice,'" Aimee informs me, "the one he uses for male visitors. He thinks it sounds tough."

When she tells him that I've written books, he says distinctly, "Jane wrote a book."

"He's friends with Jane Goodall," she explains. N'kisi hoots like a chimp. "Jane taught him the chimpanzee greeting." She tells N'kisi I've written books about medicine and healing.

"You had to go to the hospital," he says to her.

I don't see any secret hand signals. This *is* getting a little weird. Aimee explains that N'kisi's been very concerned about her health: She has been struggling with breast cancer. He sometimes seems as concerned about her as a child, a parent, a friend. Once when she was lying down on the couch, trying to rest, she reports he said in gentle tones, "Hey, baby, are you tired? Want me to put the light out?"

Normally, she says, he uses the pronouns "I" and "me" for himself and "you" and "your" when referring to others. But when he is distressed about something unpleasant that is happening to her, he tends to use "I" or "we," as if it were happening to him as well. When Aimee had to go in for breast surgery, she explained to N'kisi a doctor would cut her body to take out the sick part, and then she was going to get better. N'kisi said on one occasion, "I wanna take you better. We'll cut my body there. It's okay. We're gonna cut my body, and we're gonna take it better, okay?" It could be argued he's imitating her own first-person remarks. But unless she's made the whole thing up, Aimee's painted a persuasive portrait of a tenderhearted creature capable of empathy, sympathy, and even compassion.

When she claims that N'kisi does a little mind reading on the side, even I, Cedric the Gullible, arch an eyebrow. Then she pulls out a video of a recent experiment that I'm not sure I know how to argue with.

In the experiment, photos illustrating words from N'kisi's vocabulary were sealed in opaque envelopes and randomized by an outside party so that no one knew which image each envelope contained. Then, in a series of trial runs, Aimee was independently videotaped as she opened the envelopes behind closed doors in a room on the next floor. N'kisi, who remained in his cage downstairs, was taped by a second synchronized camera.

During one of the time-coded, two-minute sequences, Aimee can be seen sitting in her room looking at a picture of small, purple-pink flowers. N'kisi in his cage says, "We gotta go get the pictures of flowers. I gotta put pictures of flowers. Little flowers." She opens a picture of two men walking on the beach in skimpy, Speedo-style bathing suits. "Look at my pretty naked body!" N'kisi exclaims. She looks at a picture of a man talking on the phone— "Whatcha doin' on the phone?" N'kisi asks—and then a photo of two people hugging: "Can I give you a hug?" A panel of outside scorers determined that N'kisi had made 23 "hits" out of 71 sessions, far above chance.

Aimee says the strong results are due to the fact that, not to mince words, they love each other. I hear him call out to her: "I love you, weirdo, don't worry!" Is N'kisi compassionate? He talks the talk, and I imagine he'd walk the walk if he had proper feet. N'kisi means the "spirit of the thing": the soul, the mystery of the subjective (or *inter*subjective) life. Koko the gorilla signs "hug" by clasping herself around the shoulders with a rocking motion; Washoe the chimp gestured "Please Person Hug" in American Sign Language; Kanzi the bonobo pokes at his "Hug" lexigram and grins. N'kisi says, "Can I have a kiss? Hurry up, I can't reach you!"

*I*F NATURE HAS A FEELING-LIFE, AND WE ARE PART OF ITS VAST webbing, are there subtler ways in which we too reach out to one another? Could it be that, though we think ourselves sovereign individuals, we are swimming in an unsuspected sea of empathy? I pay a visit to Dean Radin, a former Bell Labs scientist and the author of *The Conscious Universe,* to see for myself. A diminutive man with a balding pate, his face framed by small wire-rims and a big moustache, the image on his T-shirt a wildly colored tree frog, Radin cuts a distinctly hobbity figure as we amble down to his laboratory at the rural Institute of Noetic Sciences (IONS) in Petaluma, California.

"Watch out for critters," he cautions as he unlocks the sliding glass door and a small lizard tries to skitter inside. His lab, a modest affair ("held together with spit and sealing wax," he says) consisting of a few computers, has one impressive central feature: a real Faraday cage, a gleaming steel vault lined with copper shielding against any magnetic, electrical, or radio interference. Radin plans to isolate me from another experimental subject in a separate building—Rose, a jolly, red-haired, matronly IONS staffer who's volunteered to act as the "sender"—and test whether I can somehow distantly feel what she feels.

Radin points out that though the term *telepathy* became popularly known in the nineteenth century as "thought transference," the coinage literally means "far-feeling" or "feeling at a distance."

Our experiment, he explains, will be literally testing for a transfer of "gut feelings": Rose and I will have electrodes attached to our abdomens to pick up electrical impulses from the dense concentration of neurons of the "enteric nervous system" (often called the "belly-brain"). Radin asks us to exchange a personal object to help us tune in. I give Rose my watch; she takes a Celtic cross from around her neck and folds it into my hand. We hug and head off, like 1950s quiz show contestants, to our separate isolation booths.

Radin hands me a blue plastic razor to rasp off some abdominal hair, leaving me not only feeling like a lab animal but, with a neat bald patch in my fur, looking like one. He attaches electrodes to my skin, their wires leading to a computer that will record my electrogastrogram, or EGG. The theory is that my unconscious "visceral perception" of Rose's feelings as she is shown a series of emotionally charged images may influence my readings. I recline comfortably in a chair, a set of earphones playing a soothing neutral tone stuck on my head.

I haven't been told how many images Rose will be seeing or at what intervals they will be presented to her. Holding her talisman, I try to "feel into" her feelings—"get a gut hunch" as Radin suggested. I do a little meditation: *Einfuhlung,*" I repeat to myself as a mantra. *"Einfuhlung mit Rose."* It's cozy in here. I sink into my padded chair. I get a fleeting image of a soldier with a gun; a little later, a clear, pacific sensation washes over me. I have no idea how much time passes until the door abruptly swings open and Radin pops his head in to tell me it's over, setting about freeing me from the Laocoönian tangle of wires.

We cluster around the monitors as he examines our graphs, which compare, second by second, our patterns of physiological arousal. I'm surprised that during a series of violent images—a soldier with a gun (a standard image, after all), starving Africans, killer sharks, all accompanied by a screeching soundtrack from the death-metal band Rammstein—neither I nor Rose show much agitation. Radin says this is common. "For sections that are negative or sad, volunteers' physiology typically becomes really quiet, as if they're holding their breath, waiting for it to be over. Maybe it's like animals whose nervous systems 'play dead' under threat."

I'm embarrassed when Radin points out that, according to the lines on my chart, toward the end of the session I had fallen fast asleep. "But look here," he says, sounding, in his imperturbable way, excited. "There's a *huge* rise. Something fished you out in a hurry." Sure enough, at the very second that Rose was flashed a final image-and-sound stimulus, both her physiology *and* mine suddenly shot straight up, our graph lines nearly whanging off the chart in tandem.

"So what was *that*?" I ask.

He goes to his laptop, punches in the sequence, and the Beatles' "Twist and Shout" blasts out, accompanying a montage of smiling babies, bunnies, puppies, and kittens. I've been mad for the Beatles since my first high school cover band. And I do have an embarrassing weakness for baby animal pictures.

Statistically speaking, I've done better than chance, but I'm no star empath. When I ask Radin if he's had any real prodigies, he describes Steven and David, two medical students from the University of Florida who met for the first time in his lab. They were put in separate rooms, wired up to brain EEGs, and instructed only to "tune into the presence of the other person." Radin pulls up the resultant charts for me on his computer. They're uncanny: The two students' tracings mirror each other with precision *every single time*. Peak for peak, trough for trough, the "receiver's" graph line maneuvers along the "sender's" flight path like a heat-seeking missile.

I am getting the feeling we are more than just connected; maybe we are *saturated* with each other, soaked through to the skin (and under it), brain, heart, guts—*you in me, me in you,* for real. Radin's experiments certainly raise some intriguing questions. Might a compassionate doctor be directly affecting the physiology of the patients he treats? (One HeartMath experiment demonstrated how a person's "coherent" heart rate variability could entrain another's EEG in a similar pattern—from several feet away.)

Is this why Tibetan doctors are constantly reciting mantras for compassion and healing under their breath? Could a loving teacher be invisibly augmenting her students' attention spans? Is there a baseline scientific truth to "I'm picking up good vibrations"? What if our empathic sensing of another's feelings is not elicited solely by subtle facial cues, tone of voice, and body language, as social scientists believe, but by some emotional *emanation*? (Perhaps this was the mystery Edith Stein had wrestled with back in the 1920s when she posited that "true" empathy was distinguished by "immediately...reach[ing] its object directly without representation.")

If such emanations could be said to exist, Radin maintains they would be relatively weak. His instrumentation reveals that the amplitude of the receiver's response is far less than that of the sender: If the sender is engulfed by a crashing emotional wave, the receiver may only be moistened by the spray. It appears too that most people must work at staying tuned in, since we all seem to have an unconscious self-protective function (some psychologists call it an "empathic wall") that screens out others' unwanted feelings.*

---

*There may be an all-too-prosaic reason why we find it hard to remain empathically tuned in: our tendencies toward self-centeredness. As Alfie Kohn explains in his book, *The Brighter Side of Human Nature,*

> What often seems to happen is that genuine, other-oriented empathy gives way after a moment to dwelling on one's own experiences. One starts by feeling *her* joy, but this calls up a memory of the last time something unexpected and delightful happened to oneself, and soon the other's reality has slid away. [Martin] Hoffman calls this "egoistic drift," and the impact is that one's capacity for empathy is a function not only of whether one can respond to others, but whether one can continue responding to others, *persisting* in the other-orientation.

My girlfriend, knowing I'm interested in this sort of thing, occasionally springs her own pop-quiz experiments on me. Driving around in her car one mid-December day, she playfully told me, "Okay, one of your really big Christmas presents is in the trunk. If you can guess what it is, I'll give it to you right now." I tried to clear my thoughts and get into a receptive state so as not to prejudge any images that might come to mind. (Parapsychologists theorize that psi is "primary process" cognition—a form of perception that is mostly preconscious.)

A picture immediately rose in my mind: a dead, gutted, still bloody sheep carcass lying crossways in the car's trunk. I was baffled.

"You got me, uh...a year's supply of *mutton?*"

She pulled the car over, opened the trunk. In it lay a nylon garment bag. She unzipped it to reveal an ankle-length, fleece-lined coat.

"Sheepskin," she said. "Do you *love* it?"

It was hard to say. I couldn't get the emotionally charged image out of my mind. I didn't want to hurt her feelings—it was a luxurious present. But now I was thinking (oh, *please* don't laugh) of a childhood encounter with a lamb at a petting zoo, recalling that eyes-wide feeling when, flush with some camaraderie of littleness, I reached out to stroke the sweet-faced creature's warm, soft fleece. I asked apologetically if she could return the coat; I just couldn't strut around wrapped in a dead sheep. Though it had never bothered me before, the idea of turning living beings into fashion statements now seemed barbarous. It was as if my vision had been received via some other organ of perception, the heart itself, which knows better than the intellect our true relationship to the things in this world.

One translation of the Buddhist term for compassion is "resonating concern." We say, "You touched a chord in me." A cello is bowed, and a string on an instrument across the room thrums. And not just across the room. The profoundly illogical phenomenon in quantum physics known as nonlocality implies that it could be across the galaxy. It has been shown that when light particles are shot from the same source in opposite directions, each tiny photon is instantaneously affected by what happens to its twin, even if the distance that separates them is light years. This interconnection, called quantum entanglement, has startling implications. Said a recent article in *New Scientist:* "When two electrons are entangled, it is impossible even in principle to describe one without the other. They have no independent existence."

Writing about this nonlocal coherence between separate entities, physicist Henry Stapp labels it the "most profound discovery in all of science." Profound, he says, because it suggests the truth of an ancient mystical formula: "We are all one; what I do to you, I do unto myself." Can it be that *you in me, me in you* is woven with infinitesimal care into the very fabric of the cosmos? The late systems engineer R. Buckminster Fuller, who designed the first geodesic dome and christened our planet Spaceship Earth, was once asked where a proper investigation of human nature should begin. He answered, as if it were plain as the nose on your face, "Why, you start with the *universe.*"

*W*HICH IS WHERE THE ORGANIZATION KNOWN AS SETI (Search for Extraterrestrial Intelligence) comes in. Based in Mountain View, California, the fertile delta of dot-com civilization, SETI has been deploying the world's largest radio telescope to scan a thousand sunlike stars—a quest that, thanks to vast increases in computational power, is trillions of times more effective than SETI's first hesitant census-taker's knock on heaven's door back in 1960.

SETI has now turned its attention to an overlooked contingency in the alien contact scenario—not just what message they might be trying to send us but how we should reply. Years ago, when *Pioneer 10* took its baby steps into the cosmos, we sent out an invitation of sorts: an embossed golden map of our solar system (along with a sort of Earth's Greatest Hits compilation that included Chuck Berry's rocket-in-my-pocket rave-up, "Johnny B. Goode"). Carl Sagan, who designed the messages, later mused that any civilization advanced enough to produce detectable signals must be cooperative enough to produce large-scale technology—and, if they were still out there, to have survived its Faustian consequences. They would therefore, he surmised, also prize altruism—something he'd neglected to stress in his cosmic care package.

Taking his cue, the Mountain View scientists are crafting what amounts to a new Human Manifesto. Our message to the stars, they've decided, should not just be that we're such almighty big-brains (the cosmic equivalent of cocktail party bores) but that we have hearts of gold. SETI hopes to encode, in the universal language of math and science, that humankind is, well...*kind*.

The idea that there could be intelligent beings on other worlds is no longer far-fetched. Almost every other week, astronomers announce the discovery of a new extrasolar planet (more than a hundred out of potential billions). For years now the thousand-foot dish antenna at Arecibo Observatory in Puerto Rico has sat receptive, its petals opened heavenward, awaiting a precious drop of intelligent communication amid the random patter of galactic rainfall. SETI has outsourced the processing of the enormous data stream via a computer program called SETI@Home, which runs as a screensaver in the computers of 4 million volunteers in more than two hundred countries, quietly crunching numbers in the machines' downtime, scanning for pattern. SETI managed to cull 166 candidate stars that *could* be sending out signals, to which they added five observed extrasolar planetary systems, thirty-five proximate sunlike stars, and fifteen nearby galaxies.

In March 2003, SETI scheduled a rare block of fifteen hours of precious radio-telescope time to reexamine the most promising sectors of the sky in hopes of finally making contact. That same week a small group of scientists gathered in Paris to discuss what could potentially become a pressing question: If someone *had* sent us a message, what should we say back?

It was a muted, murky springtime in the City of Lights. The first laser-guided smart bomb had just ploughed headfirst into a Baghdad bunker. The French president had reiterated his opposition to the war, and in Washington's congressional kitchens Earth's first Freedom Fries received their baptism by hot grease. Even as we inclined an ear toward the heavens, we had ceased listening to each other. The planet's airwaves were thick with discussions of acceptable collateral damage, not an auspicious time to persuade alien ham radio enthusiasts to be humankind's new best friend.

None of this fazed the hardy band of international scientists scattered on antique floral print couches in a grand *maison,* its stucco walls decorated with modern art and Hubble blow-ups. The meeting had been convened by SETI's "Interstellar Message Group Leader," Douglas Vakoch. A calm, alert man with a trim beard and an endearing air of humility, he opened by summarizing the protocols of the International Academy of Astronautics: If a strong candidate signal were identified (as it could be at any moment), the policy would be to immediately announce first contact to the world.

The gravitas of the meeting duly noted, he shifted to the task at hand, posing a pointed question: "Why should we think we have an ultimate understanding of compassion, given how poorly we act upon it? Maybe we'd best imagine we're speaking to a slightly older civilization than our own, one that's gotten through this phase and come out the other side."

What *would* we say to them? I ask Vakoch later. "Maybe we'd first talk about relationships between creatures in the language of biology, of kin selection and DNA transmission," he suggests, sipping his Darjeeling. "Based on that, we could try to convey something about reciprocal altruism: 'We'll be nice to you if you're nice to us.'"

But what if they find mere conditional niceness hopelessly primitive? Shouldn't we show that we can be generous to someone even if they don't deserve it? That we can be kind beyond calculation, forgive when we've been wronged?

When Vakoch replies that they are devising computer algorithms to express that very thing, I catch some of the excitement of this project: to lift ourselves for a moment above the muck of earthly affairs and put our best foot forward to the stars; to announce, officially, that we're not just a species mired in quotidian callousness and endless tribal squabbles; to tell Someone Out There that we're becoming what we aspire to be—Really Good People—and maybe convince ourselves in the process.

It's an exercise in perspective-taking. By reimagining altruism through ET's eyes, can we find new ways of thinking about compassion itself? It is less a question about deep space than the deeper recesses of the human heart. Would discovering some alien Other, as the old sci-fi premise has it, render trivial the differences among us, so we would finally regard each other as fellow Earthlings worthy of mutual terrestrial mercies?

Vakoch has been seeing the world through this exotic lens all his life. He decided early in sixth grade that it was only rational to assume ET was out there somewhere. His high school science fair project was titled "Encoding Interstellar Messages," and he has never strayed far from his original path, though his ideas of how to get where he's going have diverged. At first he thought we should trumpet our scientific strengths to the stars. Now, he muses, if we want to get a compassionate response from a more mature civilization, we might tell them how fragile we are.

"When we think of representing ourselves in interstellar messages," he says, "we usually think of how we can show we're great and powerful. But what makes us potentially unique in this galaxy is that we're so *young*. Maybe our most interesting characteristic to a civilization that's thousands or even millions of years more advanced is that we're still frail and mortal creatures. We can't download our consciousness or continually back ourselves up. Death *means* something to us. The sense of personal finitude, that we each will end, tends to overcome egotism. It can be an opening to care for the other."

I'm moved: If this is the applause line for our galactic debut, it could be a big opening night.

But how do we know how advanced *their* compassion is? Should we broadcast our vulnerabilities willy-nilly to the whole universe, let everyone in hailing range know what a wussy little orb we really are? Although a predisposition to cooperate is genetically encoded in our species—and is probably a trait of civilized creatures anywhere—there could be crucial differences in degree. "Maybe *they've* only gotten as far as kin-selected altruism. Then they may be ethnocentric like we are," says one scientist. But here on Earth, he adds, "the definition of the in-group is malleable— sometimes it's your immediate family, sometimes it's all your uncles and cousins, sometimes your whole village, or everyone who speaks your language. We'd better find a way to convince them, 'Hey, we're your relatives; we're like you.'"

Or maybe out there in the galaxy, he posits, the in-group consists of any intelligent species. That could be good—or maybe not. What if the intergalactic smart set didn't agree we make the cut?

Or what if, as another scientist queries, they'd want to see "a moral imperative, something we strive to attain rather than possess automatically as a species"? How to convey the sincerity of our striving was the subject of intense discussion. Religious imagery, it was suggested, embodies the human aspiration toward compassion and virtue. On the other hand, religions' centuries of sectarian strife show that one group's standard of virtue is another's definition of moral turpitude. There seems to be no limit to how badly "universal truths" can be mishandled.

To say nothing of visual imagery, another messaging strategy. I've wondered how Sagan's image of the man with the upraised hand, our classic we-come-in-peace gesture, has been received across the parsecs (after all, the V-for-victory sign in some cultures is a crude sexual insult). One message designer shows an animation of a spindly biped carrying a similarly shaped but differently colored creature in its arms. The idea, he says, is to signal that we care for our injured, a compassionate human trait going back to the fossil evidence. But it occurs to me an alien might think, *It's only protecting its mate, its kin, its tribesman;* or, worse, *It's bringing home the groceries.*

It's proposed that a Madonna and Child image would be the most universal way of conveying the value we place on parental care of infants. "This is almost surely a trait of all intelligent species," notes a scientist. "At the very least, some transgenerational bonding necessary for the emergence of culture." But is this enough to demonstrate compassion? We love our own children and our brother's kids and even the next-door neighbor's, but what about the stranger's children? What about the children of our enemies? There were uneasy jokes about hoping the aliens didn't get cable, so they wouldn't see any CNN images of child victims of famine and war (in which case, sending our message of peace and love might result in our being designated on all star charts as the Planet of the Big Fat Liars).

A few days into the event, the question (at least the "out there" part of it) was mooted, at least for now. There had been no gush of eager cosmic chatter at Arecibo. The search, at least this phase of it, had drilled another dry hole. Humanity would have a little more alone time to get its act together, though who knows for how long. Vakoch points out that SETI will be ramping up its search to include a hundred thousand stars in the Milky Way, a locale where, as another SETI-ite put it, "planets are as common as phone poles."

"If there is life out there, we'll have a reasonable chance of detecting it," says Vakoch. Contact within twenty-five or at most fifty years is the number commonly bandied about.

Decades ago, in this Parisian house built by a Portuguese sculptor, where pulleys that once hoisted the blank marble blocks still dangle from the ceiling, Soviet cosmonauts and American astronauts had met at the peak of the Cold War to seek commonality across what seemed an unbridgeable gulf. I can sense the same wistful hankering for human harmony beneath all this passion for galactic dialogue. If we can figure out how to describe lovingkindness to an alien, why can't we manifest it here on Earth, a place where, despite a bravura bit of celestial PR, we are increasingly alienated from one another? Are we really capable of becoming one people, one world? Can we create a global civilization based on compassion and stewardship—the kind we'd like to imagine might be out there among the stars—here on the home planet, before it really is too late?

CONCLUSION

And the day came when the risk it took to remain closed in a bud became more painful than the risk it took to blossom.

—Anaïs Nin

HERE, THERE, EVERYWHERE: IS THERE SOMEPLACE COMPASsion is contraindicated? It's good for body, mind, and spirit; good for loved ones and total strangers; good for creatures great and small (I draw the line at spiders, but I've joined Arachnophobes Anonymous).

I do know for a plausible fact that people change for the better—and incrementally change others. I know that compassion is a grace of sorts: It inheres in the nature of things, but it's brought forth by a certain exertion, as butter emerges from cream by the labor of the churn.

So I labor, little by little. I've started volunteering at a home for mentally disabled adults. A few are functional enough to hold down a janitor's job, while others are too impaired to talk. When we go on field trips to the bowling alley, half the balls roll into the gutter. When we play laser tag, the beams bounce anywhere but the target. We win some, lose most, but who cares? I like making my way in the world with them. Their need draws out, as if by capillary action, a flow of affection. It makes so-called charity mutual.

Sometimes I help out at a local family assistance center, stacking the cans, doing intake; or I fill in a shift now and again at the homeless shelter. I don't do all that much, dear reader, probably less than *you* do. But I've noted that simple kindness never fails to live up to its billing. That trick that's no trick at all works as advertised:

Amaze your friends and confound your enemies. The instructions are basic. When your heart feels empty, try filling someone else's. What's in it for you? Nothing but love's infinite debt.

Pierre Teilhard de Chardin took the infinite part seriously. He insisted that compassion is—must be—endlessly extensible. "We are often inclined to think," he wrote, "that we have exhausted the various natural forms of love with a man's love for his wife, his children, his friends, and to a certain extent for his country. Yet a universal love is possible; it is the only complete and final way in which we are able to love."

Polls show that most people in the world favor humbler, more compassionate solutions to our common problems. They not only favor them but, resolving to love in a more complete and final way, try to put them into action. A society based on universal kindness is not just our best hope; it is an evolutionary imperative.

Teilhard de Chardin, for one, believed that our entire species is heading, eventually, toward some new and improved version— and why not? Evolution reveals that we've *come from* somewhere; we must be *going* somewhere. Some of our woes seem to stem from quirks of our brain's evolutionary history: We are wired, neurobiologist Joseph LeDoux points out, for "emotional arousal to dominate and control thinking." But the story's not over. LeDoux also notes that in higher primates the neural connections between cognitive and emotional areas have, in a mere eyeblink of eons, grown so extensively that it could be said our species is fairly racing toward "a more harmonious integration of reason and passion."

Darwin himself was certain of it. "Looking to future generations," he wrote in a burst of optimism, "the struggle between our higher and our lower impulses will be less severe, and virtue will be triumphant." I spoke to one leading evolutionary biologist who affirmed it (though he cautiously refused to elaborate): "Recent evidence for directional trends in evolution involve increases in empathy, affectionate attachment, and intersubjective awareness."

In 2003 it was discovered that humans and African apes, alone among the mammals, have large, specialized neurons called spindle cells. (Bonobos have two thousand of them; an adult human has more than eighty thousand.) These cells, which have been called the "air-traffic controllers for emotion," show up in the fronto-insular cortex, an area that in real-time imaging of the human brain lights up on quintessentially human occasions: when we gaze lovingly at a romantic partner, feel embarrassment, perceive unfairness or deception, or respond to an infant's cry. It has been speculated that this area might be the biological seat of the moral sense.

It is located within a brain region that began an explosive growth spurt a mere hundred thousand years ago. It means that fully fledged *Homo sapiens sapiens*—noble not only in form but in sensibility—may have popped onto the stage in what is very nearly historical time. What we think of as our most human characteristics are so brand-new they're practically in beta-testing. It's hard to imagine there won't be future upgrades.

There are mutterings among some geneticists that we should do the work ourselves. With the forward leaps following the sequencing of the 3 billion base-pairs of our genome, the audacity of tinkering with human nature is no longer just a sci-fi premise. Scientists like DNA co-discoverer James Watson are already chafing at the restraints: "Sure, we talk about making better plants and making better animals," he fumed recently, "but you're not allowed to talk about making *better humans.*"

But what *is* a better human? In Watson's estimation, smarter, to be sure, but not necessarily kinder. He has opined that the "two stupidest sentences" in the English language are "love thine enemy" and "the meek shall inherit the Earth." (Interestingly, biblical scholars translate "the meek" as "the humble-minded" or "the peacemakers"; and my dictionary defines meek as "not inclined to anger or resentment." For my money, they can't inherit the Earth soon enough.)

So flash-forward, if you will, to the not-too-distant future. You're shopping for your kid, literally: perusing the aisles for those genes that will best enhance your progeny. You've scrimped and saved for that premium value-pack of brilliance, good looks, disease resistance, and athleticism. You can afford one more selection: that ambition gene everyone's been talking about, or an altruism gene. Which are you going to pick? Do you want your kid to have Mengzi's "mind that is unable to bear the suffering of others"? How will that work out on the playground of the future, when he's surrounded by genetically turbocharged kids whose parents didn't prioritize tenderheartedness? Will genes for empathy and altruism wind up as K-Mart blue-light specials, right next to the laser pruning shears?

In his novel *Brave New World*, Aldous Huxley, intellectual godfather of human genetic engineering, conceived of a society dominated by specimens factory-bred for dazzling intellectual gifts and cold, calculating hearts. But this common portrait of the superbrainy is completely at odds with contemporary studies of gifted children. Educators have observed in them an acute moral sensitivity, a tendency to forgive easily when offended, and precocious concerns about peace and justice. They have also noted the difficulties these children have in, as one researcher put it, "continuing with the generous, compassionate, and altruistic responses of early childhood" as they go through school. (Emotionally sensitive boys may become extra-aggressive to avoid "the considerable risk for peer rejection and ridicule"; their empathic "overexcitability" makes them vulnerable.)

But also chronicled is what happens when such children are encouraged: The world becomes a kinder place. One boy, with his parents' bemused support, had decided at age five that he had a personal mission to protect the rights of children and began speaking at public events. By the time he was ten, he had formed his own national organization. A four-year-old, upset at seeing a flood on the news, packed up his toys to send to the disaster zone and then persuaded other kids to do the same, until the town's children (and some inspired adults) filled a semi-trailer for the victims.

I recently met a seven-year-old girl, call her Cicely, with an off-the-charts IQ. She ran into the room like a ray of light. She had large, bright blue eyes, like a Keane painting. She's an unquestionably smart kid. (Her mother, a former bar waitress, remembers her as "this talking infant who startled people: Did that *baby* just say that?")

To make me feel at home, Cicely proposed a tea party, serving me on a little tray she'd set with her miniature cups and saucers. "To put a fish in a pond to be caught for sport," she observed, making rather pointed teatime chitchat, "that's rather cruel, don't you think?" Most certainly, I agreed, pretend-sipping as she regarded me gravely.

Cicely is ferociously articulate, but her mother has been most astonished by her acute empathy. "When she was little, she'd bring in leaves at the end of fall 'so they won't be cold all winter.' If even a cartoon character gets into trouble, she can't stand it. She'll chant, 'Oh, no, oh, no,' and breathe real fast." When someone in Cicely's class refused to sit next to the most unpopular kid, she ran over and threw an arm over the rejected girl's shoulder, repeating with great feeling, "I really, *really* like you." One Halloween, said her mother, "We ran out of candy and she told me, 'Mom, just put all the stuff I got in *their* bags.' I would never have given away my Halloween goodies when I was kid—*never*."

For all that, Cicely's a well-balanced, even merry child. When I discovered a tiny hair in my little cup, we sleuthed from its blonde color it was her eyelash.

"Eyelash tea, how delicious!" she exclaimed, grinning at me as she mimed another pour.

I occasionally wonder if those most gifted with "caring thinking" aren't early harbingers of our human future, of some kinder, gentler *homo noeticus.* But we don't need a new set of genes or extra smarts to share our candy. Something within us already conduces toward heartfulness and when nurtured has a tendency to flourish. Asked on his deathbed to sum up what he had learned in his eventful life, Aldous Huxley reportedly said, "It's embarrassing to tell you this, but it seems to come down mostly to just learning to be kinder." And though I set out to write a more hardheaded, less softhearted (and perhaps less soft*headed*) book, I can only conclude the same.

People living in arid countries have found a simple method of collecting water. They spread out sheets of fabric at night and siphon off the dew that condenses on them each morning. Like moisture, love really *is* in the air. It will settle upon the thinnest reed, scintillate on a bare tip of grass, free for the taking. It is an elixir that can heal, drop by drop, all the sorrow and separation in the world. It changes pretty much everything.

EPILOGUE

Enough words have been exchanged;
Now at last let me see some deeds!...
Something useful should transpire...
So get on with it!

—Johann Wolfgang von Goethe

*I*N THE YEARS SINCE I WROTE THIS BOOK, MY LIFE HAS changed more radically than I could have imagined. The words I set on the page eventually got under my skin. Hanging out with the folks who do the heart's heavy lifting confirmed a hypothesis: Do-gooding is contagious. Suddenly, being a writer, the literary equivalent of a UN observer, was no longer enough. I wanted to go out into the world and get my arms around it.

My mother died as I was finishing the book tour. She was the secret solar center of my life, a maternal personality so giving that, in truth, I'd sometimes wished she'd dim her brights (her typical epistolary closing: *love, love, love*, three exclamation points). After she died people kept coming up and telling me things she had done for them: little things, big things, always specific, usually unasked. She'd done a final boon for me too, leaving me enough money to pay down my debts and take some time off. I'd needed that time— to mourn the loss of her, to reassess my life. As the hiatus stretched into months, I'd told my friends I was practicing *wu wei*, the Taoist art of not-doing. This was, I explained, not the same as doing nothing. I hoped I was right.

I felt I was emptying out my preconceptions. I didn't want to make another move until I knew it would tangibly help the world. It became a personal experiment: What would happen, really, if I just planted a seed of good intention and waited to see what came up?

A few months later, at a friend's cliffside home in Malibu, I met an elderly forestry expert who had been planting trees across the globe for most of his life. As we talked through the afternoon, with the blue Pacific murmuring rumors of the world's vastness and nearness, he explained how trees were the ecological equivalent of one-stop shopping. They could restore degraded soil and increase crops, feed livestock, restore biodiversity, bring dormant aquifers back to life, and help destitute villages to thrive—all while hoovering tons of CO_2 from the atmosphere.

Trees, it seemed, could take care of everything from earth to sky, from people to planet. I had a minor epiphany: *green compassion*! I envisioned a collective class project to color those brown, barren swatches of the map green again. I called my notion the Green World Campaign. I had no idea what I was getting myself into.

My Malibu friend, who happened to be a philanthropist, offered me a small start-up loan. My kitchen table became the Campaign's world headquarters. One day, computer-phoning partners in Ethiopia while a friend sat next to me at his laptop working with a Web designer in Japan, I had to pause in amazement at our twenty-first-century power to change the world through mouse-clicks.

I'd resolved that I'd work for free. When my savings were depleted and I began to doubt my sanity, a Hollywood director astonished me by writing a check to support me for six months. ("I like the idea of planting trees," he told me, "but first I want to water the tree-planter.") More people soon showed up, offering time, know-how, and talent. When a few more donations came in, I funded a project in Ethiopia to plant calliandra trees, which anchor the soil and put forth blossoms for bees to forage, prospering the village honey hives. The next year someone gave me a plane ticket to see the program firsthand. I was shown around a verdant outpost in the arid countryside of the Gurage Zone, made by villagers who had spent patient years sowing a paradise-in-the-making.

They pointed out the thousands of holes they had dug for the calliandra saplings and walked me through rows of buzzing, Kenyan-designed beehives. A few days later, I found myself the only foreign face among ten thousand Muslim pilgrims at a backcountry religious festival. Families set up campsites bounded by sheets, chanting and clapping through the night, their silhouettes backlit by smoky orange fires. The next morning, sitting as an honored guest at an ancient coffee ritual, I was no longer a stranger in a strange land but just another global citizen, permanent home address Earth.

The circle grew. In Addis Ababa I made an alliance with a group working with indigenous tribes to heal the degraded land around the ancient Menegasha Forest. Soon after coming home, I was approached by a Mexican organization helping the Tlahuica villagers of San Juan Atzingo to restore their forestland, and suddenly there was a Green World Mexico. I heard from another group that was planting trees to protect India's sacred Arunachala Mountain and from an agronomy professor in Zambia who had a plan to reverse the dwindling of his nation's tree cover.

"The moment one definitely commits oneself," wrote Scottish mountaineer William H. Murray, "then Providence moves, too... raising in one's favor all manner of unforeseen incidents and meetings and material assistance..." I can attest to it. As of this writing, still reliant on volunteers, still running lean, the Green World

Campaign is the hub of a far-flung network of global citizens finding new ways to care for our world. We're scaling up our efforts, convinced we can play a role in restoring the economy and the ecology of some of the planet's poorest places.

I've come to admire the metaphoric elegance of a tree: donating free oxygen, running on solar energy, sheltering all creatures, making a quiet, tenacious display of life's generativity. People have always gathered beneath trees to parley and to palaver, to picnic and to play. Every faith has a Great Tree rooted in its narrative. I imagine each sapling we plant as a resurrection of hope, an emissary to the future. A tree seems an apt emblem of the interdependent, ecology-based global order so many are working to bring to fruition. I made up a slogan, a mantra I apply to both daily increments and grand gestures: *It's amazing what one seed can grow.* Sown in the ground, planted in the heart, each day it feels more true.

Acknowledgments

$\mathcal{T}$ HIS BOOK IS THE PRODUCT OF MANY HELPING HANDS AND steadfast hearts.

My late mother, Gloria Barasch, was a loving compassion master to her slow student.

My agent, Richard Pine, was as always keen and kindly. My friend and editor Annie Gottleib made the sparks fly with hammer-and-tong smithing on moonless nights. Editor Mariska van Aalst displayed unexpected talents as a muleteer. My assistant, Dana McDowell, showed supernal diligence, helping me find what I didn't know I was looking for. Researcher Claudia Robinson helped me stockpile an indispensable Alexandrian library.

Ginny Jordan's early belief and unswerving faith in this book were its genesis and exodus. John and Margo Steiner were fully and generously present, helping when I most reluctant to ask, the sign of true friendship. Neva Newman was tried-and-true through thick and thin, her heart never far from her hand.

Hector Black, Harold Mintz, Steve Aman, Pete Dobrovitz, Aimee Morgana, and Joseph Sebarenzi welcomed me into their homes, opening their lives with unstinting honesty. They were among the many others who gave me their stories, holding nothing back, asking nothing in return. I wish I could have included them all.

There were those who shared with me the bounty of their life's work: Courtney Cowart of Nine-Twelve; Bill Fields of the University of Georgia's Language Research Lab; Doug Vakoch of SETI; Dean Radin of IONS; Doc Childre and Rollin McCraty of Heart-Math; Linda Silverman of the Gifted Development Center; Fleet

Maull of the Zen Peacemaker Order; Toni Henderson of the British Columbia Transplant Society; Melodye Feldman of Seeking Common Ground; Robin Casarjian of the Lionheart Foundation; Frans de Waal of the Yerkes Primate Center; Susan Hepburn of the University of Colorado Health Sciences Center; and many others who provided me with generous access and crucial insights.

Most essential were those who gave friendship new meaning (actually, its oldest one, selfless affection): Michele Correy, whose deep caring was never in doubt. Maryse Elias, whose doting friendship more than once kept this vessel from capsizing in high seas. The Buckley family, who taught me about "making relatives" and gave me warm shelter from the storm. Tano Maida, ever available to share his lucid "tea mind" and infallible sense of direction. Jill Satterfield, who provided unflagging good cheer and a sun-drenched perch in New York. Lynne and Bill Twist, who offered their unassuming friendship and the insight that those who set out to save the world can still belt out a mean show tune.

And my family: my daughter, Leah, who has for every day of her life brought me more joy; her mother, Latha, who showed up for some timely interventions; my brother, Doug, who was a stalwart supporter; and my father, Norman, who taught me a writer's tenacity.

There were those who were bearers of special gifts: Mark Gerzon, Sharon Salzberg, and Rabbi Zalman Schachter gave me crucial early encouragement. Angeles Arrien, Georgia Kelly, and David and Lila Tresemer provided the means to attend a pivotal conference that helped set this work on its course. Dr. Mark Renneker offered the sustenance of his healer's craft, along with instructions how to surf in all circumstances. Robin Temple kept healing front and center. Jamie Pendell gave me lessons in *metta* engraved forever within. Donna Zerner furnished shrewd advice and keen counsel. Larry Laszlo looked at me, as he looks at life, through a compassionate lens. Nyoman and his family in Ubud, Bali, allowed me to work on my final galleys in paradise. Khenpo Tsultrim Gyamtso pulled me out of a tailspin with eight words of pith-instruction ("Scared mind comes from nowhere and goes nowhere"). Chögyam Trungpa Rinpoche revealed to me, unforgettably, the reality of the path.

Then there were those who showed me their love when I didn't ask and were kind when I couldn't see why they'd bother. This book would not exist—nor could I—without the givers in my life. You know who you are. You have my heart.

Notes

1. The Circle of Compassion

3 *read thyself* Thomas Hobbes, *Leviathan,* ed. Michael Joseph Oakeshott (New York: Simon and Schuster, 1997), p. 20.

3 *one can have that feeling toward oneself as well* Richard J. Davidson and Anne Harrington, *Visions of Compassion: Western Scientists and Tibetan Buddhists Examine Human Nature* (New York: Oxford University Press, 2002), p. 98.

4 *self-love but serves the virtuous mind to wake* Alexander Pope, *An Essay on Man* (New York: Routledge, 1982), p. 164.

4 *as with a pick, wrenches open the lock of self-love* Søren Kierkegaard, *Works of Love,* ed. and trans. Howard V. Hong and Edna H. Hong (Princeton, NJ: Princeton University Press, 1995), p. 17.

5 *openness to mutual influence* Janet L. Surrey, "The Self-in-Relation," in *Women's Growth in Connection: Writings from the Stone Center,* eds. Judith V. Jordan et al. (New York: Guilford Press, 1991), pp. 51–66. Surrey critiques D. W. Winnicott's model of "object relations," citing its "basic assumption of narcissism and human separateness."

5 *self-actualized person* Abraham Maslow, "Health as Transcendence of Environment," in *Toward a Psychology of Being* (New York: Van Nostrand Reinhold, 1968), p. 180.

6 *the American way is to first feel good about yourself* Father Thomas Keating, personal interview with the author, Snowmass, Colorado, April 2003.

6 *for attractive lips, speak words of kindness* Sam Levenson, "Time Tested Beauty Tips," in *In One Era and Out the Other* (New York: Simon and Schuster, 1973), p. 176.

8 *spiritual practice is not just about feeling peaceful* Dzongsar Khyentse Rinpoche, personal interview with the author, 2003.

9 *all, everything that I understand* Leo Tolstoy, *War and Peace,* trans. Aylmer Maude (New York: Oxford University Press, 1991), p. 1051.

9 *sealed and locked from all the world save her alone* Gottfried Von Strassburg, *Tristan: Translated Entire for the First Time,* trans. Arthur Thomas Hatto (New York: Penguin Classics, 1967) p. 145.

9 *the very peak of self-esteem* Kierkegaard, *Works of Love*, p. 56.

10 *love to faults is always blind* William Blake, *The Complete Poetry and Prose of William Blake*, ed. David V. Erdman and Harold Bloom (Berkeley: University of California Press, 1982), p. 472.

11 *like a mother who protects her child* The Buddha in the *Metta Sutra* (Discourse of Lovingkindness), quoted in *The Mystic Vision* by Andrew Harvey and Anne Baring (San Francisco: HarperSanFrancisco, 1995).

11 *our brains are physically wired to develop in tandem* Allan N. Schore, *Affect Dysregulation and Disorders of the Self* (New York: W. W. Norton, 2003), p. xv.

12 *love of humanity* UCLA researcher Belinda Campos found that "love of humanity" correlated negatively with other kinds of love. Romantic love, for example, had only a 0.23 correlation, with family love and friendship scoring marginally higher. Interestingly, the low correlation with romance implies that the form of relatedness most associated with genetic replication is at the farthest removed from universal love. Belinda Campos, "The Love of Humanity: Evidence for Prosocial Collective Emotion." Short research summary available at http://www.ppc.sas.upenn.edu/institute2002 shortsummaries.htm.

12 *like the love of lovers* Ibn El-Arabi, "My Heart Can Take On Any Appearance." Available online at http://www.rumi.org.uk/sufism/ibnarabi.htm.

13 *this brand of beneficent love* The term *generativity* is credited to psychoanalyst Erik H. Erikson, from whom it denotes a stage of personal development extending beyond care of the family to future generations and society as a whole. It is addressed in his works *Childhood and Society* (New York: Norton, 1950) and *Identity and the Life Cycle* (New York: International Universities Press, 1959). Generativity was also extensively treated by Pitirim Sorokin, a Russian Orthodox sociologist who led the Harvard Research Center for Creative Altruism and wrote *The Ways and Power of Love* (1954).

17 *where you find no love, put love* Saint John of the Cross, quoted in *By Little and by Little: The Selected Writings of Dorothy Day*, ed. Robert Ellsberg (New York: Knopf, 1983), p. 40.

2. Roots, Branches, and the Clear Blue Sky

19 *only two entries for "survival of the fittest"* David Loye, *Darwin's Lost Theory of Love: A Healing Vision for the New Century* (Lincoln, NE: iUniverse.com, 1998), p. 5. Loye also notes 24 entries for *mutual aid* versus 9 entries for *competition*, 61 for *sympathy*, and 91 for *moral*. It was Darwin's contemporary,

Herbert Spencer, who in his 1851 work *Social Statistics* on free-market economics coined the term *survival of the fittest*. This is claimed by American
sociologist Richard Hofstadter, among others, to have underpinned a philosophy of "Social Darwinism" that justified market-driven social inequity,
though Russian anarchist Peter Kropotkin used it to support the idea that
cooperative societies can be more "fit" than competitive ones. Although
Darwin later adopted the term in the fifth edition of *The Origin of Species*,
modern biologists view it as a tautology and tend to use the original term
natural selection. In some scientific circles, this includes *group selection* (or
multilevel selection), which looks at the group, not just the "selfish gene," as a
determinant unit of evolutionary biology (see Elliott Sober and David Sloan
Wilson, *Unto Others: The Evolution and Psychology of Unselfish Behavior*,
Cambridge, MA: Harvard University Press, 1998).

19 *strong sexual, parental, and social instincts*   Charles Darwin, quoted in
Robert J. Richards, *Darwin and the Emergence of Evolutionary Theories of
Mind and Behavior* (Chicago: University of Chicago Press), 1989, p. 119.

19 *only slightly remodeled chimpanzee-like apes*   2003 report to the National
Academy of Sciences, quoted in "Chimps Belong on Human Branch of Family Tree, Study Says," by John Pickrell, *National Geographic News*, May 20,
2003.

20 *extending the circle of compassion*   Alex Kirby, "Apes in Line for Legal
Rights," BBC News, February 11, 1999.

20 *a banana's got 30 percent of human DNA*   Kate Prendergast, "Updating Our
Origins; Biology, Genetics and Evolution: An Interview with Steve Jones,"
Science and Spirit 10, no. 5 (2000): 24.

24 (footnote) *full-body hugging*   Thomas H. Huxley, *Evolution and Ethics*
(New York: D. Appleton, 1894), p. 81.

25 *ruthless self-assertion*   Huxley, *Evolution and Ethics*, p. 86.

25 *curbing the instincts of savagery*   Ibid.

26 *psychiatrists at Northwestern University trained rhesus monkeys to pull a
chain*   Stanley Wechkin, Jules H. Masserman, and William Terris Jr., "Shock
to a Conspecific as an Aversive Stimulus," *Psychonomic Science* 1 (1964):
47–48; and "'Altruistic' Behavior in Rhesus Monkeys," *American Journal of
Psychiatry* 121 (1964): 584–85.

26 *Italian neuroscientists pinpointed a mechanism in the primate brain*   Vittorio
Gallese and Alvin Goldman, "Mirror Neurons and the Simulation Theory of
Mind-reading," *Trends in Cognitive Sciences* 12 (1998): 493–501.

27 *they will provide a unifying framework for a host of mental abilities* Vilayanur S. Ramachandran, "Mirror Neurons and Imitation Learning as the Driving Force behind 'The Great Leap Forward' in Human Evolution," quoted in "Read My Mind" by Alison Motluk, *New Scientist* 169 (January 27, 2001): 22. Ramachandran article available online at http://www.edge.org/documents/archive/edge69.html.

27 *mirror neurons suggest that an archaic kind of sociality* Leslie Brothers, "A Biological Perspective on Empathy," *American Journal of Psychiatry* 146, no. 1 (1989): 10–19.

27 *emotional contagion* Brothers, "Biological Perspective."

28 *if I pretend to be crying* Frans de Waal, *The Ape and the Sushi Master: Cultural Reflections of a Primatologist* (New York: Basic Books, 2001), p. 326.

29 *because it makes them realize the same may happen to themselves* Saint Thomas Aquinas, *Summa Theologica*, Vol. 3 (Part II, Second Section) (New York: Cosimo Classics, 2007), p. 1312.

29 *giving her a hug while making consoling sounds* Carolyn Zahn-Wexler and Marian Radke-Yarrow, "The Origins of Empathic Concern," *Motivation and Emotion* 14, no. 2 (1990): 107–30.

29 *indiscriminate emotional contagion is superseded by cognitive empathy* Zahn-Wexler and Radke-Yarrow, "Empathic Concern."

29 *archaic sociality which does not distinguish between self and other* Brothers, "Biological Perspective."

30 *the other is also a self* Paul Ricoeur, *Oneself as Another*, trans. Kathleen Blamey (Chicago: University of Chicago Press, 1992).

30 *I feel myself inside of him* Edith Stein, *On the Problem of Empathy*, trans. Waltraut Stein (The Hague: Martinus Nijhoff, 1964). The term *empathy* was first introduced into the American intellectual lexicon by psychologist Edward Titchener. See Edward B. Titchener, *A Textbook of Psychology*, New York: Macmillan, 1909).

30 *inner participation in foreign experiences* Stein, *Problem of Empathy*.

31 *Kanzi tried to wash her wound* Sue Savage-Rumbaugh, Stuart G. Shanker, and Talbot J. Taylor, *Apes, Language, and the Human Mind* (New York: Oxford University Press, 1998).

31 *we also differ from the lower animals in the power of expressing our desires by words* Charles Darwin, *The Descent of Man, and Selection in Relation to Sex* (Chapter 21) (Princeton, NJ: Princeton University Press, 1981).

35 (footnote) *all animals are competitive* Frans de Waal, "Bonobos, Left & Right: Primate Politics Heats Up Again as Liberals and Conservatives Spindoctor Science," *eSkeptic,* August 8, 2007. http://www.skeptic.com/ eskeptic/07-08-08.html#feature.

35 (footnote) *a 2007 experiment in which apes were presented with a platform* For the study de Waal cites, see Brian Hare et al., "Tolerance Allows Bonobos to Outperform Chimpanzees on a Cooperative Task," *Current Biology* 17, no 7 (2007): 619–23.

35 (footnote) *the presence of food normally induces rivalry* De Waal, "Bonobos, Left & Right."

38 (footnote) *a cultural swing toward pacifism* Natalie Angier, "No Time for Bullies: Baboons Retool Their Culture," *New York Times,* April 13, 2004.

38 (footnote) *an attitude…the social ethos of the group* Angier, "No Time for Bullies," quoting Dr. Andrew Whiten.

3. Empathy: You in Me, Me in You

44 *some kids can't do that* Dennis Krebs and Christine Russell, "Role-taking and Altruism: When You Put Yourself in the Shoes of Another, Will They Take You to Their Owner's Aid?" in *Altruism and Helping Behavior,* eds. J. Philippe Rushton and Richard M. Sorrentino (Hillsdale, NJ: Lawrence Erlbaum, 1981), p. 137.

44 *a 2003 UCLA study* Belinda Campos, "The Love of Humanity: Evidence for Prosocial Collective Emotion." Short research summary available at http://www.ppc.sas.upenn.edu/institute2002shortsummaries.htm.

45 *a king who looked out from his balcony* Franklin Perkins, "To Be Human Is to Be Humane," *Parabola* 28, no. 1 (2003): 14–15.

46 *guilt-proneness* Karen Leith and Roy F. Baumeister, "Empathy, Shame, Guilt, and Narratives of Interpersonal Conflicts," *Journal of Personality* 66 (1998): 1–37.

46 *do not do to others what would cause pain if done to you* Mahābhārata 5:1517 (http://www.religioustolerance.org/reciproc.htm) and *Anusasana Parva,* Section CXIII, verse 8.

46 *what I do not wish men to do to me* Confucius, *The Analects,* XV.24, tr. David Hinton. The same idea is also presented in V.12 and VI.30.

46 *therefore all things whatsoever ye would that men should do to you* Matthew 7:12.

46 *none of you truly believes until he wishes for his brother* Mohammed, quoted in Number 13 of *Al-Nawawi's Forty Hadiths.* Available online at http://www .iiu.edu.my/deed/hadith/other/hadithnawawi.html#hadith13.

47 *do not do unto others as they should do unto you* George Bernard Shaw, *Man and Superman: A Comedy and a Philosophy* (Whitefish, MT: Kessinger, 2005), p. 227. See also George Bernard Shaw, *Maxims for Revolutionists* (1903).

47 *somatic quieting* Elliott Sober and David Sloan Wilson, *Unto Others: The Evolution and Psychology of Unselfish Behavior* (Cambridge, MA: Harvard University Press, 1998), pp. 235–36.

48 *be kind, for everyone you meet is fighting a great battle* The quote is most commonly attributed to the Jewish Hellenist legal scholar Philo of Alexandria (13 B.C.E.–45-50 C.E.) and less commonly to Plato. The authorship is uncertain.

48 *when I condole with you for the loss of your only son* Adam Smith, *The Theory of Moral Sentiments* (Cambridge: Cambridge University Press, 2002), p. 374.

49 *alterity* This concept was developed by Emmanuel Levinas in a series of essays collected under the title *Alterity and Transcendence* (New York: Columbia University Press, 2000). It is most often used in the context of exchanging one's own perspective for another's.

49 *this sacred mystery* Shantideva, *The Way of the Bodhisattva,* trans. Padmakara Translation Group (Boston: Shambhala Press, 1997). See also Dilgo Khyentse Rinpoche, *Enlightened Courage,* trans. Padmakara Translation Group (Ithaca, NY: Snow Lion, 1993).

50 *a great relation exists only between real persons* Martin Buber, quoted in *The Brighter Side of Human Nature: Altruism and Empathy in Everyday Life* by Alfie Kohn (New York: Basic Books, 1990), p. 153.

50 *affective resonance* Freudian analyst Michael Franz Basch, for example, regarded it as the "primitive empathy" of childhood and suggested that its persistence into adulthood is psychologically damaging if not displaced by a more-regulated "mature empathy." See M. F. Basch, "Empathic Understanding," *Journal of the American Psychoanalytic Association* 31 (1983): 101–26.

50 *one must feel sufficiently unthreatened* Kohn, *Brighter Side,* p. 101.

51 *a famous Ray Bradbury story* Ray Bradbury, *The Martian Chronicles* (New York: Bantam/Doubleday, 1967), pp. 119–31.

51 *an early "Star Trek" episode* "The Empath," *Star Trek,* Season 3, Episode 12, NBC, December 6, 1968.

52 (footnote) *two chimps named Austin and Sherman* Sanjida M. O'Connell, "Empathy in Chimpanzees: Evidence for Theory of Mind?" *Primates* 36, no. 3 (July 1995): 401.

52 *the Chameleon Effect* Tanya L. Chartrand and John A. Bargh, "The Chameleon Effect: The Perception-behavior Link and Social Interaction," *Journal of Personality and Social Psychology* 76, no. 6 (1999): 893–910. See also M. Iacoboni et al., "Cortical Mechanisms of Human Imitation," *Science* 286 (1999): 2526–28.

52 *those who do this most readily also rate highest on the empathy scale* Chartrand and Bargh, "Chameleon Effect."

54 *hypersociability* Wendy Jones et al., "Hypersociability in Williams Syndrome," *Journal of Cognitive Neuroscience* 12 (2000): S30–S46.

56 *they have exaggerated emotional contagion* Susan Hepburn, personal communication with the author, March 2004.

56 *mindblind* Simon Baron-Cohen, *Mindblindness: An Essay on Autism and Theory of Mind* (Cambridge, MA: MIT Press, 1997).

56 *tone of voice, facial expression, body language* Anna Hayward, "Alien with Aspergers." Available online at http://www.ratbag.demon.co.uk/anna/autism/Huntsnews.htm.

57 *lack of empathy is not psychopathy* Ibid.

57 (footnote) *one study he performed with Cambridge students* Simon Baron-Cohen, Annual Disability Lecture (St. John's College, Cambridge, UK, 2006). See also Simon Baron-Cohen et al., "Autism Occurs More Often in Families of Physicists, Engineers, and Mathematicians," *Autism* 2 (1998): 296–301.

59 *interbeing* Thich Nhat Hanh, *Interbeing* (Berkeley: Parallax Press, 1993). Nhat Hanh founded the Order of Interbeing between 1964 and 1966.

59 *their empathy makes them too vulnerable* Susan Hepburn, personal communication with the author, March 2004.

59 *the sense of self must be protected by an empathic wall* Donald L. Nathanson, MD, "The Empathic Wall and the Ecology of Affect," *Psychoanalytic Study of the Child* 41 (1986): 171–87. Nathanson suggests that a child must learn to block "primitive empathy" with an "empathic wall" to form an adult personality. He writes in "From Empathy to Community" (*The Annual of Psychoanalysis*, Vol. 25, edited by Jerome A. Winer for the Chicago Institute for Psychoanalysis): "An adult who walked through life always vulnerable to the affect being broadcast into the local environment would be unable to maintain personal boundaries, just as an adult who admits no information from the affect broadcast by others is truly isolated. The empathic wall

must be strong when necessary, but possess doors and windows that can be opened when necessary and optimal."

59 *I often have a feeling of wanting to just protect their naiveté*   Susan Hepburn, personal communication with the author, March 2003.

59 *connect, only connect*   E. M. Forster, *Howard's End* (New York: Penguin Classics, 2000), p. 159.

60 (footnote) *intersubjectivity, a sort of self-and-otherhood*   Vittorio Gallese, "The 'Shared Manifold' Hypothesis: From Mirror Neurons to Empathy," *Journal of Consciousness Studies* 8, no. 5–7 (2001): 33–50.

60 *you need to love all persons as yourself*   Meister Eckhart, quoted in *A Spirituality Named Compassion: Uniting Mystical Awareness with Social Justice* by Matthew Fox (Rochester, VT: Inner Traditions/Bear, 1999), p. 88.

60 *one will come to care for them as much as one now cares for oneself*   Shantideva, *Way of the Bodhisattva*, p. 182.

60 *there is no I or you*   Pablo Neruda, *100 Love Sonnets* (*Cien Sonetos de Amor*), ed. Stephen Tapscott (Austin: University of Texas Press, 1986), "Sonnet XVII: Love," p. 39.

60 *to cut the sky in two with a knife*   Shantideva, *Way of the Bodhisattva*, pp. 180–81.

61 *put your right hand on the back of your left*   Ruben L. F. Habito, "Being and Emptiness: Buddhist Perspectives on Compassion," *Science and Spirit* 11, no. 1 (2000): 46.

61 *a kind of optical delusion of consciousness*   Albert Einstein, quoted in *Mathematical Circles Adieu* by Howard Whitley Eves (Boston: Prindle, Weber, and Schmidt, 1977).

63 *charity extends the privileges of insiders to outsiders*   Ted Peters, "Altruism: A Theological Perspective," *Science and Spirit* 12, no. 5 (2001).

64 *he who would do good to another*   William Blake, *The Complete Poetry and Prose of William Blake*, eds. David V. Erdman and Harold Bloom (Berkeley: University of California Press, 1982), p. 205.

4. Street Retreat: The Debt of Love

66 *the most dangerous acquaintance love can make*   Søren Kierkegaard, *Works of Love*, ed. and trans. Howard V. Hong and Edna H. Hong (Princeton, NJ: Princeton University Press, 1995), p. 186.

68 *who thinks he exists only for the distinguished*   Ibid., p. 75.

68 *unknowing*   Bernie Glassman, personal communication with the author, November 2003.

69 *when we bear witness*   Bernie Glassman, *Bearing Witness: A Zen Master's Lessons in Making Peace* (New York: Bell Tower–Random House, 1999), p. 84.

70 *here I was in Denver*   Jack Kerouac, *On the Road* (New York: Penguin Classics, 2003), p. 85.

70 *pay homage to a life of exuberant discovery*   Sales brochure for Jack Kerouac Lofts, 3100 Huron Street, Denver, Colorado.

70 *suffer the little children to come unto me*   Mark 10:14.

71 *by loving some people*   Kierkegaard, *Works of Love*, p. 62.

72 *root out all equivocation and fastidiousness*   Ibid., p 166.

72 *when I see beings of a negative disposition*   *Eight Verses of Thought Transformation.* Available online at http://www.archive.org/details/ Tse_Chen_Ling_GD_8_Verses_Transformation_20070819.

74 *do not judge your fellowman*   Rabbi Hillel the Younger, quoted in *Dictionary of Jewish Biography* by Geoffrey Wigoder (New York: Simon and Schuster, 1991), p. 207.

79 *touched with compassion, changed clothes with him*   Alban Butler, *Butler's Lives of the Saints: Concise Edition, Revised and Updated* (New York: Harper-Collins, 1991), p. 315.

79 *when I left them*   Saint Francis, *Testament*, quoted in *The Ways and Power of Love: Types, Factors, and Techniques of Moral Transformation* by Pitirim Aleksandrovich Sorokin (West Conshohocken, PA: Templeton Foundation Press, 2002), p. 157.

79 *O, Divine Master, grant that I may not so much seek to be consoled*   Saint Francis, quoted in *Love Never Faileth* by Eknath Easwaran (Tomales, CA: Nilgiri Press, 1996), p. 20.

80 *careless of the day*   *The Writings of St. Francis of Assisi* (Charleston, SC: Forgotten Books), p. 60.

81 *when we don't ask*   Glassman, *Bearing Witness*, pp. 201–2.

81 *reminiscent of an actual bookkeeping arrangement*   Kierkegaard, *Works of Love*, p. 176.

83 *concerned with matters of consequence*   Antoine de Saint-Exupéry, *The Little Prince* (New York: Harcourt, Brace, and World, 1943), p. 70.

85 *the great Hasidic sage Reb Nachman* Story told to the author by Rabbi Zalman Schachter, Boulder, Colorado, May 2003. Rebbe Nachman of Reslov was the great-grandson of the Baal Shem Tov and was said to possess "the good eye."

5. The Good Eye

87 *on the scales of merit* Quote from the *Pirkei Avot,* in "Sweetening the Judgements: The Kabbalah of Compassion" by Estelle Frankel, *Parabola* 28, no. 1 (2003): 14–15.

87 *to intentionally focus on what is most pure* Ibid.

88 *until I remove the threat of hatred from my heart* Samuel H. Dresner, *Levi Yitzhak of Berditchev: Portrait of a Hassidic Master* (New York: Shapolsky, 1986), p. 49.

89 *if we treat people as if they were what they ought to be* Johann Wolfgang von Goethe, *Wilhelm Meister's Apprenticeship and Travels,* cited in *Goethe* by Jeanne Ancelet-Hustache (New York: Grove Press, 1960), p. 132.

90 *optical delusion of consciousness* Albert Einstein, quoted in *Mathematical Circles Adieu* by Howard Whitley Eves (Boston: Prindle, Weber, and Schmidt, 1977).

90 *the Activity of Being in Crowds* Ninth Karmapa Wang-ch'ug Dorje, *The Mahamudra: Eliminating the Darkness of Ignorance,* trans. Alexander Berzin (Dharmsala, India: Library of Tibetan Works and Archives, 1978), p. 101.

92 *transform jealousy to admiration* Yoko Ono, "Revelations" (song lyrics). © 2007 Yoko Ono under exclusive license to Astralwerks.

93 *people you think are your friends* Donald Trump, quoted in "Trump: Paranoia Good for Business," *USA Today,* March 12, 2004.

97 *intersubjectivity* Discussed by the philosophers from Martin Buber to phenomenologist Edmund Husserl (*Intersubjektivität*), it has been elaborated by psychotherapist Daniel Stern in such books as *The Present Moment in Psychotherapy and Everyday Life* (New York: W.W. Norton, 2004).

100 *cease to be aware of yourselves* Martin Buber, *Tales of Hassidim: The Early Masters,* trans. Olga Marx (New York: Schocken Books, 1947), p. 107.

101 *thrones of compassion* Zos Imos, "Sufi Traditions." Available online at http://www.gnosis.org/sufi.mystica.html.

101 *the real heart is that heart which is neither on the right nor on the left* Ibid. The Prince of the Illumined was Hazrat Khwaja Moinuddin Hasan Chishti of Ajmer.

104   *changed god…Now he counsels "peace of soul"*   Friedrich Wilhelm Nietzsche, "The Anti-Christ," in *The Portable Nietzsche* (New York: Viking Press, 1969).

105   *it is only with the heart that one can see rightly*   Antoine de Saint-Exupéry, *The Little Prince* (New York: Harcourt, Brace, and World, 1943), p. 70.

105   *we all carry with us our places of exile*   Albert Camus, *The Rebel: An Essay on Man in Revolt,* trans. Anthony Bower (New York: Vintage Books, 1984), p. 13.

6. Heart Science, Heart's Mystery

107   *what is the heart, but a spring*   Thomas Hobbes, *Leviathan,* ed. Michael Joseph Oakeshott (New York: Simon and Schuster, 1997), p. 10.

107   *when psychologist Carl Jung visited Chief Mountain Lake*   Carl Gustav Jung and Aniela Jaffe, *Memories, Dreams, Reflections* (New York: Pantheon Books, 1973), p. 247.

108   *the power of perception and the soul's ability to nourish itself*   Aristotle, *De Anima,* quoted in *Introduction to Aristotle,* ed. Richard McKeon (New York: Modern Library, 1992).

108   *a widely reported 1986 experiment*   David C. McClelland, "Some Reflections on the Two Psychologies of Love," *Journal of Personality* 54, no. 2 (June 1986): 344–49.

112   *emotionally tinged intuition*   Jonathan Haidt, "The Emotional Dog and Its Rational Tail: A Social Intuitionist Approach to Moral Judgment," *Psychological Review* 108, no. 4 (2001): 814–34.

112   *it is the heart that always sees*   Thomas Carlyle, *Chartism,* excerpted in *Selected Writings by Thomas Carlyle,* ed. Alan Shelston (New York: Penguin Books, 1971), p. 179.

113   *our heart is the place of the rational faculty*   Saint Gregory Palamas (1296–1359), discussing Makarios in *Gregory Palamas: The Triads* (New York: Paulist Press, 1983), p. 43.

113   *this spiritual heart located in the bodily heart*   Greg Cook, "The Jesus Prayer," *Parabola* 26, no. 4 (Winter 2001).

113   *self-luminous Being who swells within the lotus of the heart*   Brihadaranyaka *Upanishad* in *The Upanishads: Breath from the Eternal,* trans. Swami Prabhavananda and Frederick Manchester (New York: Signet Classic, 2002), p. 104. See also the *Mundaka Upanishad* 2:2:7.

116   *the heart is a tomb*   Saint Markarios of Egypt, *The Philokalia* 3, quoted in *Parabola* 26, no. 4 (Winter 2001): 70.

117 *a practice called the Prayer of the Heart*   *The Way of a Pilgrim*, in *Pilgrim Souls: An Anthology of Spiritual Autobiographies*, eds. Amy Mandelker, Elizabeth Powers, and Madeleine L'Engle (New York: Simon and Schuster, 1999), p. 238. For a more complete edition, see *The Way of a Pilgrim* and *The Pilgrim Continues His Way*, trans. R. M. French (Hope Publishing House, 1993).

117 *the Pilgrim claims he was taught by an old cleric*   Ibid.

118 *the strength of a man's virtue*   Blaise Pascal, *Pensees* (1670), quoted in *Wisdom for the Soul*, ed. Larry Chang (Washington, DC: Gnosophia, 2006), p. 339.

119 *a redistribution of gray matter*   Eleanor A. McGuire, Kate Woollett, and Hugo J. Spiers, "London Taxi Drivers and Bus Drivers: A Structural MRI and Neuropsychological Analysis," *Hippocampus* 16 (2006): 1091–1101.

119 *if you do something for twenty years*   Stephen Kosslyn, quoted in "Is Buddhism Good for Your Health?" by Stephen S. Hall, *New York Times*, September 14, 2003, sec. 6, p. 46.

120 *let there be only compassion and love in the mind for all beings*   Daniel Goleman, *Destructive Emotions: How Can We Overcome Them?* (New York: Bantam Books, 2003), p. 6.

120 *caring and concern, mixed with a not unpleasant strong, poignant sadness*   Goleman, *Destructive Emotions*, pp. 11–27.

120 *a warm response to others' suffering had become so ingrained as to be automatic*   Summarized by research psychologist Paul Ekman (Human Interaction Laboratory at the University of California at San Francisco): "His thoughts were about human suffering and how to relieve it; his feelings were a sense of caring and concern, mixed with a not unpleasant strong, poignant sadness....When he spontaneously felt compassion during the burn film, his physiological signs reflected relaxation even more strongly than they had when the signs had been measured during a resting state."

120 *a 2003 conference at the Massachusetts Institute of Technology*   DVD footage of the Investigating the Mind Conference (Massachusetts Institute of Technology, Cambridge, MA, September 14, 2003), furnished to the author courtesy of Mind and Life Institute.

123 *a recent animal experiment*   Michael J. Meaney, "Maternal Care, Gene Expression, and the Transmission of Stress Reactivity across Generations," *Annual Review of Neuroscience* 24 (2001): 1161–92; and in Frances A. Champagne et al., "Variations in Maternal Care in the Rat as a Mediating Influence for the Effects of Environment on Development," *Physiology and Behavior* 79, no. 3 (2003): 359–71.

124 (footnote) *a study on moral reasoning and compassionate action*   Albert Erdynast and Logsang Rapgay, "Developmental Levels of Conceptions of Compassion in the Ethical Decision-Making of Western Buddhist Practitioners, *Journal of Adult Development* 1573-3440 (online), November 23, 2008. Available online at http://www.springerlink.com/content/538252728m02848 7/?p=9087bad73b3d428a8493065eddf18283&pi=0.

127 *my crown is in my heart, not on my head*   William Shakespeare, *Henry VI, Part III*, Act III, scene 1, line 62.

7. The Giveaway

129 *to the virtuous, no suffering exists but that of others*   For the story of the Bodhisattva King Sivi, see H. T. Francis and E. J. Thomas, *Jataka Tales*. Available online at http://www.archive.org/stream/jatakatalesoofran/jataka talesoofran_djvu.txt.

134 *the humblest man alive must confess*   Bernard Mandeville, *The Fable of the Bees: And Other Writings* (Indianapolis: Hackett, 1997) p. 44.

135 *the sacrifices that Joseph made on Robert's behalf*   Deborah Solomon, *Utopia Parkway: The Life and Work of Joseph Cornell* (New York: Noonday Press, 1998).

139 *positive emotional benefits, with no regrets*   H. Sadler et al., "The Living, Genetically Unrelated Kidney Donor," *Seminars in Psychiatry* 3 (1971): 86. See also C. H. Fellner and S. H. Schwartz, "Altruism in Disrepute: Medical versus Public Attitudes Toward the Living Organ Donor," *New England Journal of Medicine* 284 (1971): 582; and A. Matas et al., "Nondirected Living Kidney Donation," *New England Journal of Medicine* 343 (2000): 433-36.

140 *reported intentions are not necessarily highly correlated with actual behaviors*   Monica A. Landolt et al., "They Talk the Talk....Surveying Attitudes and Judging Behavior about Living Anonymous Kidney Donation," *Transplantation* 76, no. 10 (2003): 1437-44.

142 *cannot bear another's suffering*   Antonia J. Z. Henderson et al., "The Living Anonymous Kidney Donor: Lunatic or Saint? *American Journal of Transplantation* 3, no. 2 (2003): 203-13.

143 *embark on a larger-scale study*   Landolt, "Talk the Talk," p. 1440-41.

144 *a highly integrated spiritual belief system*   Henderson, "Lunatic or Saint?" pp. 206-7.

145 *truth is handsomer than the affectation of love*   Ralph Waldo Emerson, *Selected Essays, Lectures, and Poems* (New York: Random House, 1990), p. 154.

8. The Altruist

150 *evolution can honestly be described as a process for maximizing short-sighted selfishness*   Philip Clayton and Jeffrey Schloss, eds., *Evolution and Ethics: Human Morality in Biological and Religious Perspective* (Grand Rapids, MI: Wm. B. Eerdmans, 2004), p. 240.

150 *kin-directed altruism*   David M. Buss, *The Handbook of Evolutionary Psychology* (New York: Wiley-IEEE Press, 2005), p. 29.

150 *conspecifics*   John F. Dovidio et al., *The Social Psychology of Prosocial Behavior* (New York: Routledge, 2006), p. 49. See also Nancy L. Segal, "Evolutionary Studies of Cooperation, Competition," in *Evolutionary Perspectives on Human Development* by Robert G. Burgess, Kevin B. MacDonald (Thousand Oaks, CA: Sage, 2005).

150 *for the good of another would annihilate my theory*   Charles Darwin, quoted in *Altruism and Altruistic Love: Science, Philosophy, and Religion in Dialogue* by Stephen Garrard Post et al. (New York: Oxford University Press, 2002), p. 214.

150 *we are facing the profound paradox*   Frans de Waal, *Good Natured: The Origins of Right and Wrong in Humans and Other Animals* (Cambridge, MA: Harvard University Press, 1997), p. 5.

151 (footnote) *the easy altruism is kinship altruism*   Richard Dawkins, BBC Radio Current Affairs, "Scratch My Back," November 23, 2000, presenter Alan Dilnot.

152 *this line of research was begun by Samuel Oliner*   Samuel Oliner and Pearl Oliner, *The Altruistic Personality: Rescuers of Jews in Nazi Europe* (New York: Free Press, 1988).

153 *when someone comes and says, "I escaped from the camp"*   Oliner and Oliner, *Altruistic Personality*, p. 175. The Oliners add, "Rescuers thus did not differ from others with relation to the type of empathy called 'emotional contagion'—that is, a general susceptibility to others' moods. Rescuers did not any more than non-rescuers become worried just because others were worried or get upset just because a friend was upset. Nor did they differ from non-rescuers with respect to being moved by others' positive emotional experiences."

153 *what distinguished rescuers from nonrescuers*   Oliner and Oliner, *Altruistic Personality.*

153 *an extraordinary empathy*   Monica A. Landolt et al., "They Talk the Talk.... Surveying Attitudes and Judging Behavior about Living Anonymous Kidney Donation," *Transplantation* 76, no. 10 (2003): 1437–44.

154 *trying to stuff a fat lady in a corset*   Kristen Renwick Monroe, BBC Radio Current Affairs, "Scratch My Back," November 23, 2000, presenter Alan Dilnot.

155 *August Comte, the eccentric nineteenth-century French visionary*   Mary Pickering, *Auguste Comte: An Intellectual Biography,* Vol. 1. (Cambridge: Cambridge University Press, 1993), p. 315.

155 (footnote) *the debate over whether it is thought or feeling*   J. D. Greene et al., "An fMRI Investigation of Emotional Engagement in Moral Judgment," *Science* 293 (2001): 2105–08.

155 *we address ourselves not to their humanity*   Adam Smith, *The Wealth of Nations, Books I–III* (New York: Penguin Classics, 1999), p. 119.

156 *dramatic refutation of the kin selection hypothesis*   Kristen Renwick Monroe, *The Heart of Altruism: Perceptions of a Common Humanity* (Princeton, NJ: Princeton University Press, 1996), p. 165.

157 *I had to convince them I was doing it*   Dan Majors, "The Gifted Who Keeps on Giving," *Pittsburgh Post-Gazette,* July 23, 2003.

157 *his brand of altruism borders on obsession*   Stephanie Strom, "An Organ Donor's Generosity Raises the Question of How Much Is Too Much," *New York Times,* Health Section, August 17, 2003.

158 *I would go through fire for my kids*   Zell Kravinsky, online blog (accessed October 2003; site now discontinued).

159 *love of humanity*   Belinda Campos, "The Love of Humanity: Evidence for Prosocial Collective Emotion." Short research summary available at http://www.ppc.sas.upenn.edu/institute2002shortsummaries.htm.

159 *no man is an island, entire of itself*   John Donne, "Devotions upon Emergent Occasions, Meditation XVII," in *No Man Is an Island: Selected from the Writings of John Donne,* ed. Keith Fallon (New York: Random House, 1970).

159 *all human beings belong to one family*   Kristen Renwick Monroe, "John Donne's People: Explaining Differences between Rational Actors and Altruists through Cognitive Frameworks," *Journal of Politics* 53, no. 2 (1991): 428.

160 *self-contained and solitary as an oyster*   Charles Dickens, *A Christmas Carol and Other Christmas Writings* (New York: Penguin Classics, 2004), p. 34.

160 *all men have a mind which cannot bear to see the suffering of others* Mengzi, quoted in *The Origins and Diversity of Axial Age Civilizations: 1st Conference: Papers* by Shmuel Noah Eisenstadt et al. (Albany, NY: SUNY Press, 1986), p. 340.

161 *personalistic or empathic ties to family* Kristen Renwick Monroe, *The Heart of Altruism: Perceptions of a Common Humanity* (Princeton, NJ: Princeton University Press, 1996).

161 *Q: Would you help somebody you don't like?* Ibid., p. 201.

161 (footnote) *not even empathy was necessary for pure altruists* Ibid., p. 203.

161 *boundless impartiality* Patrul Rinpoche, *The Words of My Perfect Teacher: A Complete Translation of a Classic Introduction to Tibetan Buddhism*, trans. Padmakara Translation Group (Lanham, MD: Rowman Altamira, 1998), pp. 196 and 202.

162 *there are such helpers in the world* Jelaluddin Rumi, quoted in *Mathnawi II*, lines 1932–1942, in *Delicious Laughter: Rambunctious Teaching Stories from the Mathnawi of Jelaluddin Rumi*, trans. Coleman Barks (Athens, GA: Maypop Books, 1990).

162 *more crucial than the "law of mutual struggle" was "mutual aid"* Peter Kropotkin, *Mutual Aid: A Factor of Evolution* (Boston: Porter Sargent, 1976).

162 *unconscious recognition* Ibid., pp. 21–22.

162 *it is not love of my neighbor* Kropotkin cited in Daniel Batson, *The Altruism Question: Toward a Social Psychological Answer* (Hillsdale, NJ: Lawrence Erlbaum, 1991), p. 40.

163 *self-sacrifice is counterbiological* Christopher Ringwald, "Encoding Altruism," *Science and Spirit* 12, no. 5 (2001).

163 *those communities which included the greatest number of the most sympathetic members* Charles Darwin, *On the Origin of Species by Means of Natural Selection* (Broadview Press, 2003), p. 529.

163 (footnote) *a team of Israeli scientists* R. Bachner-Melman et al., "Dopaminergic Polymorphisms Associated with Self-report Measures of Human Altruism: A Fresh Phenotype for the Dopamine D4 Receptor," *Molecular Psychiatry* 10 (2005): 333–35.

163 (footnote) *in 2007 another study* A. Knafo et al., "Individual Differences in Allocation of Funds in the Dictator Game Associated with Length of the Arginine Vasopressin 1a Receptor RS3 Promoter Region and Correlation between RS3 Length and Hippocampal mRNA," *Genes, Brain and Behavior* 7, no. 3 (2008): 266-75.

164 *children who are shown TV programs with positive messages* Alfie Kohn, *The Brighter Side of Human Nature: Altruism and Empathy in Everyday Life* (New York: Basic Books, 1990). Kohn quotes George Gerbner and colleagues at the Annenberg School of Communication at the University of Pennsylvania. George Gerbner, "The Politics of Media Violence: Some Reflections" in *Mass Communication Research: On Problems and Policies: The Art of Asking the Right Questions,* eds. Olga Linné and Cees J. Hamelink (Norwood, NJ: Ablex, 1994).

164 *in a small town, three-quarters of passersby stopped to help* Alfie Kohn, "Beyond Selfishness," *Psychology Today,* October 1998, pp. 34–38.

164 *(footnote) the social ethic is so pervasive* South African Governmental White Paper on Welfare, Government Gazette (February 2, 1996), no. 16943, p. 18, para. 18.

164 *role models who had transmitted virtually identical moral messages* Monroe, *Heart of Altruism,* p. 184.

165 *children classified as highly gifted also used a higher level of moral reasoning* Lawrence Kohlberg, "Development of Moral Character and Moral Ideology," in *Review of Child Development Research,* Vol. 1., eds. M. Hoffman and L. Hoffman (New York: Russell Sage Foundation, 1964).

165 *he was wont to scatter half the seed over the land of the poor* Alban Butler, *Butler's Lives of the Saints: Concise Edition, Revised and Updated* (New York: HarperCollins, 1991), p. 40.

166 *we have dozens of cases on record of gifted children* Linda Silverman, "The Moral Sensitivity of Gifted Children and the Evolution of Society," *Roeper Review* 17, no. 2 (1994): 110–16.

166 *she describes Sara Jane* Ibid.

167 *a qualitatively different new intelligence* "Caring thinking" was introduced by Matthew Lipman at the Sixth International Conference on Thinking in Boston in 1994.

167 *advanced cognitive abilities* Ibid.

167 *such individuals are loving and friendly from childhood* Pitirim Aleksandrovich Sorokin, *The Ways and Power of Love: Types, Factors, and Techniques of Moral Transformation* (West Conshohocken, PA: Templeton Foundation Press, 2002), p. 147.

167 *seized with horror, at having killed an innocent creature* John Woolman, "A Strange Deed and a Guilty Dream," in *The New Oxford Book of English Prose,* ed. John Gross (New York: Oxford University Press, 1998), p. 242.

168 *the hand of compassion* Kristen Renwick Monroe, *The Hand of Compassion: Portraits of Moral Choice during the Holocaust* (Princeton, NJ: Princeton University Press, 2006), p. 55.

168 (footnote) *the greater strength of the social or maternal instincts* Charles Darwin, *The Descent of Man, and Selection in Relation to Sex* (Princeton, NJ: Princeton University Press, 1981), p. 87.

168 *the "egoistic" hypothesis was not borne out by scientific evidence* C. Daniel Batson, *The Altruism Question: Toward a Social Psychological Answer* (Hillsdale, NJ: Lawrence Erlbaum, 1991); and C. D. Batson and L. Shaw, "Evidence for Altruism," *Psychological Inquiries* 2, no. 2 (1991): 107–22.

168 *concern for the welfare of others is within the human repertoire* Ibid.

169 *where id was, ego shall be* In German: *Wo Es war, soll Ich werden,* in "The Dissection of the Psychical Personality" by Sigmund Freud, *New Introductory Lectures on Psychoanalysis,* SE XXII (1933a), p. 80.

169 *only a small number of Holocaust rescuers* Samuel P. Oliner, *Do unto Others* (Boulder, CO: Westview Press, 2004), p. 108.

169 *I see the whole world as one living body* Monroe, *Heart of Altruism,* p. 205.

170 *seeing-good* Charles Taylor, *Sources of the Self: The Making of Modern Identity* (Cambridge, MA: Harvard University Press, 1989), p. 516.

170 *radical energy* Pierre Teilhard de Chardin, *The Phenomenon of Man* (New York: HarperPerennial, 1976), chapter 2: "Love as Energy," p. 264ff. Teilhard de Chardin called this radical energy "amorization."

170 (footnote) *Sorokin proposed five factors* Sorokin, *Ways and Power,* pp. 15–17.

171 *only slightly better than those of an average American congressman* Monroe, *Heart of Altruism,* p. xi.

171 *a woman named Margo* Ibid.

171 *humble and self-effacing* Monica A. Landolt et al., "They Talk the Talk…. Surveying Attitudes and Judging Behavior about Living Anonymous Kidney Donation," *Transplantation* 76, no. 10 (2003): 1437–44.

171 *altruism's dark side* Elliott Sober, "The ABCs of Altruism," in *Altruism and Altruistic Love: Science, Philosophy and Religion in Dialogue* by Stephen Garrard Post el al. (New York: Oxford University Press, 2002), pp. 25–26.

175 *saved the concept of the human being as capable of goodness* Patrick Gerard Henry, *We Only Know Men: The Rescue of Jews in France during the Holocaust* (Washington, DC: Catholic University of America Press, 2007), p. 168.

175   *poignant isolation*   Kristen Renwick Monroe and Connie Eperson, "But What Else Could I Do?": Choice, Identity, and a Cognitive-Perceptual Theory of Ethical Political Behavior," *Political Psychology* 15, no. 2 (1994): p. 202.

9. The Elixir of Forgiveness

179   *fantasies about killing people they don't like*   Douglas Kenrick and David Buss in *The Blank Slate: The Modern Denial of Human Nature* by Steven Pinker (New York: Viking, 2002), pp. 316–17.

180   *in those who harbor such thoughts*   The Dhammapada, quoted in *Forgiveness: Theory, Research, and Practice,* eds. Michael E. McCullough et al. (New York: Guilford Press, 2000), p. 27.

180   *ordinarily, if your enemy harms you, you will feel anger*   Garchen Rinpoche, "On Meditation," lecture (Ratnashri Tibetan Meditation Center, Lidingo, Sweden, September 15, 2001).

187   *social scientists talk of "grudge theory"*   McCullough, *Forgiveness.*

187   *forgiveness increases self-esteem*   Everett L. Worthington, *Handbook of Forgiveness* (Boca Raton, FL: CRC Press, 2005), pp. 396–99.

187   *men in a drug and alcohol treatment program*   Ibid.

187   *cardiac patients who blame others for their initial heart attack*   Carl F. Thoreson, Alex H. S. Harris, and Frederic Luskin, "Forgiveness and Health: An Unanswered Question," in *Forgiveness: Theory, Research, and Practice,* eds. Michael E. McCullough et al. (New York: Guilford Press, 2001), p. 257.

187   *positive emotions like forgiveness*   Charlotte VanOyen Witvliet et al., "Granting Forgiveness or Harboring Grudges: Implications for Emotion, Physiology, and Health," *Psychological Science* 12, no. 2 (2001): 117–23.

187   *as important to the treatment of emotional and mental disorders*   Richard Fitzgibbons, "Anger and the Healing Power of Forgiveness," in *Exploring Forgiveness,* eds. Robert D. Enright and Johanna North (Madison: University of Wisconsin Press, 1998), p. 71. Lamb and Murphy (see next note, p. 86) respond: "Not all patients who are treated with penicillin or sulfa drugs are necessarily getting the treatment they should be given."

188   *in a recent poll of the profession*   Sharon Lamb and Jeffrie G. Murphy, eds., *Before Forgiving: Cautionary Views of Forgiveness in Psychotherapy* (New York: Oxford University Press, 2002), p. 67.

188   *forgiving means to write the person off*   Fitzgibbons, "Anger and Healing," p. 100.

188 *to forgive, one must have the capacity to identify with others* Robert A. Emmons, "Personality and Forgiveness," in McCullough, *Forgiveness*, p. 166.

188 *a flaw in a narcissistically perceived reality* John Patton, "Forgiveness: Pastoral Care and Counseling," in McCullough, *Forgiveness*, p. 289.

188 *the most extensive scientific investigation of forgiveness to date* Robert Enright, *Forgiveness Is a Choice* (Washington, DC: American Psychological Association, 2001), p. 36.

189 *Enright concluded that there is a deeper level of forgiveness* Enright and North, *Exploring Forgiveness*, p. 20.

189 *an attitude of compassion, generosity, and even love* Ibid., p. 151.

189 *some counselors have worked with parents who forgave the behavior of drug-addicted youth* Lamb and Murphy, *Before Forgiving*, p. 89.

189 *it is important that I do all I can to restore relationship* Desmond Tutu, lecture (University of Colorado, Boulder, March 29, 2004).

191 *a ferryman is taking a rich nobleman across a river* Author's variant of a Zen parable traceable to a famous analogy by Chuang Tzu: See Thomas Merton, ed. and trans., *The Way of Chuang Tzu* (New York: New Directions, 1965), pp. 168-171.

191 *it is the way of the Tao to recompense injury with kindness* Lao Tzu, *Tao Te Ching*, verse 63 (1).

192 *my Raphael knows how to love the most wicked evil-doers* Martin Buber, *Tales of Hassidim: The Early Masters*, trans. Olga Marx. (New York: Schocken Books, 1947).

192 *forgiveness means reconciliation in spite of estrangement* Paul Tillich, *The New Being* (New York: Charles Scribner's Sons, 1955), pp. 7–9.

10. Loving the Monster

199 *for Jesus had commanded the evil spirit to come out of the man* Luke 8:29.

199 *those who, maddened by the demons of delusion, commit violent negative actions* The XIVth Dalai Lama, in *Life Prayers from Around the World: 365 Prayers, Blessings, and Affirmations to Celebrate the Human Journey*, eds. Elizabeth Roberts and Elias Amidon (New York: HarperOne, 1996), p. 122.

199 *what is the essence of the cycle of violence* The Honorable Robert Yazzie, "Navajo Justice," *Yes Magazine*, Fall 2000.

202   *higher morality is written on the heart*   Saint Paul, quoted in Romans 2:14–15. See also J. Budziszewski, *Written on the Heart: The Case for Natural Law* (Downers Grove, IL: InterVarsity Press, 1997).

202   *I felt pity to see this man destroyed*   Jason Horowitz, "Pity for Hussein at the Vatican," *New York Times,* December 17, 2003, A20.

203   *De Kock surprised everyone by asking to meet the widows*   Pumla Gobodo-Madikizela, *A Human Being Died That Night: A South African Story of Forgiveness* (Boston: Houghton Mifflin, 2003), p. 47.

205   *God's forgiveness is independent of anything we do*   Paul Tillich, *The New Being* (Lincoln, NE: University of Nebraska Press, 2005), p. 9.

207   *generativity*   Pitirim Aleksandrovich Sorokin, *The Ways and Power of Love: Types, Factors, and Techniques of Moral Transformation* (West Conshohocken, PA: Templeton Foundation Press, 2002).

215   *I tell you, not seven times but seventy-seven times*   Matthew 18:22.

215   *Tutu had to sit and listen to a police torturer*   Desmond Tutu, lecture (University of Colorado, Boulder, March 29, 2004).

11. A Little Peace of the Heart

219   *history is a nightmare from which I am trying to awake*   Stephen Daedelus in James Joyce, *Ulysses* (Charleston, South Carolina: Forgotten Books, 1925), p. 31.

224   *dependence on negative memory*   Yitzhak Mendelsohn, personal communication with the author, November 2004.

224   *Buddhas see delusion as the enemy*   Aryadeva (second century C.E.), the *Chatu-Shataha Shastra,* in *Fundamentals of Tibetan Buddhism* by Rebecca McClen Novick (San Francisco: Crossing Press, 1999), p. 127.

225   *self-esteem is in large measure a function of the esteem accorded to groups*   Donald L. Horowitz, *Ethnic Groups in Conflict* (Berkeley: University of California Press, 2000), p. 143.

228   *people would often rather die than live with a sense of shame*   Neil Altman, "Humiliation, Retaliation, and Violence," *Tikkun* 19, no. 1 (January–February 2004): 17.

229   *there is a lasting form of shame associated with having been vulnerable*   Ibid.

230   *each group nourishes its own pride and vanity*   William G. Sumner and Albert G. Keller, *Folkways: A Study of the Sociological Importance of Usages, Manners, Customs, Mores and Morals* (Boston: Ginn, 1906), p. 13.

230 (footnote) *a poll taken in Kosovo in 1997*   Blaine Harden, "Playing Chicken with Milosevic," *New York Times Magazine,* April 25, 1999, p. 13, quoting a 1997 poll published in the Belgrade magazine *Vreme.*

231 *we are men, the rest are something else*   William G. Sumner, *War and Other Essays* (New Haven, CT: Yale University Press, 1911).

231 *their belief that they were the first, finest, and most refined form of man*   Johan M. G. Van der Dennen, "Of Badges, Bonds and Boundaries: Ingroup/Outgroup Differentiation and Ethnocentrism Revisited," Proceedings of the Fifth Annual Meeting of the European Sociobiological Society, St. John's College, Oxford, UK, January 5–6, 1995, referring to *A History of Warfare* by John Keegan (London: Pimlico, 1993), p. 97.

231 *rival tribes were linguistically lumped with game animals*   R. F. Murphy, "Intergroup Hostility and Social Cohesion," *American Anthropologist* 59 (1957): 1018–35. See also R. F. Murphy, *Headhunter's Heritage* (Berkeley: University of California Press, 1960).

232 *never shall I forget the little faces of the children*   Elie Wiesel, *Night* (New York: Hill and Wang, 1960), p. 9.

234 *if we could read the secret history of our enemies*   Henry Wadsworth Longfellow, *The International Thesaurus of Quotations,* ed. Rhoda Thomas Tripp (New York: Thomas Crowell, 1970), p. 186.

234 *I did think, when I saw a picture on the TV of an old woman on all fours*   James Bennet, "Israeli Official Offers Empathy but Hits a Nerve," *New York Times,* May 24, 2004.

234 *the injury cannot be healed*   Erroll McDonald, ed., *The Drowned and the Saved,* trans. Raymond Rosenthal (New York: Random House, 1988), p. 12.

241 *irrational beliefs serve the purpose far better than rational ones*   Robert Bigelow, *The Dawn Warriors: Man's Evolution towards Peace* (Boston: Little Brown, 1969), p. 246.

245 *give, then, Your servant a listening heart*   I Kings 3:9. In virtually all English Bible translations, Solomon asks God for an "understanding mind." However, the original Hebrew term, *lev shome'a,* would translate more closely as "receptive heart," considered in ancient times an organ of perception.

12. The Beloved Community

247 *the victorious weight of innumerable little kindnesses*   Stephen Gould, "A Time of Gifts," *New York Times,* Opinion, September 26, 2001.

247 *you will get more with a kind word and a gun* Donald Rumsfeld frequently quoted this line from Al Capone, even before 9/11, e.g., quoted in "Meanwhile, at the Pentagon..." by Mark Thompson, *Time,* December 31, 2000.

249 *theologian Courtney Cowart* Courtney Cowart, *An American Awakening: From Ground Zero to Katrina the People We Are Free to Be* (New York: Seabury Books, 2008).

254 *as I stood with them and saw white and Negro* Martin Luther King Jr., *Where Do We Go from Here: Chaos or Community?* (New York: Harper and Row, 1967), p. 284.

256 *no hint of genuine clarity* Michael Ghiselin, *The Economy of Nature and the Evolution of Sex* (Berkeley: University of California Press, 1974), p. 247.

257 *he quotes an interview with a woman* Jonathan Haidt, "Elevation and the Positive Psychology of Morality," in *Flourishing: Positive Psychology and the Life Well-lived,* eds. Corey L. Mikeyes and Jonathan Haidt (Washington, DC: American Psychological Association, 2003), pp. 283–87.

264 *men will die like flies* E. M. F. Durbin and John Bowlby, *Personal Aggressiveness and War* (New York: Columbia University Press, 1939), cited in Johan M. G. Van der Dennen, "Of Badges, Bonds and Boundaries: Ingroup/Outgroup Differentiation and Ethnocentrism Revisited," Proceedings of the Fifth Annual Meeting of the European Sociobiological Society, St. John's College, Oxford, UK, January 5–6, 1995.

269 *our loyalties transcend our race* King, *Chaos or Community?,* p. 9.

13. All My Relations

272 *a motion and a spirit that rolls through all things* William Wordsworth, "Lines Composed a Few Miles above Tintern Abbey, on Revisiting the Banks of the Wye during a Tour, 13 July 1798." Available online at http://www.nbu.bg/webs/amb/british/3/wordsworth/abbey.htm.

272 *the cavesnail was dying off in large numbers* U.S. Fish and Wildlife Service, Tumbling Creek Cavesnail (*Antrobia culveri*) Fact Sheet. Available online at http://www.fws.gov/midwest/endangered/Snails/tcca-fctsht.pdf.

273 *beyond the world of human beings to include all living things* Kristen Renwick Monroe, *The Heart of Altruism: Perceptions of a Common Humanity* (Princeton, NJ: Princeton University Press, 1996), pp. 206–7.

273 *the force that through the green fuse drives the flower* Dylan Thomas, *The Poems of Dylan Thomas,* ed. Daniel Jones (New York: New Directions, 2003), p. 90.

275 (footnote) *in one of Braud's studies* William G. Braud, PhD, "Distant Mental Influence of Rate of Hemolysis of Human Red Blood Cells," *Journal of the American Society for Psychical Research* 84 (1990), pp. 1–24.

275 (footnote) *consciousness, he has concluded, produces verifiable biological effects* William G. Braud, PhD, "Psychokinesis in Aggressive and Nonaggressive Fish with Mirror Presentation Feedback for Hits: Some Preliminary Experiments," *Journal of Parapsychology* 40 (1976), pp. 296–307. See also William G. Braud, "On the Use of Living Target Systems in Distant Mental Influence Research," in *Psi Research Methodology: A Re-examination,* eds. B. Shapin and L. Coly (New York: Parapsychology Foundation, 1993), pp. 149–88.

276 *he once remarked that animals had no feelings whatever* René Descartes, "Discourse on Method," Part V (1637) in *The Philosophical Writings of Descartes,* 3 vols., trans. John Cottingham, Robert Stoothoff, and Dugald Murdoch (Cambridge: Cambridge University Press, 1991). The same idea was advanced by Nicholas Malebranche, who declared that animals were insentient machines that "eat without pleasure, cry without pain." Nicholas Malebranche, quoted in *Oeuvres Complètes,* ed. G. Rodis-Lewis (Paris: J. Vrin. 1958–70), II, p. 394, cited in "Descartes on Animals" by Peter Harrison, *The Philosophical Quarterly* 42, no. 167 (April 1992): 219–27.

284 *one HearthMath experiment* Rollin McCraty et al., "The Electricity of Touch: Detection and Measurement of Cardiac Energy Exchange between People," in *Brain and Values: Is a Biological Science of Values Possible,* ed. Karl H. Pribram, International Neural Network Society (Hillsdale, NJ: Lawrence Erlbaum, 1998), pp. 359–79.

284 *true empathy was distinguished by immediately reaching its object* Edith Stein, *On the Problem of Empathy,* trans. Waltraut Stein (The Hague: Martinus Nijhoff, 1964), p. 24.

284 *empathic wall* Donald L. Nathanson, MD, "The Empathic Wall and the Ecology of Affect," *Psychoanalytic Study of the Child* 41 (1986): 171–87.

284 (footnote) *what often seems to happen is that genuine, other-oriented apathy gives way* Alfie Kohn, *The Brighter Side of Human Nature: Altruism and Empathy in Everyday Life* (New York: Basic Books, 1990), referencing *Empathy and Moral Development: Implications for Caring and Justice* by Martin L. Hoffman (Cambridge: Cambridge University Press, 2001) p. 56.

286 *when two electrons are entangled* Hans Christian von Baeyer, "In the Beginning Was the Bit," *New Scientist,* February 17, 2001.

286 *we are all one* Henry Stapp, cited in *Entanglement: The Greatest Mystery in Physics* by Amir D. Aczel (New York: Four Walls Eight Windows, 2002). See also Henry Stapp, "Bell's Theorem and World Process," *Il Nuovo Cimento* 29B (1975): 271; and Henry Stapp, "Einstein Locality, EPR Locality, and the Significance for Science of the Nonlocal Character of Quantum Theory," in *Microphysical Reality and Quantum Formalism*, Vol. 2, eds. A. van der Merwe et al. (Dordecht: Kluwer, 1988), pp. 26–78.

286 *once asked where a proper investigation of human nature should begin* R. Buckminster Fuller, *Synergetics 2: Explorations in the Geometry of Thinking* (New York: Macmillan, 1983), p. 61.

Conclusion

294 *we are often inclined to think that we have exhausted the various natural forms of love* Pierre Teilhard de Chardin, *The Phenomenon of Man* (New York: Harper and Brothers, 1959), p. 266.

294 *emotional arousal to dominate and control thinking* Joseph LeDoux, *The Emotional Brain: The Mysterious Underpinnings of Emotional Life* (New York: Simon and Schuster, 1998), p. 21.

294 *looking to future generations* Charles Darwin, *The Descent of Man, and Selection in Relation to Sex* (Princeton, NJ: Princeton University Press, 1981), p. 104.

296 *continuing with the generous, compassionate, and altruistic responses* Linda Silverman, "The Moral Sensitivity of Gifted Children and the Evolution of Society," *Roeper Review* 17, no. 2 (1994): 110–16.

296 *the considerable risk for peer rejection* Ibid.

Epilogue

301 *the moment one definitely commits oneself* William H. Murray, *The Himalayan Scottish Expedition* (London: J. M. Dent and Sons, 1951). The entire quote is often attributed to Goethe due to Murray's citation of one of the poet's couplets as his personal inspiration: "Whatever you can do, or dream you can, begin it; boldness has genius, power, and magic in it."

Select Bibliography

Books

Aczel, Amir D. *Entanglement: The Greatest Mystery in Physics.* New York: Four Walls Eight Windows, 2002.

Batson, C. Daniel. *The Altruism Question: Toward a Social Psychological Answer.* Hillsdale, NJ: Lawrence Erlbaum, 1991.

Bigelow, Robert. *The Dawn Warriors: Man's Evolution towards Peace.* Boston: Little Brown, 1969.

Buber, Martin. *Tales of Hassidim: The Early Masters.* Translated by Olga Marx. New York: Schocken Books, 1947.

Cory, Gerald A., and Russell Gardner Jr., eds. *Evolutionary Neuroethology of Paul MacLean: Convergences and Frontiers.* Foreword by Jaak Panksepp. Westport, CT: Praeger, 2002.

Damasio, Antonio. *Looking for Spinoza: Joy, Sorrow, and the Feeling Brain.* Orlando, FL: Harcourt, 2003.

Davidson, Richard J., and Anne Harrington. *Visions of Compassion: Western Scientists and Tibetan Buddhists Examine Human Nature.* New York: Oxford University Press, 2002.

De Waal, Frans, and Frans Lanting. *Bonobo: The Forgotten Ape.* Berkeley: University of California Press, 1997.

De Waal, Frans. *The Ape and the Sushi Master: Cultural Reflections of a Primatologist.* New York: Basic Books, 2001.

Dorje, Wang-ch'ug. *The Mahamudra: Eliminating the Darkness of Ignorance.* Translated by Alexander Berzin. Dharmsala, India: Library of Tibetan Works and Archives, 1978.

Dresner, Samuel H. *Levi Yitzhak of Berditchev: Portrait of a Hasidic Master.* New York: Shapolsky, 1986.

Emmons, Robert A. "Personality and Forgiveness." In *Forgiveness: Theory, Research, and Practice,* edited by Michael E. McCullough, Carl E. Thoresen, and Kenneth I. Pargament. New York: Guilford Press, 2001.

Enright, Robert. *Forgiveness Is a Choice.* Washington, DC: American Psychological Association, 2001.

Fuller, Robert W. *Somebodies and Nobodies: Overcoming the Abuse of Rank*. Gabriola Island, B.C., Canada: New Society, 2004.

Ghiselin, Michael. *The Economy of Nature and the Evolution of Sex*. Berkeley: University of California Press, 1974.

Glassman, Bernie. *Bearing Witness: A Zen Master's Lessons in Making Peace*. New York: Bell Tower–Random House, 1999.

Gobodo-Madikizela, Pumla. *A Human Being Died That Night: A South African Story of Forgiveness*. Boston: Houghton Mifflin, 2003.

Goleman, Daniel. *Destructive Emotions: How Can We Overcome Them?* New York: Bantam Books, 2003.

Haidt, Jonathan. "Elevation and the Positive Psychology of Morality." In *Flourishing: Positive Psychology and the Life Well-lived,* edited by Corey L. Mikeyes and Jonathan Haidt. Washington, DC: American Psychological Association, 2003.

Hobbes, Thomas. *The Elements of Law Natural and Politic: Part I, Human Nature, Part II, De Corpore Politico; with Three Lives*. Edited with an introduction by J. C. A. Gaskin. New York: Oxford University Press, 1994.

Horowitz, Donald L. *Ethnic Groups in Conflict*. Berkeley: University of California Press, 2000.

Kierkegaard, Søren. *Works of Love*. Edited and translated by Howard V. Hong and Edna H. Hong. Princeton, NJ: Princeton University Press, 1995.

King, Martin Luther Jr. *Where Do We Go from Here: Chaos or Community?* New York: Harper and Row, 1967.

King, Rachel. *Don't Kill in Our Names*. New Brunswick, NJ: Rutgers University Press, 2003.

Kohn, Alfie. *The Brighter Side of Human Nature: Altruism and Empathy in Everyday Life*. New York: Basic Books, 1990.

Krebs, Dennis, and Christine Russell. "Role-taking and Altruism: When You Put Yourself in the Shoes of Another, Will They Take You to Their Owner's Aid?" In *Altruism and Helping Behavior,* edited by J. Philippe Rushton and Richard M. Sorrentino. Hillsdale, NJ: Lawrence Erlbaum, 1981.

Kropotkin, Peter. *Mutual Aid: A Factor of Evolution*. Boston: Porter Sargent Publishers, 1976.

Lamb, Sharon, and Jeffrie G. Murphy, eds. *Before Forgiving: Cautionary Views of Forgiveness in Psychotherapy*. New York: Oxford University Press, 2002.

Levi, Primo. *The Drowned and the Saved*. Edited by Erroll McDonald. Translated by Raymond Rosenthal. New York: Random House, 1988.

Loye, David. *Darwin's Lost Theory of Love: A Healing Vision for the New Century*. Lincoln, NE: iUniverse.com, 1998.

McCullough, Michael E., Kenneth I. Pargament, and Carle E. Thorsen, eds. *Forgiveness: Theory, Research, and Practice*. New York: Guilford Press, 2000.

Monroe, Kristin Renwick. *The Heart of Altruism: Perceptions of a Common Humanity*. Princeton, NJ: Princeton University Press, 1996.

Oliner, Samuel P. *Do unto Others*. Boulder, CO: Westview Press, 2004.

Oliner, Samuel, and Pearl Oliner. *The Altruistic Personality: Rescuers of Jews in Nazi Europe*. New York: Free Press, 1988.

Peterson, Dale, and Richard Wrangham. *Demonic Males: Apes and the Origins of Human Violence*. Boston: Mariner Books–Houghton Mifflin, 1997.

Pickering, Mary. *Auguste Comte: An Intellectual Biography*. Vol. 1. Cambridge: Cambridge University Press, 1993.

Piechowski, M. M. "Emotional Giftedness: The Measure of Interpersonal Intelligence." In *Handbook of Gifted Education*, edited by Nicholas Colangelo and Gary A. Davis. 2nd ed. Needham Heights, MA: Allyn and Bacon, 1997.

Pinker, Steven. *The Blank Slate: The Modern Denial of Human Nature*. New York: Viking, 2002.

Post, Stephen Garrard, Lynn G. Underwood, Jeffrey P. Schloss, and William B. Hurlbut. *Altruism and Altruistic Love: Science, Philosophy, and Religion in Dialogue*. New York: Oxford University Press, 2002.

Rose, Hilary, and Steven Rose. *Alas Poor Darwin: Arguments against Evolutionary Psychology*. New York: Harmony Books–Random House, 2000.

Rushton, J. Philippe, and Richard M. Sorrentino, eds. *Altruism and Helping Behavior*. Hillsdale, NJ: Lawrence Erlbaum, 1981.

Savage-Rumbaugh, Sue, and Roger Lewin. *Kanzi, the Ape at the Brink of a Human Mind*. New York: John Wiley and Sons, 1994.

Schwartz, Jeffrey M., and Sharon Begley. *The Mind and the Brain: Neuroplasticity and the Power of Mental Force*. New York: Regan Books–HarperCollins, 2003.

Shantideva. *The Way of the Bodhisattva*. Translated by Padmakara Translation Group. Boston: Shambhala Press, 1997.

Smith, Adam. *The Theory of Moral Sentiments*. Cambridge: Cambridge University Press, 2002.

Sober, Elliott, and David Sloan Wilson. *Unto Others: The Evolution and Psychology of Unselfish Behavior.* Cambridge, MA: Harvard University Press, 1998.

Stein, Edith. *On the Problem of Empathy.* Translated by Waltraut Stein. The Hague: Martinus Nijhoff, 1964.

Sumner, William G. *War and Other Essays.* New Haven, CT: Yale University Press, 1911.

Surrey, Janet L. "The Self-in-Relation." In *Women's Growth in Connection: Writings from the Stone Center*, edited by Judith V. Jordan, Alexandra G. Kaplan, Jean Baker Miller, Irene P. Stiver, and Janet L. Surrey. New York: Guilford Press, 1991.

Teilhard de Chardin, Pierre. *The Phenomenon of Man.* New York: Harper-Perennial, 1976.

Thoreson, Carl E., Alex H. S. Harris, and Frederic Luskin. "Forgiveness and Health: An Unanswered Question." In *Forgiveness: Theory, Research, and Practice,* edited by Michael E. McCullough, Kenneth I. Pargament, and Carl E. Thoresen. New York: Guilford Press, 2001.

Ury, William. *The Third Side: Why We Fight and How We Can Stop.* New York: Penguin, 2003.

Von Kreisler, Kristin. *Beauty In the Beasts: True Stories of Animals Who Choose to Do Good.* New York: Jeremy P. Tarcher, 2002.

Wright, Robert. *The Moral Animal: The New Science of Evolutionary Psychology.* New York: Pantheon Books–Random House, 1994.

Articles/Papers

Altman, Neil. "Humiliation, Retaliation, and Violence." *Tikkun* 19, no. 1 (January–February 2004): 17.

Brothers, Leslie. "A Biological Perspective on Empathy." *American Journal of Psychiatry* 146, no. 1 (1989): 10–19.

Campbell, W. K., E. Rudich, and C. Sedikides. "Narcissism, Self-esteem, and the Positivity of Self-views: Two Portraits of Self-love." *Personality and Social Psychology Bulletin* 28 (2002): 358–68.

Darren, George, Patrice Carroll, Robert Kersnick, and Katie Calderon. "Gender-related Patterns of Helping among Friends." *Psychology of Women Quarterly* 22, no. 4 (1998): 685–704.

Frankel, Estelle. "Sweetening the Judgements: The Kabbalah of Compassion." *Parabola* 28, no. 1 (2003): 14–15.

Haidt, Jonathan. "The Emotional Dog and Its Rational Tail: A Social Intuitionist Approach to Moral Judgment." *Psychological Review* 108, no. 4 (2001): 814–34.

Hall, Stephen S. "Is Buddhism Good for Your Health?" *New York Times,* September 14, 2003, sec. 6, p. 46.

Henderson, Antonia J. Z., Monica A. Landolt, Michael F. McDonald, W. M. Barrable, J. G. Sooz, W. Gourlay, C. J. Allison, and D. N. Landsberg. "The Living Anonymous Kidney Donor: Lunatic or Saint?" *American Journal of Transplantation* 3, no. 2 (2003): 203–13.

Kohn, Alfie. "Beyond Selfishness." *Psychology Today,* October 1998, pp. 34–38.

Levin, Jeff. "A Prolegomenon to an Epidemiology of Love: Theory, Measurement, and Health Outcomes." *Journal of Social and Clinical Psychology* 19 (2000): 117–36.

Lipman, Matthew. "Caring Thinking." Proceedings of the Sixth International Conference on Thinking, Massachusetts Institute of Technology, Boston, July 17–22, 1994.

McClelland, David C. "Some Reflections on the Two Psychologies of Love." *Journal of Personality* 54, no. 2 (June 1986): 344–49.

Murphy, R. F. "Intergroup Hostility and Social Cohesion." *American Anthropologist* 59 (1957): 1018–35.

O'Connell, Sanjida M. "Empathy in Chimpanzees: Evidence for Theory of Mind?" *Primates* 36, no. 3 (July 1995): 401.

Pinker, Steven. "Is There a Gene for Compassion?" Review of *The Moral Animal,* by Robert Wright. *New York Times,* September 25, 1994, p. BR3.

Preston, Stephanie D., and Frans B. M. de Waal. "Empathy: Its Ultimate and Proximate Bases." *Behavioral and Brain Sciences* 25, no. 1 (2002): 515–26.

Silverman, Linda K. "The Moral Sensitivity of Gifted Children and the Evolution of Society." *Roeper Review* 17, no. 2 (1994): 110–16.

Van der Dennen, Johan M. G. "Of Badges, Bonds and Boundaries: Ingroup/ Outgroup Differentiation and Ethnocentrism Revisited." Proceedings of the Fifth Annual Meeting of the European Sociobiological Society, St. John's College, Oxford, UK, January 5–6, 1995.

Zahn-Wexler, Carolyn, and Marian Radke-Yarrow. "The Origins of Empathic Concern." *Motivation and Emotion* 14, no. 2 (1990): 107–30.

INDEX

MARC IAN BARASCH

*M*ARC BARASCH'S PREVIOUS BOOK, *Healing Dreams* (2000), was hailed by the *Washington Post* as "lucid...courageous...trailblazing." It won a 2001 Nautilus Award, and is taught in universities alongside the works of Jung and Freud. His prior book, *Remarkable Recovery* (1995, with Caryle Hirshberg), a study of spontaneous remission, was a national bestseller. It was translated into a dozen languages and continues to be used in medical schools, hospitals, and healing centers worldwide.

Marc is the author of the award-winning classic *The Healing Path* (1992). Dr. Larry Dossey writes: "If you read one book about the mind-body connection, make it this one. It is a beacon of science, spirituality, and sanity."

Marc has been an editor at *Psychology Today, Natural Health,* and *New Age Journal* (which won a National Magazine Award under his tenure). In the television field, Marc was writer/producer of "One Child, One Voice," an international TV special for the Turner Broadcasting System, which aired in 150 countries. A call for global solutions to ecological and social problems, it was nominated for an Emmy and won numerous international awards. Marc has produced television specials for the Discovery Channel and England's Channel Four.

He is the founder of the Green World Campaign, a global charity helping to restore the ecology and the economy of the world's poorest places (www.greenworld.org).

His work has been featured on *Good Morning America,* the *Today Show, NBC Dateline,* and NPR's *All Things Considered.*

Marc was educated at Yale University. He has taught at Naropa University, where he was a founder of the master's program in psychology. As a hobby he has played and recorded in the "lit-rock" band the Rock Bottom Remainders. *Interview* magazine once called him "one of today's coolest grown-ups." He lives in the foothills of the Rockies.

About Berrett-Koehler Publishers

*B*ERRETT-KOEHLER IS AN INDEPENDENT PUBLISHER DEDICATED to an ambitious mission: *Creating a World that Works for All.*

We believe that to truly create a better world, action is needed at all levels—individual, organizational, and societal. At the individual level, our publications help people align their lives with their values and with their aspirations for a better world. At the organizational level, our publications promote progressive leadership and management practices, socially responsible approaches to business, and humane and effective organizations. At the societal level, our publications advance social and economic justice, shared prosperity, sustainability, and new solutions to national and global issues.

A major theme of our publications is "Opening Up New Space." They challenge conventional thinking, introduce new ideas, and foster positive change. Their common quest is changing the underlying beliefs, mindsets, and structures that keep generating the same cycles of problems, no matter who our leaders are or what improvement programs we adopt.

We strive to practice what we preach—to operate our publishing company in line with the ideas in our books. At the core of our approach is *stewardship,* which we define as a deep sense of responsibility to administer the company for the benefit of all of our "stakeholder" groups: authors, customers, employees, investors, service providers, and the communities and environment around us.

We are grateful to the thousands of readers, authors, and other friends of the company who consider themselves to be part of the "BK Community." We hope that you, too, will join us in our mission.

BE CONNECTED

Visit Our Web Site

Go to www.bkconnection.com to read exclusive previews and excerpts of new books, find detailed information on all Berrett-Koehler titles and authors, browse subject-area libraries of books, and get special discounts.

Subscribe to Our Free E-Newsletter

Be the first to hear about new publications, special discount offers, exclusive articles, news about bestsellers, and more! Get on the list for our free e-newsletter by going to www.bkconnection.com.

Get Quantity Discounts

Berrett-Koehler books are available at quantity discounts for orders of ten or more copies. Please call us toll-free at (800) 929-2929 or e-mail us at bkp.orders@aidcvt.com.

Host a Reading Group

For tips on how to form and carry on a book reading group in your workplace or community, see our Web site at www.bkconnection.com.

Join the BK Community

Thousands of readers of our books have become part of the "BK Community" by participating in events featuring our authors, reviewing draft manuscripts of forthcoming books, spreading the word about their favorite books, and supporting our publishing program in other ways. If you would like to join the BK Community, please contact us at bkcommunity@bkpub.com.